P9-AOF-975

Global Perspectives
on Social Issues

Global Perspectives on Social Issues

Juvenile Justice Systems

by Paola Zalkind and Rita J. Simon

Brooks - Cork Library
Shelton State
Community College

LEXINGTON BOOKS
Lanham • Boulder • New York • Toronto • Oxford

LEXINGTON BOOKS

Published in the United States of America
by Lexington Books
An imprint of The Rowman & Littlefield Publishing Group, Inc.
4501 Forbes Boulevard, Suite 200, Lanham, Maryland 20706

PO Box 317
Oxford
OX2 9RU, UK

Copyright © 2004 by Lexington Books

All rights reserved. No part of this publication may be reproduced,
stored in a retrieval system, or transmitted in any form or by any
means, electronic, mechanical, photocopying, recording, or otherwise,
without the prior permission of the publisher.

British Library Cataloguing in Publication Information Available

Library of Congress Cataloging-in-Publication Data

Zalkind, Paola, 1981–
  Global perspectives on social issues : juvenile justice systems / by Paola Zalkind and
Rita J. Simon.
    p. cm.
  Includes bibliographical references and index.
  ISBN 0–7391–0730–5 (cloth : alk. paper)
  1. Juvenile justice, Administration of—Cross-cultural studies. I. Simon, Rita James. II.
Title.
  HV9069.Z35 2004
  364.36–dc22   2004001755

Printed in the United States of America

♾ ™ The paper used in this publication meets the minimum requirements of
American National Standard for Information Sciences—Permanence of Paper for
Printed Library Materials, ANSI/NISO Z39.48–1992.

Contents

Preface

Global Perspectives on Social Issues: Juvenile Justice Systems joins a series of books that examines social issues the world over. Thus far, the topics covered include abortion, euthanasia, capital punishment, pornography, and marriage and divorce. Forthcoming volumes will focus on immigration and education. Further down the road we expect to produce manuscripts on the use and distribution of illicit drugs and on the rights and responsibilities of citizenship.

In this book, we characterize the status of juvenile offenders in twenty-five nations in North America, South America, Western and Eastern Europe, the Middle East, Africa, Asia, and Australia. We report the stated and actual rights of children in criminal proceedings, the age of criminal responsibility, the likely punishment for different types of offenses, and the conditions of juvenile detention facilities. Each of the chapters reports on the countries in the eight different regions of the world. Consistent with the other works in this series, *Juvenile Justice Systems* is explicitly comparative.

Rita J. Simon

1

Introduction

On November 20, 1959, the United Nations adopted the Declaration of the Rights of the Child. The charter was meant to safeguard the rights of children all over the world and protect the most vulnerable members of society from mistreatment at the hands of their parents, the government, the military, educational institutions, and any establishment capable of exerting power over children. The preamble recognizes: "the child, by reason of his physical and mental immaturity, needs special safeguards and care, including appropriate legal protection, before as well as after birth."[1] According to the United Nations, all member countries, as well as the world as a whole, should respect the rights of a child because juveniles are inherently more vulnerable than adults.

The United Nations is particularly concerned with the rights of juvenile offenders and their status under individual country's laws:

> Article 37 provides that state parties shall ensure that:
> a) No child should be subjected to torture or other cruel, inhuman or degrading treatment and punishment. Neither capital punishment nor life imprisonment without the possibility of release shall be imposed for offenses committed by persons below eighteen years of age.[2]

The United Nations states that regardless of the type of crime committed by a person defined as a juvenile, the citizen may not be subjected to the same punishments and liability as adult criminals. The organization is acting with the assumption that youths cannot be fully responsible for criminal action and that many youth crimes are committed without full understanding of the act or the consequences of criminal action for victims, society as a whole, and the offenders themselves.

Approximately forty-three years after the passage of the Declaration of the Rights of the Child, a number of United Nations member countries remain in defiance of the requirements of the United Nations. Many children well under eighteen languish in prisons across the world, at times even subjected to capital punishment. Many juvenile offenders are not appropriately informed of their rights, even to the standards of legal privileges defined by individual nations. Detention centers are often overcrowded, and instead of focusing on rehabilitation of the youth offenders and continuance of education, children merely are treated with goals of penal retribution for their actions. Children are also routinely subjected to physical and emotional abuse in a variety of nations. While some countries have better records than others regarding the status of juvenile offenders, overall, the status of children who commit all forms of crime is internationally unacceptable.

This volume investigates the status of juvenile offenders in twenty-five different countries in the regions of North America, South America, Western Europe, Eastern Europe, the Middle East, Africa, Asia, and Australia. It establishes both the stated legal rights of children in the face of criminal proceedings as well as the actual experiences of children in various juvenile justice systems. Often, factors other than legal codes have an additional impact on the rights of children, including gender, ethnicity, and class. Finally, the political and cultural mindset of individual countries, particularly where juvenile crime is on the rise, has a powerful effect on the treatment of juvenile offenders. This study compares a variety of issues, including the age of criminal responsibility, the court system for juvenile offenders, the rights of juveniles in conflict with the law and any differentiation from adult rights, and finally, the conditions and goals of punishment.

The United Nations has attempted to instill a uniform system for offenders by classifying a "juvenile" as anyone under the age of eighteen. But few member countries of the United Nations actually follow their guidelines. Internationally, the age at which a child is considered a juvenile varies. The term "juvenile" affords special status of limited liability and, at times, proceedings in the juvenile court. While many countries agree with the United Nations and list eighteen as the age when a juvenile becomes a legal adult, other factors such as severity of crime and maturity play a role, and eighteen is a number often subject to change.

The age of criminal responsibility is defined as the age at which children can be fully subjected to penal laws for the commission of a crime; it is the time in their lives in which they are considered to fully understand the implications of their actions. In terms of how a juvenile is defined, the age of criminal responsibility is the year in a child's life that he or she is afforded the status of juvenile. The United Nations has not specified a specific age at which it thinks children should become criminally liable for their actions. However, the "committee responsible for monitoring compliance with it [the Convention on the Rights of the Child] has criticized jurisdictions in which the minimum age is twelve or less."[3]

The laws of many individual nations and comparable international standards for the treatment of children believe that the turning point in which an offender is criminally accepted as an adult should be based on other factors. For instance, the Beijing Rules recommend that: "The age of criminal responsibility be based on emotional, mental, and intellectual maturity, and that it not be fixed too low."[4] Some nations instead take different factors into account, legally setting a particular age at which an individual can be criminally considered an adult, but also allowing the leeway to take into account the severity of the crime.

The United Nations also recognizes the need for children in conflict with the law to be treated by a separate judicial system. Many countries have allotted space, funds, and manpower for juvenile courts. The rules in the juvenile system are often different from the expectations and goals of the adult proceedings. It is expected that juvenile offenders will be heard by judges in a different physical setting than adults, and by specially trained jurists who understand that many juvenile offenders are afforded a limited liability for the offenses they commit. Article 40 of the Convention on the Rights of the Child states that, in relation to the need for special court proceedings for juvenile offenders, children have the right to:

> have the matter determined without delay by a competent, independent, and impartial authority or judicial body in a fair hearing according to law, in the presence of legal or other appropriate assistance. . . . State Parties shall seek to promote the establishment of laws, procedures, authorities, and institutions specifically applicable to children alleged as, accused of, or recognized as having infringed the penal law.[5]

International organizations believe that children in conflict with the law are ultimately in need of a separate judicial body to provide them with judicial treatment that recognizes their unique needs in the face of criminal liability. For the purposes of this study, the references to the individual juvenile courts will refer to what each specific nation deems the ages and offenses that apply to their individual definition of juvenile.

Various justice systems throughout the world also afford specific rights to citizens in conflict with the law. For instance, many nations operate their courts under the assumption that anyone charged with a violation of the law is innocent until proven guilty. Other countries require that an offender is afforded the right to an attorney in the quest to prove his innocence or guilt. In 1948, the United Nations passed the Universal Declaration of Human Rights, hoping that all member countries would recognize legal systems that afford dignity and civil privileges to citizens around the world. In reference to violations of penal codes, Article 11 states, "Everyone charged with a penal offense has the right to be presumed innocent until proved guilty according to law in a public trial in which he has had all the guarantees necessary for his defense."[6] Fifty years later, many nations fail at providing even the most basic rights to their citizens.

In regard to children charged with penal offenses, both the United Nations and various member countries require a higher standard of protection of legal rights. While adult trials are held in a public setting to assure community participation, trials in which a minor is the defendant often include a right to closed hearings. This precaution is taken under the assumption that many young offenders are first-time delinquents, and that protecting the child from the social backlash of being seen as a lawbreaker in his or her community will aid the youth in rehabilitation. In addition, even nations that refuse to provide an attorney for the average citizen are more inclined to do so when a child faces criminal penalties. The United Nations also requires a higher standard of protection for youth offenders versus their adult counterparts. In the Convention on the Rights of the Child, Article 37 states: "Every child deprived of his or her liberty shall have the right to prompt access to legal and other appropriate assistance, as well as the right to challenge the legality of the deprivation of his or her liberty before a court or other competent, independent and impartial authority and to a prompt decision on any such action."[7]

The notable difference between the United Nations' requirements for adult and juvenile offenders is the necessity of legal assistance for youths. This study will compare juvenile liberties both with the rights of adults within each nation, as well as with the rights deemed necessary by international organizations. It will discuss the right to legal defense, the regulations regarding parental and guardian involvement in any proceedings, and the right to privacy from public knowledge of the crime.

Finally, the purpose of separating juvenile delinquents from adult offenders is both to protect children and take advantage of their greater capacity for rehabilitation. International legal standards and a majority of nations in this study accomplish this goal in a number of ways. For instance, juveniles often have separate courts, are afforded distinctive rights, and hold limited liability for their crimes. The United Nations Convention on the Rights of the Child furthers the separation between juvenile and adult offenders by requiring that any sanctions placed upon youths convicted of crimes will be different from the punishment of adults sentenced for the same crime.

Finally, the United Nations provides detailed guidelines for the punishment of convicted juvenile offenders. Article 37 of the Convention on the Rights of the Child states the following:

> State Parties shall ensure that:
> a. No child should be subjected to torture or other cruel, inhuman, or degrading treatment or punishment. Neither capital punishment nor life imprisonment without possibility of release shall be imposed for offenses committed by persons below eighteen years of age;
> b. No child shall be deprived of his or her liberty unlawfully and arbitrarily. The arrest, detention or imprisonment of a child shall be in conformity with the law and shall be used only as a measure of last resort and for the shortest appropriate period of time;
> c. Every child deprived of liberty shall be treated with humanity and respect for the inherent dignity of the human person, and in a manner [that] takes into account the needs of persons his or her age. In particular, every child deprived of liberty shall be separated from adults unless it is considered in the child's best interest not to do so and shall have the right to maintain contact with his or her family through correspondence and visits, save in exceptional circumstances.[8]

Most importantly, international standards require that minors may never be sentenced to death. While a number of nations, particularly in Europe, have outlawed capital punishment all together, some nations that continue to employ the death penalty ban the execution of minors. The decision to do so is a reflection of the acceptance of limited liability crimes committed under the age of majority, regardless of the seriousness of the crime.

In addition, while imprisonment is used as a punitive measure for a number of adult criminal actions, the United Nations insists that juveniles can only be detained as a last resort, and only in specific circumstances. Adult prison facilities are meant generally to weed offenders from society and to punish them for their actions, but juvenile detention facilities are meant to rehabilitate youth offenders, providing them with therapy, education, and health care during any period of detainment. Basically, any sanction used against youth criminals must be supported by the underlying notions of juvenile justice; rehabilitation, not punitive action. The study also investigates which nations around the world follow international standards for juvenile punishment. Are any death sentences laid down for youth offenders? Are juveniles detained often for less serious crimes, or are courts inclined to utilize alternate sentences? When children are confined, is it required that they must be separated from adult criminals? Finally, what are the conditions of juvenile detention facilities, and are the individuals in charge of such places attempting to better the lives of delinquent children?

NOTES

1. Alemika, E. E. O., and I. C. Chukwuma. *Juvenile Justice Administration in Nigeria: Philosophy and Practice*. Lagos, Nigeria: Centre for Law Enforcement Education, 2001, 28.

2. Alemika and Chukwuma, 28.

3. Urbas, Gregory. "The Age of Criminal Responsibility." *Australian Institute of Criminology: Trends and Issues*, No. 181. Canberra: Nov. 2000.

4. UNICEF. "Special Protections: Progress and Disparity." *Progress of Nations 1997*. [Online]. Google, Internet, 15 Oct. 1995. Available: http: www.unicef.org/pon97.p56a.htm.

5. United Nations. "Convention on the Rights of the Child." 2 Sept. 1990. Provided by UNICEF. [Online]. Available: http://www.unicef.org/crc/fulltext.htm.

6. Office of the High Commissioner for Human Rights. "Universal Declaration of Human Rights." United Nations Department of Human Rights. 10 Dec. 1948. [Online]. Available: http://193.194.138.190/udhr/lang/eng.htm.

7. United Nations. "Convention on the Rights of the Child." 2 Sept. 1990. Provided by UNICEF. [Online]. Available: http://www.unicef.org/crc/fulltext.htm.

8. United Nations. "Convention on the Rights of the Child." 2 Sept. 1990. Provided by UNICEF. [Online]. Available: http://www.unicef.org/crc/fulltext.htm.

2

North America

The two countries included in this portion of the investigation are similar. Both Canada and the United States have a democratic history, and a large and diverse population. In regards to their criminal justice systems, a rise in juvenile crime in the past few decades has led both nations to enforce stricter guidelines in the youth courts, while prior to that shift, both nations had been matched in their social welfare programs for youths in conflict with the law.

UNITED STATES

The United States, unlike many countries, is a confederation of states that holds its own body of criminal law. Thus, while the nation is coalesced under one federal constitution, each state has a separate body of law to determine the age in which a child can be held criminally responsible for his or her actions. Oklahoma has the lowest age of criminal responsibility, listed at seven years. Nevada and Washington do not lag far behind, holding children responsible for crimes at eight. Colorado lists the age of criminal responsibility as ten, with Oregon at twelve; Georgia, Illinois, New Hampshire, and New York at thirteen; and finally, California, Idaho, New Jersey, Texas, and Utah deem all youths above the age of fourteen as responsible for their criminal actions. It is important to note, however, that states with extremely low ages of criminal responsibility require prosecutors to prove that children knew, at the time of the commission of the crime, that the action was wrong. In addition, while Washington lists the age of criminal responsibility as eight, the law presumes that children aged eight to twelve are incapable of committing a crime. The majority of states in America do not specify an age within their criminal statutes, including states in completely different regions, such as Alabama, New Mexico, Vermont, and Montana.[1]

Many states without a minimum age of criminal responsibility instead set a maximum age at which an offender can still be tried within the juvenile justice system rather than as adult criminals. For example, Connecticut, New York, and North Carolina set the age at which an offender must be tried as an adult in criminal proceedings at sixteen. Georgia, Louisiana, Massachusetts, Michigan, Missouri, New Hampshire, South Carolina, Texas, and Wisconsin allow offenders to remain within the juvenile justice system if their crime is committed before the age of seventeen. But, the age requirements of adult court proceedings are not entirely inflexible. Instead, "juvenile court judges have had the discretion to waive jurisdiction to the criminal court. These waivers generally fit one of three case types: serious offense, extensive juvenile record, or juvenile near the age limit."[2]

Basically, while a variety of jurisdictions in the United States have chosen to set a minimum or maximum age in which an offender can be prosecuted as an adult rather than a juvenile, other factors allow individual jurists to take an offender under the legal limit and send them to adult court. For instance, if a sixteen-year-old offender in Wisconsin is charged with murder and also has an extensive record of escalating crime, a judge will most likely send the offender to adult court for trial. In the United States, this transfer can occur by three processes: "judicial waiver, prosecutorial direct file, and statutory exclusion."[3] Judicial waiver involves a jurist's decision to transfer the offender. Prosecutorial direct file occurs when the transfer to adult court is made by the officer prosecuting the case, but still involves the factors of seriousness of offense, previous record, and age at commission of crime. Finally, statutory exclusion refers to the legal definition of certain offenses as adult crimes. "For example, in New Mexico a child who is at least 15 years of age and is accused of first-degree murder is excluded from juvenile court jurisdiction. Mississippi excludes all felonies committed by juveniles who are 17 years of age."[4]

The United States has wide variance in the age of criminal responsibility based on the state in which a juvenile offender commits a crime. If a juvenile in one state commits a crime in which he or she can be prosecuted as an adult, an offender in another state committing a similar crime may be tried as a juvenile, even if both offenders are the same age. American statutory law provides for a large amount of leeway concerning which factors, other than age, can reassign a youth into adult criminal proceedings.

The diversity within the United States has not effected the formation of juvenile courts in the same way that it has the age of criminal responsibility. While there is some differentiation in the juvenile court proceedings in various states, there is more uniformity in understanding the need for a separate court for offenders under the age of eighteen. The origins of the juvenile court in America occurred in the late nineteenth century through the beginning of the twentieth century. Reformers were astounded to find that juveniles charged with minor offenses were not afforded any protection by the legal system and faced an adult criminal judge. "Progressive reformers . . . created the juvenile court as an informal welfare system and an alternative to the criminal process. Rather than punishment for crimes, juvenile court judges made dispositions in the child's 'best interests' and the state functioned as *parens patriae*, as a surrogate parent."[5] The progressive reformers launched a national trend. At the end of the nineteenth century, Illinois instituted the first separate juvenile court in the nation. Within twenty-five years, all but two states in the country had followed its lead.[6]

The original goals of the juvenile court were for it to become an alternative to criminal proceedings and to care for youth whose parents were unable to control them. To avoid the notion of criminalizing youth, the juvenile court in America created a separate system of terms that are used to differentiate the process from adult criminal courts. "They employed a euphemistic vocabulary and initiated proceeding by 'petitions' rather than 'indictments' or 'complaints,' 'adjudicated' youths for 'delinquency' rather than conducting criminal 'trials,' and imposed 'dispositions' that could include commitment to 'training schools' rather than 'sentencing hearings' that could result in confinement in prison."[7] Even in wording, the American reformers were attempting to make a divergent system for minors in conflict with the law, hoping that children would not be stigmatized for offenses early in life. Also, the formation of a separate system would allow for more rehabilitation rather than punitive measures against youths.

While each state in America now has a juvenile court system, the national ideology behind the original ideals has shifted substantially over the past three decades. Instead of a system in which the court becomes comparable to that of a parent of the child offender, juvenile courts have shifted to becoming simply a criminal proceeding with outcomes for juveniles similar to what they would receive in adult criminal court: "court decisions, statutory amendments, and administrative changes have transformed the juvenile court from a social welfare agency into a scaled-down, second-class criminal court for young offenders."[8] The shift is reflected in the number of offenders across the nation under the age of eighteen who are transferred into the adult court systems for their crimes.

In a 1998 study released by the Office of Justice Programs at the U.S. Department of Justice, data compilers found that in 1994 almost 70 percent of the responding prosecutor's offices admitted to charging a youth as an adult in that year.[9]

Across the United States, there has recently been a great increase in the desire to treat children, who legally have juvenile status, with the codes and penalties applicable to the adult court system, rather than utilizing the rehabilitative youth courts formed with the notion of a social welfare program. One explanation for this shift has been the increase in crime, particularly since the 1970s. While the crime rate officially began to fall in the 1990s, legislators and the judiciary have continued to treat juvenile crime as acts that require adult consequences. A related explanation is the escalation in the seriousness of crimes committed by juveniles. Many of the offenders who have been transferred out of the juvenile court have been reassigned by the commission of violent felonies. One investigation in the 1990s found that, of the juveniles transferred to adult court, 11 percent were charged with murder, 34 percent with robbery, and 15 percent charged with felony assault.[10]

Changes have also occurred to the rights that juveniles are afforded when in conflict with the law. The basis of all rights in America was the rebellion against the lack of rights in British colonies; the most important privileges were recognized in the first ten amendments to the Constitution. The Bill of Rights assures all Americans that they will be afforded due process, an attorney to help with their legal defense, the right to indictment, formal court procedures to determine guilt or innocence, the right to a speedy public trial, the ability to participate in legal proceedings, and the option to face any witnesses testifying against them. While many of these rights apply to juveniles in conflict with the law, the original formation of the juvenile court system is based on the necessity of treating juvenile delinquents differently than their adult counterparts. Thus, many of the rights embodied in the American Constitution in regard to conflict with the law are not experienced by minors.

In a way, the decision to treat children differently because of their age was as harmful as it was helpful. Initially, the guarantees of the Bill of Rights were ignored when the criminal defendant was a youth. "Because the [juvenile court] judge was to act in the best interests of the child, procedural safeguards available to adults, such as the right to an attorney, the right to know the charges brought against one, the right to trial by jury—and the right to confront one's accuser—were thought unnecessary. Juvenile court proceedings were closed to the public and juvenile records were to remain confidential so as not to interfere with the child's or adolescent's ability to be rehabilitated and reintegrated into society."[11] The rights considered necessary by the founders of America have been denied to children in conflict with the law under the guise that it is in their best interest. Throughout the evolution of the youth court, minors have earned rights more in line with adult offense guarantees, while at the same time keeping a number of their own special protections.

In the landmark 1967 *Gault* case, the Supreme Court overrode multiple state procedures and declared that the Fourteenth Amendment right to equal protection and the entire Bill of Rights extended to juveniles in the same way as adults. All due process rights, particularly the right to an attorney, were henceforth considered mandatory for juveniles as well. However, "state statutes and court rules vary in their strategies to deliver legal services. Some provide that the right to counsel attaches when police take a juvenile into custody, at a detention hearing, and 'at all stages of court proceedings, unless the right to counsel is freely, knowingly, and intelligently waived by the child.'"[12]

Over thirty years have passed since the issuance of *Gault*, yet many states remain in violation of the right to an attorney for minors. Many states allow juveniles to make their own decision about the necessity of legal assistance. Throughout the 1980s and 1990s, investigations revealed that a *majority* of youth offenders were not represented at all.[13] The purpose of the formation of the juvenile court system in America was meant to recognize a higher level of vulnerability for youth offenders. If youths are meant to have special protections, should they really be able to independently decide that they are not in need of an attorney, particularly considering the improbability that any juvenile offender has dabbled in legal studies? The High Court has recognized the importance of legal representation for juvenile delinquents, yet this basic right guaranteed to their adult counterparts over two hundred years ago is often denied children in conflict with the law.

The right to private legal proceedings has evolved differently than the right to an attorney in America. Traditionally, the underlying ideologies of the juvenile justice system forged a system of confidentiality whenever a minor faced criminal charges. Originally, "proceedings were closed to the public. The identity of juveniles was not disclosed. . . . These measures were aimed at minimizing the stigma attached to court involvement and promoting the goal of rehabilitation."[14]

The rise in crime rates, particularly in severe and violent felonies, has led to a national shift toward the end of rehabilitative ideologies for juvenile offenders. Among the many changes has been a limitation in the once guaranteed right to private proceedings. By the mid-1990s, approximately 50 percent of youth criminal proceedings allowed public attendance, either unconditionally, or if the severity of the crime called for it.[15] Throughout the late 1990s, the shift continued toward greater publicity for juvenile offenders. "For example, in 1997, Idaho added language to its statute requiring open hearings for all juveniles fourteen or older charged with an offense that would be a felony if committed by an adult. . . . At the end of 1997, forty-two states allowed the release of a minor's name or picture under certain conditions, such as being found guilty of serious or violent offenses."[16]

National sentiment shifted one of the basic tenets of the juvenile justice system in opening information about minors to the public, and has simultaneously impacted the involvement of parents and alternative guardians in the court system when children are charged with a crime. Presently, no federal statutes require parent or guardian involvement in proceedings. Many courts and judges recommend that anyone with a vested interest in the future of the offender attend hearings to both give input about the child and provide a support system for the youth. While parental involvement is not often codified into law, certain states are beginning to subpoena parents to the court. In 1997, the California State Legislature debated the importance of parent involvement. In a press release regarding the bill, state senator Tom McClintock stated that, "It is important that parents understand the crime their child has been charged with committing, as well as the legal ramifications involved. . . . Requiring parents to attend court hearings also gives parents an opportunity to learn about community resources available to them."[17]

The United States continues to refuse to incorporate the Convention on the Rights of the Child into federal law because of their ongoing use of the death penalty for minors. America leads the world in juvenile executions. At present, over thirty inmates on Texas's death row were sentenced to execution for crimes that they committed before the age of eighteen. In January 2003, the Supreme Court refused to hear the case of an Oklahoma man convicted of kidnapping, robbery, and murder that occurred when the appellant was seventeen. This rebuff was merely the latest in the Supreme Court's string of refusals to impede state decisions to execute offenders that committed crimes when they were sixteen or seventeen.[18]

Based on the severity of their crime, children are waived to adult court and subsequently become subject to all adult penalties for their crime. While the national laws regarding mandatory appeals for death sentences ensure that no offender is put to death under the age of eighteen, many of the youth offenders face the death chamber before they reach the age of thirty. The decision to allow the death penalty is a state decision, and almost half of the states in the nation allow the death penalty for children under eighteen. At present, twenty-three states in America allow capital punishment for juveniles, with eighteen states setting a minimum age of sixteen and five setting it at seventeen.[19] In this respect, the United States is in serious violation of international standards on the administration of juvenile justice.

In regard to sentencing for less serious crimes, there are few federal guidelines applicable to states that declare how a juvenile should be reprimanded and rehabilitated for criminal action. Sentences meted out for similar crimes in different states will vary; any laws regarding mandatory minimum sentences are decided by jurisdiction, and are additionally left up to the discretion of individual judges. That being said, it is important to note that the ideals underlying the juvenile justice systems in America have been on a trend toward punitive sentences rather than rehabilitative measures as a response to a rise in crime. The Panel on Juvenile Crime reports that while there is a difference in whether the welfare of the juveniles or the protection of society inspires juvenile sentencing decisions in each jurisdiction, overall, the nation has become more punitive. The overall rise in juvenile crime in the 1980s and 1990s, especially more serious crimes that cause physical harm and death, has led many judges to become more concerned with punishment and the acceptance of responsibility. Presently, the concern for rehabilitation has virtually died out.[20]

Juvenile judges in America are faced with a variety of options when sentencing youths. Relying on prepared court guidelines and their own preferences, judges can dismiss charges, sentence the youth to probation, place the youth in treatment that occurs while the offender remains at home, or confine the individual in some form of juvenile detention or mental rehabilitation facility.[21] Judges make a decision based on a combination of factors, including severity of crime, past criminal activity, and the recommendations of adults regarding the individual minor. For instance, probation was the sentence of choice by juvenile judges in over half of juvenile crime cases in 1999, and this statistic does not include offenders charged by police but let off with warnings for the insignificance of the offense. The choice to utilize probation and diversion is left to individual police officers or judges, because again, there are no superceding federal guidelines regarding judicial decisions.[22]

Throughout the 1990s, independent researchers found data regarding the number of detained juveniles, and it appears that the rhetoric of justice has shifted from rehabilitation to punishment. For instance, in 1995, 28 percent of the juveniles convicted of crimes were sentenced to out-of-home placement, most often in a secure correctional facility. The alteration in punitive policy is more noticeable in the crimes for which children were imprisoned. In Georgia in 1996, researchers found that an eleven-year-old male was imprisoned for threatening his teacher, that a thirteen-year-old female was detained for stealing approximately one hundred dollars from her mother, and that a fourteen-year-old female was imprisoned for painting graffiti on public property.[23] Each of these actions are violations of the law, but they are nonviolent, and not serious enough to merit detention.

According to a number of independent commissions, conditions in juvenile facilities across the United States are deplorable, and little effort has been made to alter them. These studies have shown immense problems including lack of adequate space, lack of mental and physical health care, and an ongoing inability to hold offenders in a safe and healthy environment. Crowded conditions are widespread in juvenile training and reform schools, and inspectors have made a connection between the numbers of youths over the capacity to the problems.[24] The crowding of facilities has been directly linked to higher incidences of risk for juveniles and staff alike.

The findings of Amnesty International's investigation into America's juvenile detention facilities are much worse. While juvenile facilities are built with the intention of rehabilitation and the provision of a safe space for youths that lack proper care at home, the study found rampant abuse and a lack of educational and rehabilitative services. The study includes both personal statements from incarcerated individuals, as well as a collection of state-by-state information. From a U.S. Department of Justice Inquiry into Louisiana juvenile detention facilities, investigators noted that a female juvenile was found in solitary confinement with a bloody and bruised eyeball. A guard attacked her face with keys when she was found talking at an inappropriate time, which health care documents were able to verify. At the four juvenile facilities in Louisiana, investigators found that children were habitually physically punished by staff.[25]

Abuse is often also psychological, and is found in facilities all over the nation. While solitary confinement is prohibited for punitive use, in Illinois in 1998, an independent inquiry found that it is instead often overused. In one facility, one-tenth of the juvenile inmates were placed in isolation for over twenty-four hours. The listed infractions were insignificant, including violations such as impertinence.[26]

The conditions of detention for juveniles in youth facilities are despicable, but youth offenders subjected to the adult prison system are even worse off. The practice of placing children in confinement with adult offenders begins when a child is arrested. If the offense is serious, a youth can be jailed with adults while awaiting court proceedings. The practice of integrating youth offenders into the general prison population continues after sentencing. "In a 1997 to 1998 survey of state adult correctional systems undertaken by Amnesty International, forty states reported that they house children in the general population and had more than 3,700 children in custody. Twelve states (including some in the previous group) reported that they house children with inmates up to age twenty-one and there were nearly 2,000 children in this situation."[27] Many juveniles imprisoned with adults are afforded no special treatment when behind bars. In the twelve years between 1985 and 1997, juvenile offenders sent to state prisons more than doubled. In an exacerbation of an already serious problem, the actual offenses for which juveniles were sent to adult facilities became less serious. Instead of reserving imprisonment with adults for crimes that mandate adult penalties, the incidence of nonviolent juveniles in adult prisons continues to increase.[28]

The decision to incarcerate youth offenders with adult criminals is a state choice, and no federal guidelines declare the practice illegal. The reasons for the integration of adult and juvenile offenders vary. For instance, violent crime in certain regions will transfer a juvenile from youth courts to adult courts, and any youth offender sentenced by an adult court judge will automatically be sent to adult prison facilities. On the other hand, in smaller rural areas, jurisdictions might not have the funding or need for juvenile facilities, and any minor convicted of a crime and sentenced to detention will have to be integrated into an adult penal institution.

But, the consequences of the assimilation of youths into adult prison facilities are detrimental to the children. Youths are likely to become targets for bigger, stronger, more violent adult offenders. If they miraculously survive adult prison physically unscathed, juvenile delinquents will carry knowledge gained from the more experienced offenders. The practice of juvenile detention falls short of the stated goals of the juvenile justice system. Confinement in substandard conditions with abusive staff or integration into adult populations will not aid the youth in learning to abide by the law.

The incorporation of youth offenders into adult prisons brings to light another major issue in American juvenile justice, the problem of discrimination based on race and gender. Males have a greater likelihood of receiving an incarceration sentence than female delinquents, even when studies have matched offenders of both genders for seriousness of crime and any past deviance.[29] But the differentiation in treatment based on race is much worse than the divergence between male and female sentencing. In the late 1990s, three-fourths of juveniles sent to adult prisons were minorities, and almost 100 percent of those juveniles were male.[30]

The Amnesty International report supports the conclusion that sentencing in American juvenile courts is inherently racist. It states that black males make up less than one-fifth of the total juvenile population, but account for half of all cases sent to criminal court and two-fifths of the children detained in juvenile facilities across the nations. Including other minorities only aggravates the statistics. Overall, minority children account for three-fifths of the juvenile detention population, while they make up less than one-third of the American youth population.[31] Racial discrimination, the penchant to imprison children with adults, and the abuse that occurs in such facilities are rapidly worsening problems of the American juvenile justice system.

CANADA

Canada has set a uniform national age at which juveniles can be held criminally responsible as well as an age at which juvenile offenders can be prosecuted as adults. Like its southern neighbor, Canada's statutory definition of criminal responsibility is much lower than the United Nations charter and other international standards demand. In 1984, Canada passed the Young Offenders Act into law because of a rise in juvenile delinquency. The stated goal of the act is to provide some interventions, albeit without the use of criminal sanctions, to deal with children who commit crimes below the age of criminal responsibility: "Those [offenders] under the age of twelve who commit crimes cannot be prosecuted and must be dealt with under the child welfare and mental health laws."[32]

In the mid-1990s, an investigating committee was intending to recommend to the Canadian government that the age of criminal responsibility be lowered to ten. Apparently, a number of incidents across the nation led to the movement. These include "the gang rape of a young Toronto girl led by an eleven-year-old who allegedly proclaimed 'you can't arrest me, I'm not twelve yet.'"[33] While debate ensued regarding whether children under twelve years of age could be liable for their crimes, the most recent amendments to the Young Offender's Act, in the form of the New Youth Criminal Justice Act, have left the age of criminal responsibility at twelve. The latest version of juvenile justice was proposed in 1999 and came into effect in 2003.[34]

The Young Offenders Act includes other provisions besides the age of criminal responsibility. According to Section 16 of the Act, youths can be tried in adult court if they meet the following prerequisites: "(1) The youth must be at least 14 years old at the time of the alleged offense. (2) The crime must have been a serious indictable offense such as murder, manslaughter, armed robbery, break and enter, or sexual assault."[35] Like the United States, Canada allows for the type of offense to lower the age at which a juvenile can be prosecuted as an adult. When crimes committed by juveniles do not involve any of the above-listed offenses, the children between twelve and seventeen are under the authority of the juvenile court.[36]

Canada instituted a separate juvenile justice system only shortly before the United States. In 1893, the federal government instituted *parens patriae*, which, as in America, affords a child legal proceedings that are supposed to include parties concerned with the rights of the child. In the same year, the nation guaranteed that juveniles would be processed through a separate juvenile system that expects that the state will join the court in working on behalf of the youth, rather than treating the court as an adversarial proceeding.[37] For almost a century, the juvenile court in Canada remained a separate and distinct proceeding from the adult criminal trial. Juveniles in conflict with the law were expected to be surrounded by concerned adults, including their attorneys, the attorneys for the state, and the trier of fact, all of whom would be invested in working together to set the child back onto the right path in the hopes of averting a life of crime at an early age.

But, the rise in crime in Canada had revolutionary impacts on the juvenile court system. As in America, the goals of the juvenile justice system shifted, and while some juveniles remained in the juvenile court, others were transferred into adult proceedings, and in both locales, children were treated as criminals. Instead of investigating the root of the problem, or questioning what in the youth's life was leading him to crime, Canada shifted the purpose of its policy. The 1999 New Youth Criminal Justice Act states the new ideologies of the youth justice system: "The principles also say that protection of society is the primary objective of the youth justice system and is best achieved through prevention, meaningful consequences for youth crime (in proportion to the seriousness of the offence) and rehabilitation and social reintegration."[38]

While the preamble mentions rehabilitation of youths as a goal, it does so only after the original goal of protection of society. The juvenile court supposedly remains invested in the betterment of juvenile offenders, yet instead of assigning it as the primary purpose, Canada elevates the needs of the rest of society to a higher standing. This shift in goals limits the ability of the juvenile justice system to ascertain explanations for an individual juvenile's delinquent behavior. Other factors in a juvenile's life that might lead to crime have become less important, while the consequences for minors convicted of crimes is now the primary purpose of the juvenile court.

The change in name of the amended legislation indicates the criminalizing inclination of the Canadian juvenile court system. Over a century ago, Canada promised their troubled youth separate protections in an attempt to limit criminal action against children. The upsurge of public opinion has altered their laws, and added the terms "criminal justice" to youths who are only supposed to be subjected to limited justice procedures.

The rise and fall of youth crime over the past few decades in Canada mirrors the American statistics, which the government describes as the reasons for the new legislation. According to government-compiled data, "the overall youth crime rate is declining. Between 1991 and 1997, the charge rate for young people dropped from 643 to 495 per 10,000 youth in the population—a 23 percent decrease, mostly in property crimes. However, the rate of young people charged with violent crimes increased over this same period from 83 to 91 per 10,000 youth."[39] Like America, the shift in goals of the juvenile courts is based on a rise in juvenile crime, particularly violent offenses, leading Canada to abandon the original tenets of the juvenile court system with the New Youth Criminal Justice Act.

Another difference between the 1999 amendments and the previous Youth Offenders Act are the statutory requirements to transfer youths to adult courts for certain crimes. The provisions include adult sentencing and adult proceedings for an offense that can be punished with two or more years in jail, at the discretion of the court.[40] In both Canada and the United States, a legal juvenile court system instituted in the late nineteenth and early twentieth century remains physically intact. Yet the underlying goals of the separate institution have shifted from attempting to understand outside factors leading a child toward crime to stricter punishments, guidelines, more liability, and an overall objective to protect society.

The Canadian legislature has also taken similar steps to America in the shifts in allocation of juvenile rights when in conflict with the law. The juvenile law includes an entire section on the right to counsel, stating numerous times that a delinquent has a right to an attorney at all stages of contact with the justice system, including any contact with police. The right to counsel is initially stated by whichever authority first comes into contact with the youth: "Every young person who is arrested or detained shall, forthwith on his arrest or detention, be advised by the arresting officer or the officer in charge, as the case may be, of his right to be represented by counsel and shall be given an opportunity to obtain counsel."[41]

Canadian law also requires that any youth who is unable to afford an attorney will be provided one by the state. In addition, while the youth is afforded the option to waive his right to counsel, he must be reinformed of his right at any hearing or meeting with authorities. Youth offenders are also given the option by the juvenile court judge to allow any alternate adult deemed suitable to advise them during proceedings if they choose to waive their right to counsel.[42] While changes in juvenile law in the past few decades are generally looked upon as a reflection of the shift in the Canadian justice system toward a more punitive juvenile justice, the right to counsel continues to be an important support for children in conflict with the law.

But, in regard to the privacy of juveniles and the right to keep all proceedings closed to the public, the Young Offenders Act mirrored the latest trends in American law. While the law stipulates that for most matters all hearings shall be private and no information regarding a juvenile can be released, the Canadian legislature has added a number of exceptions. For instance, a judge can order that information about the defendant be released if "there is reason to believe that the young person is dangerous to others."[43] Critics of the legislation feel that the alteration in the previously absolute right to shield the juvenile from the public eye will be detrimental to the rehabilitation of offenders. The latest amendments to the law altered the juvenile's right to privacy only slightly. The new law permits "the publication of names of: (i) all youth who receive an adult sentence; (ii) fourteen- to seventeen-year-olds given a youth sentence for murder, manslaughter, aggravated sexual assault or repeat serious violent offenses, unless a judge decides to maintain publication ban based on rehabilitation and public interest considerations."[44] While the amendments continue to allow for judicial discretion, many children convicted of serious and adult crimes are often responding to unstable environments, and the notion that those children will be further outcast from society and labeled as delinquents is not a step toward rehabilitation.

On the other hand, the Young Offenders Act continues to protect the privacy of children by keeping all proceedings closed to the public. According to Section 39, "the court or justice may exclude any person from all or part of the proceedings if the court or justice deems that person's presence to be unnecessary to the conduct of the proceedings."[45] The amendments to the law have not altered this practice, and the nation continues to recognize the importance of the right of privacy of the offender during proceedings. Anyone who does not have a viable and dedicated interest in the life of the offender or in the crime cannot be present.

The Young Offenders Act also includes resolutions that change the status of parental involvement in juvenile justice proceedings. The legislation requires that both police and the court notify parents and guardians by any means possible regarding the crime and circumstances of judicial proceedings. It is notable that while children in conflict with the law are experiencing a limitation of their rights to privacy and have had information released to the public for more serious crimes, their rights to stand alone in front of the judicial system are not recognized. While parental involvement can be helpful on the road to rehabilitation, it is interesting that the same juvenile will be treated as an adult in regard to one of their legal rights, yet treated as a child in terms of parental notification.

The transfer of information is not the only realm of required parental involvement. Canadian law leaves it to the discretion of the judge whether to force parents and alternate guardians to attend proceedings. Section 10 of the Young Offenders Act states: "Where a parent does not attend proceedings before a youth court in respect of a young person, the court may, if in its opinion the presence of the parent is necessary or in the best interest of the young person, by order in writing require the parent to attend at any stage of the proceedings."[46] While at times it is in the best interest of guardians to present themselves and participate in court proceedings, if a juvenile has the capacity to understand his or her crime and be subjected to judicial processes, an offender should also be afforded an amount of discretion as to whether his family should attend court proceedings. Basically, as the ideology of the Canadian juvenile justice system shifts toward a stricter outlook and the divide between treatment measures for youth and adult offenders shrinks, it is ironic that in regard to the rights of independence from parental figures, juvenile delinquents continue to be treated like children.

The similar rise in crime rates in the United States and Canada has led the neighboring nations to make analogous changes to juvenile rights when in conflict with the law. Both North American nations have begun to require parental involvement in the justice process and have altered the absolute right to privacy of an offender, previously considered an integral tenet of juvenile rehabilitation. At the same time, the right to counsel, at least in the written law, remains an imperative part of the experience of a juvenile charged with a criminal offense.

Canada's punishment ideology used to lead to different outcomes from the decisions of American juvenile judges in regard to youth sentences. First, the decision to detain youth offenders occurred much less frequently. In the timeframe between 1997 and 1998, a little less than half of juvenile dispositions included some form of probation, and less than one-fifth of offenders were placed in any kind of detention. Other possible sanctions were similar to the United States, including fines and service to the community. At times, Canadian judges incorporate more than one measure together. For instance, a youth on probation could also be required to either pay a fine or provide community service.[47]

Like the United States, the use of incarceration as a response to the rise in crime increased recently, and presently Canada has one of the highest rates of juvenile imprisonment in the world. The increase in custodial sentences is unacceptable, but Canada has made some improvement by combining detention with shorter punishments.[48] The rise in crime initially triggered an upsurge in juvenile incarceration, but hopefully, the latest amendments to juvenile justice legislation will return to a trend of limiting the use of incarceration. The committee debating the New Youth Criminal Justice Act, coming into effect in 2003, recognized that penalties relying on detention were not the type of guidelines they were looking to institute.[49]

Also, like the United States, children in Canada can be transferred to adult court based on the seriousness and violence of their actions. However, any child facing an adult criminal judge cannot be sanctioned with the same punishments that adult criminals face. For instance, a youth accused of a crime that carries an adult sentence of twenty years to life has his sentence limited to a much shorter maximum imprisonment sentence.[50]

Canada differentiates in sentencing based on the gender of the juvenile offender. In a longitudinal study, researchers found that between 1986 and 1993, the incarceration of female youths has remained the same, but for male juveniles the number has risen from approximately one-quarter of the offense population to one-third.[51]

One of the motivating factors in implementing the changes to the Young Offenders Act with the introduction of the New Youth Criminal Justice Act was the lack of federal guidelines in sentencing, coupled with the overuse of custodial sentences for nonviolent and less serious crimes. For instance, the Canadian Department of Justice released information claiming that the rate of youth incarceration exceeded the rate of imprisoned adults. While the above-mentioned statistics are still the norm and the new legislation came into effect in 2003, the legislative change provides juvenile judges with a distinct sentencing outline that will alter the way in which juvenile offenders are punished. The goal of the additions to Canadian juvenile law is to give more definitive guidelines to juvenile judges so that discretion and the circumstances of the individual case have less influence. The new law has a goal of striking a balance between competing concerns; juveniles will be punished for their actions and learn to take responsibility for their crimes, but at the same time, rehabilitation will be key in their transformation into law-abiding citizens.[52]

In regard to custodial detention, the new legislation specifies requirements that judges must follow. For instance, the offense must be violent and the juvenile must have a history that includes a pattern of offenses. If a judge declares that the circumstances of a crime are exceptional and the only applicable sentence must be detention, jurists are required to provide explanations as to why they came to their decision. Finally, while alternate sentences are generally less punitive, this legislation has made it clear that even detention must be rehabilitative. A youth cannot be sentenced only to detention, but must also have a period of community supervision upon his release. The underlying reasoning behind this decision supports the legislative goal that all measures must be rehabilitative in some form. It is left to the discretion of the judge as to which segment of the sentence will involve custody and which will be completed while free.[53]

In addition to using custodial detention as a last resort, Canadian legislators have strengthened rules so that juveniles in detention will never be detained with adult offenders. Unlike the United States, the Canadian government is dedicated to making juvenile detention both an educational and safe experience. The summary of the new legislation holds as one of its major principles that juveniles must always be detained separately from adults. This rule applies throughout the justice system. For instance, juvenile offenders who reach the age of adulthood in a juvenile facility, but still have time to serve, must be transferred to adult prisons for the protection of the younger juvenile offender.[54]

NOTES

1. Office of Juvenile Justice and Delinquency Prevention. *Trying Juveniles As Adults in Criminal Court: An Analysis of State Transfer Provisions.* Washington, D.C.: U.S. Government, December 1998. [Online]. Available: http:ojjdp.ncrjs.org/pubs/tryingjuvasadult/table8.htm.

2. McCord, Joan, Cathy Spatz Widom, and Nancy A. Cromwell, eds. *Juvenile Crime, Juvenile Justice: Panel on Juvenile Crime: Prevention, Treatment and Control.* Washington, D.C.: National Academy Press, 2001.

3. McCord et al., 207.

4. McCord et al., 209.

5. Field, Barry C. *Juvenile Justice Administration: In a Nut Shell.* Minneapolis, Minnesota: West Group, 2003, 1.

6. McCord et al., 157.

7. Field, 7.

8. Field, 16.

9. Office of Justice Programs, U. S. Department of Justice. "National Survey of Prosecutors, 1994: Juveniles Prosecuted in State Criminal Courts." March 1997. [Online] 30 Oct. 2002. Available: http://www.ojp.usdoj.gov/bjs/pub/ascii/jpscc.txt.

10. Strom, Kevin J., Steven K. Smith, and Howard N. Snyder. "Juvenile Felony Defendants in Criminal Courts: State Court Proceeding Statistics, 1990–1994." Office of Justice Systems, U.S. Department of Justice. September 1998. [Online] 30 Oct. 2002. Available: http://www.ojp.usdoj.gov/bjs/pub/ascii/jfdcc.txt.

11. McCord et al., 154.

12. Field, 276.

13. McCord et al., 166.

14. McCord et al., 212.

15. Field, 250.

16. McCord et al., 212.

17. McClintock, Tom. "Senate Public Safety Committee Approves McClintock's Parental Involvement Bill." Press release, 17 Jul. 1997. [Online]. Available: http://republican.sen.ca.gov/web/mcclintock/article_detail.asp?PID=127.

18. Lane, Charles. "Justices Spurn Case on Juvenile Executions: Action Suggests Five Back Current Laws." *The Washington Post*, 28 Jan. 2003.

19. "Juvenile Death Penalty Facts." Juvenile Justice Advisory Committee. 19 June 2002. [Online]. Available: http://www.jjac.state.ky.us/JDP_Facts.htm.

20. McCord et al., 154.

21. Field, 334.

22. McCord et al., 182.

23. Amnesty International. "Betraying the Young: Human Rights Violations against Children in the U.S. Justice System." New York: Amnesty International. November 1998.

24. McCord et al., 188.

25. "Betraying the Young," 19.

26. "Betraying the Young," 29.

27. "Betraying the Young," 39.

28. McCord et al., 220.

29. McCord et al., 204.

30. McCord et al., 220.

31. Betraying the Young," 57.

32. Bindham, Stephen. "Age of Criminal Responsibility to Go Down." *Southam Newspapers*, 18 April 1997. [Online]. 15 Oct. 2002. Available: http://web.amnesty.org/libary/Index/ENGAMR510571998?open&of=ENG-USA. Accessed March 24, 2004.

33. Bindham, 2.

34. Harris, David Allen. "A Layperson's Guide to the Young Offenders Act and the Youth Criminal Justice Act, 1999." Ontario, Canada. [Online]. Available: http://lawyers.ca/dharris/yoaycja.htm.

35. Goff, Colin, and Cindy Jarigan. "Criminal Justice in Canada." [Online]. Available: http://liad.gbrownc.on.ca/crime&punishment/hw13.htm.

36. Lescheid, Alan. "The Young Offenders Act in Review: A More than Modest Proposal for Change." *Young Offenders and Corrections*. [Online]. Volume 7, January 1995. Available: http:www.csc-scc.gc.ca/text/pblct/forum/e07/e071k_e.shtml.

37. Goff and Jarigan, 1.

38. "New Youth Criminal Justice Act: Canada." [Online]. Available: http://www.sen.parl.gc.ca/lpearson/htmfiles/hill/v16crim-e.htm.

39. "New Youth Criminal Justice Act: Canada," 1.

40. "New Youth Criminal Justice Act: Canada," 3.

41. Department of Justice–Canada. "Young Offenders Act." 31 Dec. 2001. [Online]. Available: http://laws.justice.gc.ca/en/Y-1/102804.html#rid-102884.

42. "Young Offenders Act."

43. "Young Offenders Act."

44. "New Youth Criminal Justice Act: Introduction." [Online] 2 Feb. 2003. Available: http://www.sen.parl.gc.ca/lpearson/htmfiles/hill/v16crim-e.htm.

45. "Young Offenders Act."

46. "Young Offenders Act."

47. Goff and Jarigan.

48. Alan.

49. Bindham, Stephen.

50. Winterdyk, John (ed.). 2002. *Juvenile Justice Systems: International Perspectives*, 2nd ed. Toronto: Canadian Scholars' Press Inc. P. 165.

51. Winterdyk, *Juvenile Justice Systems*, 156.

52. Department of Justice–Canada. "The Proposed Youth Criminal Justice Act: Summary and Background." 20 Dec. 2002. [Online] Available: http://Canada.justice.gc.ca/en/ps/yj/legis/explan.html.

53. "The Proposed Youth Criminal Justice Act: Summary and Background."

54. "The Proposed Youth Criminal Justice Act: Summary and Background."

3

South America

While previous decades in South American history have been plagued by violence, dictatorships, and military power, in recent years most of the continent has begun a trend toward democratic leadership. These changes have also led to the installation of modernized legal systems with statutory descriptions of criminal proceedings. Both Chile and Colombia are charter members of the United Nations, and both have been reviewed extensively by the Committee on the Rights of a Child.

CHILE

In Chile, "criminal law and procedure for adults can also be applied to children between the age of sixteen and eighteen who acted with discernment."[1] In addition, the minimum age of criminal responsibility "is specifically excluded in cases in which defendants are insane or less than ten years of age. The responsibility of minors ten to sixteen years of age is also excluded unless it can be proven that they acted with full understanding of their acts."[2] Basically, Chile operates its juvenile justice system through a three-tiered structure. The youngest offenders, those under the age of ten, can have no criminal responsibility. Between the ages of ten and sixteen, criminal responsibility is assigned to a child, but the prosecution has an additional burden of proof to show that the child understood his or her acts. If the child comprehends his or her crime and its implications, that child can be prosecuted by the juvenile justice system. Offenders between the ages of sixteen and eighteen can be legally prosecuted either as adults or children depending on the severity of their offense.

The Juvenile Act of 1967 specifically established juvenile courts in Chile to hear all civil and criminal cases involving juveniles. But, in 1994, a national representative admitted to a United Nations investigating committee that there were no established guidelines or procedures regarding a juvenile court. When one committee member asked the representative why a child facing a juvenile court would feel that the court was working for or against him, Chile's representative replied that the processing of a youth must be confusing to the minor. The lack of procedural rules allowed for decisions to vary extensively between jurisdictions and also depended on the individual adjudicator. In their defense, however, a number of social welfare workers were often present to ensure that the minor was treated properly.[3]

Unlike North America, which has debated the merits and objectives of the juvenile court system for over a century, Chile does not have a separate juvenile justice system. In reality, the only major difference between the juvenile court proceeding and the adult criminal proceeding is the age of the defendant. While the Chilean representative notes that when a juvenile faces a magistrate, a social worker and psychologist might be present, neither is a guarantee. Chile is in direct violation of international standards for the rights of a child by refusing to award them special legal treatment. While national legislation guaranteed a juvenile court over three decades ago, it has still not been implemented. The United Nations reprimanded Chile's lack of distinct juvenile courts in the same 1994 meeting. The Committee does not directly request the institution of a juvenile court, but they do recommend that, "further measures should be taken to promote public awareness of the Convention, including special information programmes for children and suitable training for all those responsible for taking decisions relating to the rights of the child."[4]

Since their first encounter with the United Nations, Chile has made various legislative alterations in an attempt to form a separate judicial system for juvenile offenders. In 2002, Chile presented its Second Periodic Report to the Committee on the Rights of the Child, including changes that the government is pursuing. First, a "national plan for children" has been implemented. In all thirteen of the regions in Chile, regional children's plans have been established with a centralized coordinating office to oversee that each locale effectively enforces the rights of juveniles. Finally, the nation has implemented a "Network of Municipalities for Children."[5] While each of the new programs creates a structure in which a juvenile court could succeed, nothing in the report mentions the implementation of a distinct juvenile justice system.

In regard to the legal rights of youths, Chile continues to operate its juvenile justice system under the Juvenile Act, passed in 1967. In a report to the United Nations, Chile contends that it does not afford minors any particular protections that are not allocated to adults when in conflict with the law. "The Constitution does not contain any provisions specifically applicable to minors. One may therefore conclude that the guarantees and rules laid down therein are applicable to all individuals, whether adults or minors."[6] In this regard, it is noted that the Chilean Constitution requires the right to legal defense for juvenile and adult offenders. In addition, the Constitution requires that those who cannot afford an attorney will be provided one free of charge.[7]

But, the Chilean government contradicts itself in the United Nation's report. National authorities claimed that all rights provided to adults would also be given to minors in the same situation, including the right to defense. Shortly thereafter, the report states the following:

> As regards appearance, a minor does not require legal counsel when appearing before a juvenile judge; but there is no obligation on the part of the judge to hear the minor before making his decision. At the same time, the Minors Act does not contemplate the possibility of the designation of counsel by the minor to defend him before a juvenile judge; likewise, it contains no specific rules permitting a minor charged with an offence to give a judicial mandate. However, the amendment to the CCP introduced in 1989 authorizes the judge to appoint a lawyer or solicitor to a minor under age eighteen who has none.[8]

While the recent amendment allows the judiciary to appoint a defense attorney, it does not appear that it is a guaranteed right to minors. In a comparison of rights, children are worse off than their adult counterparts. Adult offenders have a higher level of maturity that allows them to comprehend court proceedings, but child offenders arrive in court often knowing less about the legal process and simultaneously are denied additional protections. The lack of legal counsel puts juvenile delinquents at a serious disadvantage. In addition, when refusing to guarantee legal aid to any citizen in conflict with the law, Chile is in violation of both its own Constitution and international standards on human rights.

Chile somewhat reverses the implications that a child is not guaranteed defense by allowing parental involvement in court proceedings to include the right to exercise legal privileges for the accused offender. Amendments to the Code of Criminal Procedure in 1989, "permit a minor under age eighteen to conduct his own case in criminal proceedings, stipulating that the rights of the accused may be exercised by his parents or guardians; if they do not do so the judge may appoint defence counsel following the investigation stage. This rule should be considered as an option open to both the parents and the judge; but it does not overrule the principle that the minor may act on his own behalf."[9]

Thus, Chile looks at the right to defense as a choice needed to be given to the defendant, but reserves the right for the judge and parents to override the youth's decision in this matter. But, it still seems that children should be required to have legal aid throughout all criminal proceedings. If a child faces a juvenile judge instead of the criminal court because he has shown a limited ability to comprehend his actions, then should not the child also be guaranteed counsel because of his limited capacity to under the legal process? It is important, however, that parents are expected to help the minor in their coordination. While they are not obligated to be present or play a role in the judicial process, they do have the right to become actively involved in the case.

Finally, neither the original Juvenile Act of 1967 nor the reports to the United Nations discuss whether juvenile hearings can be closed to the public. While the reports state that all protections guaranteed in the Constitution are reserved for juveniles as well, the Constitution makes no reference to whether criminal trials must be public. The juvenile justice system has been in place for many decades, but the Constitution only came into force in 1986. Political upheavals and a violent past have forced the nation toward a democratic government that demands human rights and civil liberties. But the process is slow, and who should be given access to court proceedings, particularly when they are not an involved party, is an issue that remains undecided.

Juvenile punishment in Chile has been the subject of reports by government studies, the media, and independent organizations. Interestingly, each description of the plight of juvenile offenders is quite different from the other investigations. The United Nations initially expressed concern in their final statement to Chile regarding the changes they would like to see the government make to further align national law with the Convention on the Rights of the Child. In 2002, the Committee claimed unhappiness with the use of detention, particularly because it was more often utilized for children of lower economic status. In addition, the United Nations was displeased that Chile continued to hold youths in adult prisons.[10]

While the Chilean government does not deny the allegation that juveniles are sent to prison, the supervisor of the national prison service stated that most juveniles serving sentences are not actually imprisoned. In response to a government inquiry, "Prison Guards Director Hugo Espinoza responded Monday, saying only 9 percent of the 35,727 juveniles currently fulfilling their sentence outside of jails are under the prison system's jurisdiction. This group includes prisoners who are on conditional freedom or day release. Espinoza said 91 percent of nonjailed criminals are sentenced by judges to alternative measures such as conditional remission, supervised freedom and night imprisonment, which are merely supervised by the prison system."[11] Though the United Nations is concerned with the number of children in detention, Mr. Espinoza makes it seem as if children that are on probation and sentenced to community service are part of the prison service on paper, but in reality are not detained.

But, an American Department of State report found that the United Nations was not incorrect in their criticism, both because of the sheer number of juvenile offenders imprisoned with adults and the decision to build more juvenile detention centers. The integration of youth offenders with adult prisoners is a violation of Chilean law as well as international standards regarding methods of punishment. The United States' representatives found the numbers of juveniles in adult facilities had decreased significantly between 1992 and 1998, but still remained a problem. However, the Chilean government had committed to dealing with lack of space by building three new juvenile facilities.[12]

Almost ten years before the release of this report, the Chilean government passed a number of resolutions that they would limit the number of juveniles detained with adult offenders. In their initial report to the United Nations Committee on the Rights of the Child, authorities noted that they had formulated local and wider-level organizations whose sole purpose was to get juveniles out of adult prisons. These organizations then are required to take on partial responsibility for the juvenile offender, and are expected to make alternate recommendations to judicial bodies for placing juveniles that do not include any form of custody.[13]

Chile, however, never accomplished their goal. Instead, years later, the nation continues to build more prisons for the juvenile delinquent population, claiming that juvenile offenders had begun a trend toward violent crime. The "dangerous" younger criminals had led the nation to heighten security through staff training and implementing new technology into already established facilities. In addition, national authorities planned to complete approximately five new jails in the upcoming years.[14] Apparently, the previous commitment to alternative forms of sentencing is no longer a priority.

In a reflection of their penchant for imprisonment, Chile also employs detention centers for juvenile offenders that are reserved for youths under the age of fifteen. These centers are run by the National Minors Service and in the late 1990s had approximately two hundred detainees.[15] While the separation of some youth offenders from adult criminals is an improvement, a study of the juvenile detention centers demonstrates that they are not child friendly. Like an adult prison, security is tight, and the institution is significantly overcrowded. Independent media representatives visited *Tiempo Jovien* (Time for Youth), an institution located twenty miles south of Santiago. They found tight security, locked gates, and staffers carrying weapons. Worse, the capacity of the facility was exceeding by double the number of youths it was meant to hold.[16]

The Chilean government should consider the root of the problem of juvenile delinquency and attempt to rehabilitate their youth rather than allow their prison population to grow. The national juvenile justice system seems little concerned with the betterment of youth offenders. Instead, courts sentence youth to prison terms, which are often served with adult criminals. When children are lucky enough to be placed in detention centers reserved solely for youths, the conditions are substandard, and retain a semblance to imprisonment, rather than places of education and rehabilitation.

COLOMBIA

Colombia's legal policy is quite different than Chile's. Colombia enacted the Code for Minors in 1990. The Human Rights Watch described it as "a model of progressive thinking on children's rights, stressing rehabilitation rather than punishment for juvenile delinquents."[17] As one of the few countries in the world to enact the standards of the United Nations, Colombia lists the official minimum age of criminal responsibility as eighteen.[18] This number is usually applied to the age in which children can be prosecuted as adults. In actuality, Colombia holds children much younger responsible for their actions, but continues to prosecute them under the juvenile justice system regardless of offense, rather than transferring the offender to adult courts. The Annual Report of the Inter-American Commission on Human Rights, 1991, stated in regard to Colombia that, "minors aged twelve to eighteen are brought before juvenile courts each year for criminal offenses."[19] While twelve is a young age for a child to be held responsible for his or her criminal actions, Colombia has instilled safeguards that allow a youth to remain in the juvenile system until at least eighteen years of age. Thus, youths are minimally responsible for their actions, but Colombia's laws should be altered to reflect that the true age of criminal responsibility is twelve.

One particular issue uniquely plagues Colombia in regard to the age of criminal responsibility. Colombia has had a history of rebellion and insurgency that continues through the present. The use of children as soldiers is rampant; fighting forces kidnap children and force them into military servitude, often sacrificing the youngsters in battle before the adults. Colombia has faced the issue of how to prosecute these child soldiers and whether to hold them accountable for their actions. In 2001, the United Nations Office on Coordination of Human Affairs released a report stating:

> In Colombia, children captured from guerilla forces are considered to be in breach of the law since membership of armed oppositions groups is a major crime for adults and children alike. Following discussions with child protec-

tion and other agencies, the Colombian government acknowledged that criminalizing children for their involvement in fighting forces was hindering efforts to secure boys' and girls' release and getting in the way of their reintegration. . . . A decree has been proposed that, if passed, would allow children to leave fighting forces without being prosecuted.[20]

Colombia has furthered their goal of protecting the rights of children by deciding that all minors are not to be held accountable for war crimes. The nation effectively recognizes, in compliance with United Nation's standards, that children under the age of eighteen are often brainwashed and abused into becoming warriors. Following the inclination in their statutory definitions of children who have committed regular delinquent acts, Colombia has made the status of children at war much different than that of adult fighters.

Colombia, despite its war-torn history, surprisingly has made considerable advances in relation to juvenile courts. In 1989, Decree Laws 2737 and 2272 were enacted specifically to install judicial systems to handle any juvenile issues. The decrees include the "creation of the office of Special Attorney for Protection of Minors and Family, the specialized Family Jurisdiction Agency . . . [and] Family, Juvenile, and Errant Children Court in Colombia's major municipalities."[21] The juvenile courts are separate and distinct from adult criminal courts, with special additional actors who are required to help the jurist decide how to decide each case. Juvenile care officers are attached to each court, and study the background of each child to advise the court on how to act in the best interest of the child.[22]

In addition, while other nations in the region lack any form of juvenile court, Columbia has taken additional steps and created additional juvenile courts to deal with the younger range of children that commit criminal offenses. Colombian offenders between twelve and eighteen are seen by a juvenile court. These children appear before a special children's judge and a *defensor* that takes into account any abuse, neglect, or other factors when deciding what to do with the child. In 1964, Colombia formed the Council for the Social Protection of Minors and Their Families, specifically designating that the Minors Division of the Ministry of Justice will be responsible for all criminal offenses committed by a child under the age of twelve.[23]

It is important to note that Colombian law does not state that the goals of their juvenile courts are to revolve around punishment. Columbia adopted the policies of the United States and Canada from a century ago; they want a juvenile judiciary that will act more like a social welfare system than a criminal court. But what later occurred in the North American region is beginning to transpire in Colombia. While on paper the national policy regarding juvenile courts sounds wonderful, the system has not been functioning well. Colombia faces the serious dilemma of poverty when attempting to treat juvenile offenders as youths in need, rather than as criminals. According to a Human Rights Watch report, "the number of troubled children far exceeds state resources made available to them. Of its 5,000 staff members, IBCF [Colombian Institute for Family Welfare] employs only 350 child *defensores*. Divided among them, that means each worker has a caseload of over 20,000 children. Cali, a city of over one million, relies on four child *defensores*."[24]

In addition, juvenile crime rates are increasing. "The number of children over twelve brought to trial has tripled over the past decade, most charged with robbery or theft . . . the release of juvenile delinquents who have committed serious or repeat crimes is explicitly prohibited. . . . However, *defensores* and child advocates told Human Rights Watch/Americas that these releases are everyday occurrences because there are no facilities to accommodate the children."[25] While the paper policy at present remains the same in Colombia, it will not be surprising if both the rising crime rate and lack of staff lead to a more penal-oriented juvenile court system.

Colombia's poverty and long-standing war have done much to affect the status of children in the nation. In an attempt to improve the standards of living for Colombian citizens, the government has passed legislation placing them in compliance with international standards on human rights. Both the integration of the Convention of the Rights of the Child into law and the passage of the 1991 Code for Minors ensures sound policy that affords children the right to representation and a trial closed to the public. The Inter-American Commission on Human Rights claims that "the main international instrument that specifically governs the rights of the child is the Convention on the Rights of the Child, adopted by the United Nations in 1989, and ratified by Colombia on January 28, 1991."[26]

In general, the goals of the Colombian Constitution reflect those of an open, democratic society. Originally, legal and political rights were adopted from the French Declaration of the Rights of Man in 1789, translated from French to Spanish by Antonio Narino. The present Constitution reflects the same rights of all Colombian citizens, both adult and children. In regard to due process and conflict with the law, "everyone is presumed innocent until proven guilty. Criminal defendants enjoy the right to a defense, a public trial and a publicly appointed lawyer or one of their own choosing, during the investigation and trial stages of criminal proceedings."[27] Thus, both the adopted international laws as well as the national legislation embodies the goals of human rights protections for centuries, forging a system that holds that representation must be provided for anyone in conflict with the law and that all defendants are innocent until proven guilty.

But, a number of human rights organizations have noted that the policies regarding human rights are only present on paper. In reality, the rights of children and adults in conflict with the law are often ignored. A 1994 Human Rights Watch report opens its section regarding the Code of Minors by stating, "Within Colombia, the newly revised Constitution of 1991 is often referred to as a beautifully conceived and written document that has little to do with the way rights are actually treated. Much the same can be said of the Code for Minors."[28] The Inter-American Commission on Human Rights agrees, stating, "On the contrary, Colombia has a sound and broad international and national legislative structure that establishes detailed protective measures concerning the rights of the child. The problem is that, in practice, this series of norms is not applied to the actual situation of most children in Colombia."[29]

Whether due to the constant state of war in Colombia, including major drug trafficking issues and guerilla rebels, or the total corruptness of the governing body itself, the rights guaranteed by Colombian law to children in conflict with the law are often ignored. For instance, one Colombian citizen witnessed a vicious beating of a minor by the police. He claims he saw four policemen attack a youth that was not more than seventeen years old. The youth was obviously a street child. The authorities used their nightsticks to inflict pain on the child.[30] The basic rights of due process supposedly guaranteed under Colombian law were blatantly ignored in this scene. The child never faces a judge, is not provided with an attorney, and most importantly is never given the opportunity to prove his innocence. He is mercilessly abused in a manner completely out of bounds of Colombian law.

In reference to the rights of parental involvement, Colombia faces a unique situation in regard to children's contact and relationship with their parents. There is no documentation in written law for either the requirement of involvement of relatives in the judicial processes of a minor, but it is possible that this could be a reaction to the many children in the nation who are without parental figures. The years of war have caused both the deaths of many parents as well as the separation of a number of minors from their families. The numbers of children living on the streets and committing crimes so that they have enough food to eat are staggering. The Inter-American Commission for Human Rights claims, "There are a large number of children in Colombia who make the streets their permanent home, and many more who roam the streets by day and return home at night."[31] The lack of parent-child connection in Colombia explains the absence of any legislation regarding parental involvement in juvenile justice. If most of the street children in contact with the juvenile court come from dysfunctional families, it makes little sense to require parents to participate in court processes when they are absent for much of the rest of the juvenile's life.

A number of international rights organizations have investigated Colombia's juvenile justice system, particularly in light of the nation's ongoing lack of resources. If one were only to investigate the stated policies of the government, it would appear that Colombia is making great strides in helping young offenders. The underlying ideal of juvenile law is presented in the Code for Minors, which elevates rehabilitation over punishment for offenders. Instead of jailing delinquent youth, the government stresses the importance of treatment, possibly through specialized support systems or even placement with a new family.

But the Human Rights Watch was quite discouraged by what they encountered on a 1991 visit to juvenile treatment centers. It is not an act of malevolence that leads juvenile authorities to place youths in custody. Recently, the numbers of youths charged with crimes has tripled. The social workers are impeded in all decisions, because it is forbidden to simply release a convicted juvenile. On the other hand, all of the treatment options have been exhausted. The foster homes are filled, as are the nation's few treatment facilities. *Defensores* must make the choice to release the youth illegally or place them in detention, even if their actions do not merit such punishment.[32]

Although the state of juvenile justice is in disarray, the obstacles to a better system are not lack of desire to make change, but rather a lack of resources to make the changes. This is evident from the scene researchers found at the few existing juvenile treatment centers. The Human Rights Watch learned that children in both of the visited treatment centers regularly go to classes and therapeutic sessions. They are also allowed visits with their family and are taught skills for various types of employment. Instead of remaining with the center for a fixed time, youths are constantly examined by experienced staff to determine whether they have made any advances and are ready for release. Both international and domestic human rights organizations have praised the conditions in the available Colombian facilities.[33]

A viable explanation for the lack of resources to expand this type of treatment center is the long-term civil war that has plagued the nation. Even after children have been separated from soldiers that have forcibly recruited them and sent to treatment centers, youths continue to face risks to their lives. A 2000 Human Rights Watch report regarding children in armed conflict declared that authorities often illegally release child soldiers for their protection. While national law expects that youths in the war should be imprisoned to limit the rebellion and rehabilitate the youth, children have the added risk of harm in custody from opposing militia groups. In the mid-1990s, over one-tenth of child soldiers were killed in custody by guerillas. Thus, children are clandestinely released for their own protection.[34] The unique situation of long-term war that involves the use of children as soldiers has impacted the sentencing practices of the juvenile justice system.

For the United Nations, however, the ongoing war and lack of resources is no longer acceptable as an excuse for the deplorable state of Colombia's rehabilitation method. In a 2000 statement, the Committee on the Rights of the Child expressed concern about the extensive use of detention for juvenile offenders and the lack of finite sentences, instead leaving terms of punishment up to staff at a juvenile facility. The Committee is also unhappy with the few possibilities for disposition other than confinement, like community service and probation.[35] Colombia has a written policy that supports rehabilitative sentences for juvenile offenders and treatment, but the actuality of juvenile punishment is much harsher. Although Colombia has ratified the Convention on the Rights of the Child, children continue to be detained in large numbers and with adult criminals, issues that international standards have strictly prohibited.

Finally, Colombian police play a role in informally "punishing" children they have detained without any court involvement. The stories of abuse at the hands of authorities are deplorable. The Human Rights Watch report stated, "Although Article 170 of the Code for Minors stipulates that children can only be held in police stations under rare and exceptional circumstances, and must be put at the disposition of the defensor or the children's judge immediately, many children told us that they continue to be detained for extended periods in police cells, where they are tortured."[36]

The combination of war, poverty and lack of resources, and overall turmoil has left Colombia with a corrupt system of justice. Children must be released from detention for fear that other children will kill them, and police viciously abuse children without ever knowing if they are guilty of criminal action. While the policy of the Code for Minors and the ideal of treatment and rehabilitation are virtuous, the lack of adhesion to the law is appalling.

NOTES

1. Committee on the Rights of the Child. "Concluding Observations: Chile." [Online] 4 Mar. 2002. United Nations Publications. Available: http://www.un.org/News/Press/docs/2002/hr4578.doc.htm.

2. "Chile Criminal Justice." March 1994. [Online] Available: http:www.law.monash.edu/au/humanrts/crc/chile2002.html.

3. United Nations Convention on the Rights of the Child. "Summary Record of the 148th Meeting: Chile." Geneva: 21 Apr. 1994. [Online]. Available: http://www.bayefsky.com/summary/chile_crc_c_sr.1481994.php.

4. "Summary Record of the 148th Meeting: Chile."

5. United Nations. "Chile Presents Second Periodic Report to Committee on Rights of the Child." Press release, 23 Jan. 2002. [Online]. Available: http://www .unog.ch/news2/documents/newsen/crc0211e.htm.

6. United Nations Convention on the Rights of the Child. "Consideration of Reports Submitted by State Parties Under Article 44 of the Convention: Chile." 10 Oct. 1999. [Online].Available:http://www.unhchr.ch/tbs/doc.nsf/385c 2add1632f4a8c1265a900dc311/3310335d79a77a89c1256b49004ea93e/$FILE/G0 142913.doc.

7. "Consideration of Reports Submitted by State Parties Under Article 44 of the Convention: Chile."

8. "Consideration of Reports Submitted by State Parties Under Article 44 of the Convention: Chile."

9. "Consideration of Reports Submitted by State Parties Under Article 44 of the Convention: Chile."

10. "Consideration of Reports Submitted By State Parties: Concluding Observations of the Committee on the Rights of the Child: Chile Juvenile Justice." United Nations Convention on the Rights of the Child, 29th Session. 3 April 2002. [Online]. Available: http://www.hri.ca/fortherecord2002/documentation/tbodies/ crc-c-15-add173. htm. Accessed March 24, 2002.

11. "Prison Service Takes A Beating." CHIPS News Source: *World Reporter*. 23 Jul. 1999. [Online]. Westlaw. Available: http://web2.westlaw.com/search/ default.wl?RS=WLW2.84&VR=2.0&FN=_top&SV=Split&MT=Westlaw&DB= SANTIAGO.

12. Bureau of Democracy, Labor, and Human Rights. "Chile: Country Reports on Human Rights Practices 2001." United States Department of State. 23 Feb. 2001. [Online]. Available: http://www.state.gov/g/drl/rls/hrrpt/2000/wha/736.htm.

13. "Consideration of Reports Submitted By State Parties: Concluding Observations."

14. "Juvenile Delinquency on the Firing Line: Are More Jails Enough to Combat Youth Crime Rate?" CHIPS News Source. *World Reporter*. 27 Apr. 1999. [Online]. Westlaw. Available: http://web2.westlaw.com/search/default.wl? RS=WLW2.84&VR=2.0&SV=Split&FN=_top&MT=Westlaw&RecDB=SANTI-AGO&RFFrom=%2FDirectory%2FDefault%2Ewl.

15. "Juvenile Delinquency on the Firing Line."

16. "Chile's Forgotten Children: Young Offenders Lost in a Legal Jungle." *Le Monde Diplomatique*, Feb. 1999. [Online]. Available: http://burn.ucsd.edu/ archives/chiapas-l/1999.02/msg00215.html.

17. Human Rights Watch. "Columbia—Code for Minors." [Online]. Available: http://www.hrw.org/reports/1994/colombia/gener3.htm.

18. Partnership for Global Good Practice. "International Standards for Administration of Juvenile Justice and Examples of Good Practice." Feb. 2002. [Online]. Available: http://www.peterni.demon.nl/pggp/PGGP%20Juvenile%20Justice% 20Presentation.pdf.

19. Inter-American Commission on Human Rights. "Annual Report on Human Rights, 1991." Organization of American States. [Online]. Available: http://www.cidh.oas.org/annualrep/91eng/chap.6c.htm.

20. United Nations—Office on Coordination of Humanitarian Affairs. "Justice for Children in Fighting Forces." Chapter 11, Dec. 2001. [Online]. Available: http://www.releifweb.int/library/documents/2000/sc-eleven-dec01.pdf.

21. "Annual Report of the Inter-American Commission on Human Rights 1991." 14 Feb. 1992. [Online]. Available: http://www.cidh.oas.org/annualrep/91eng/chap.6c.htm.

22. "Annual Report of the Inter-American Commission on Human Rights," 2.

23. "Annual Report of the Inter-American Commission on Human Rights," 2.

24. Human Rights Watch. "Colombia: Code for Minors." 1994. [Online]. Available: http://www.hrw.org/reports/1994/gener3.htm.

25. "Colombia: Code For Minors," 3.

26. Inter-American Commission on Human Rights. "Third Report on the Human Rights Situation in Colombia—Chapter XIII: The Rights of the Child." Organization of American States. 26 Feb. 1999. [Online]. Available: http://www.cidh.oas.org/countryrep/Colom99en/chapter-13.htm.

27. Inter-American Commission on Human Rights. "Third Report on the Human Rights Situation in Colombia—Chapter II: Human Rights Protection in the Colombian Legal System." Organization of American States. 26 Feb. 1999. [Online]. Available: http://www.cidh.oas.org/countryrep/Colom99en/chapter-2.htm.

28. Human Rights Watch/Americas. "Generation Under Fire: Children and Violence in Colombia." Nov. 1994. [Online]. Available: http://www.hrw.org/reports/1994/colombia/gener3.htm.

29. "Third Report on the Human Rights Situation in Colombia—Chapter XIII: The Rights of the Child," 5.

30. "Generation Under Fire: Children and Violence in Colombia."

31. "Third Report on the Human Rights Situation in Colombia—Chapter XIII: The Rights of the Child," 19.

32. "Columbia—Code for Minors."

33. "Columbia—Code for Minors."

34. Children's Rights Division. "Colombia: Children Affected by Armed Conflict." New York: Human Rights Watch, 31 March 2000. [Online]. Available: http://www.crin.org/docs/resources/treaties/crc.25/colombiaNGOreport1.pdf.

35. "Colombia: Reports to Treat Bodies." United Nations Convention on the Rights of the Child. Jan. 2000. [Online]. Available: http://www.hri.ca/fortherecord2000/vol4/colombiatb.htm.

36. "Columbia—Code for Minors."

4

✛

Western Europe

The nations in this chapter, the United Kingdom, Ireland, France, Germany, and Sweden, have all made changes to their juvenile justice systems at similar times. For instance, the decision to enact legislation for separate juvenile court systems swept through Western Europe all at once, and was a result of major social and cultural changes. Industrialization and migration to the cities led to a limitation on parental control of children, many of whom were working in newly formed factories. The cultural changes, coupled with a newfound interest in social sciences, altered the attitudes toward juvenile offense from one of strict punishment to more of a social welfare approach.[1]

In the early twentieth century, juvenile courts were formed to insure that children in conflict with the law would be treated distinctively from adults in the same situation. The approach of the early 1900s called for a system that would allow for juvenile rehabilitation rather than imprisonment with little chance of reintegration into society. The similar histories and growing connections between the nations in the region explain the parallel choices. On the other hand, subtle differences can be noted in the way that the nations of the regions handle a youth offender.

UNITED KINGDOM

The United Kingdom, a nation with liberal laws and less violence than other countries, has an extremely low age of criminal responsibility. British legislation defines criminal responsibility as the age at which youths can understand what the implications of their actions are, and can be prosecuted.[2] In Britain, children who are ten years and older are expected to take on this responsibility. The Children's Society published a report on the impact of the low age on youth in the United Kingdom. They note that the age of criminal responsibility is lower than any other nation in Western Europe. They also found a correlation between the low age of responsibility and the number of youths who are prosecuted and harshly sentenced for criminal action.[3]

The report also describes the historical changes to the United Kingdom's age of criminal responsibility, and the nation's reversal of historical law. "In the 14th century the principle of *doli incapax* established that children between the ages of ten and thirteen years were presumed to be incapable of criminal intent unless the prosecution could show otherwise. The principle was abolished in 1998."[4] Like Canada, the United Kingdom has begun a trend toward tougher criminal policies for their youth, allowing children to face charges even before they have reached puberty.

On the other hand, in similar fashion to Colombia, the United Kingdom attempts to keep all minors under the age of eighteen within the juvenile justice system. There are also other attempts to provide additional protection for young offenders. For example, offenses for children between the ages of ten and eighteen are considered summary offenses and are kept in the youth court. "However, the youth court may decide that certain 'grave crimes' need to be committed to the Crown Court for trial . . . in some instances older juveniles can be dealt with in an adult court."[5] The United Kingdom allows for the severity of crime to overturn the definition of a juvenile. The offense itself has a role in deciding whether a young person is to be considered mature enough to face an adult sentence, or whether he can still be rehabilitated as a juvenile.

The United Kingdom is similar to the United States and Canada in its implementation of a juvenile court system, although it occurred slightly later. "Separate jurisdictions and penal laws for children were established in the United Kingdom in 1908."[6] The Youth Court in the United Kingdom that oversees juvenile delinquents is kept completely separate from any cases that involve juvenile neglect and abuse. An explanation of this separation can be seen in a court comparison between the United Kingdom and Colombia. In Colombia, all juvenile matters are brought before the Family, Juvenile and Errant Children Courts, meaning that children who have been abandoned by their parents, are lumped within the same system as any child charged with theft. In contrast, the British Youth Court is responsible only for criminal cases, and includes three magistrates, rather than one judge. A clerk specifically trained in juvenile legal matters assists the panel.[7]

The ideologies that uphold the juvenile court are usually reform measures, but the United Kingdom also takes into account the persistence and seriousness of the offender's delinquent acts. Like the North American countries, "the justice orientation seems to be stronger than the welfare orientation."[8] The British police have a huge role in the admission of an offender in front of the Youth Court. The prosecutor does not always decide whether a youth will be charged; instead, English police make the initial decision, deciding whether to give a juvenile delinquent an informal warning, a formal caution, or to refer the case to the prosecutor. The police also have the option of adding regulations to the warnings and cautions they administer. At times, without any involvement from the court, the police confer with social service agencies to determine the best method to supervise the offender.[9] The police are like an alternate to actual court proceedings, and they have a wide and independent, albeit informal, jurisdiction over juvenile offenders.

The United Kingdom also allows for the severity of crime to decide a transfer of an offender out of the more flexible juvenile court to an adult court. "Proceedings against children and young persons are for the most part dealt with in the youth court as summary offenses. But, the youth court may decide that certain 'grave crimes' need to be committed to the Crown Court for trial."[10] Thus, placement of a delinquent under the age of eighteen is not guaranteed in the Youth Court because the severity of the crime also plays a role. In addition, if the offender will turn eighteen shortly after the commission of the crime, the youth court, regardless of the offense, has the option of remitting the offender to the adult magistrate's court. The United Kingdom has followed the ideals set forth in the United Nations Convention on the Rights of the Child. Children are held accountable for their actions in a separate jurisdiction than their adult counterparts and the juvenile jurisdiction has more of a social welfare approach than penal influences.

Like the similarities between the North American and Western European methods of implementation of the juvenile court systems, the similarities between the regions are also reflected in the rights afforded to children in conflict with the law. The United Kingdom, for instance, affords the same rights to minors guaranteed in American legislation. In a 1998 report to the United Nations, the representatives of the United Kingdom defined the rights of delinquents. Section 104 states, "All such children have a right to legal representation, which is provided free of charge for those who cannot afford it. / Legal Aid Act 1989 Part II./ The name, address, school or any other identifying particulars of a child brought before a juvenile court may not be published in a newspaper or other media./ Summary Jurisdiction Act 1989 sect. 41."[11]

Both the right to privacy of the youth to protect against social ramifications and the right to legal aid can be found in the multiple acts that make up the body of juvenile law for Great Britain. While British adults are afforded a right to public trial and their juvenile counterparts are given privacy, the right to representation and the offer of counsel at the cost of the state is given to adults and children alike. The rules regarding parental involvement for juvenile delinquency are an issue that historically has split the nation and continues to change. As early as 1908, British Parliament debated parental responsibility for the crimes of children. At this time, Herbert Samuel introduced the "Children Bill," and one of the main tenets is that "parents should be made more responsible for the wrongdoing of their children."[12]

While the more liberal 1960s saw a shift in British policy that stressed less responsibility for both parents and children and instead treatment for the whole family to locate the root of juvenile criminal activity, legislation of the 1990s was a return to the ideals from the beginning of the century. The 1991 Criminal Justice Act, still in effect, attempts to make parental responsibility greater for the offenses of their children:

> This has been done by making stronger the requirement for parental responsibility for children's offending (especially those under the age of fifteen years). This has been done by making stronger the requirements for parents to attend the youth court whenever their children appear. In addition, it gives the court powers to bind over parents with regard to their children's future behavior, if it is satisfied that this would be 'desirable in the interests of preventing the commission by him of further offenses.' Consequently, if children continue to offend then the parents can be fined for not exercising proper control and for being in breach of the binding over condition.[13]

Like the United States, Great Britain's policy makers are using every possible power to lower the incidence of juvenile delinquency. While the rights of children, particularly to privacy and representation, are respected, the rights of parents and guardians are becoming more limited. The parents are now responsible for crimes that they did not commit, and possibly knew nothing about.

The rise in juvenile crime in the 1990s also prompted the British Parliament to institute stricter measures for youth offenders with the implementation of the Criminal Justice and Public Order Act of 1994. In summary, the four new provisions allowed the following changes to occur. A Secure Training Order was introduced, which allows detention for juveniles aged twelve to fourteen if they are repetitive offenders. This new type of sentence allows for a range of detention for six months to two years and includes a provision that all released offenders will spend half of their sentence out of treatment, but under continued supervision from authorities. But even though the statute passed, no government action has been taken to build such facilities.

The Criminal Justice Public Order Act of 1994 also allows for long-term detention for sentences applicable to juveniles aged ten to thirteen if they have been convicted of murder or manslaughter. Prior to the new law, only children aged fourteen and above could receive long term confinement. In addition, children between the ages of ten and fifteen who are convicted of any sexual assault can receive long-term detention sentences. Finally, the law raised the maximum detention for offenders aged fifteen to seventeen from one year to two.[14]

British researchers calculated changes in the youth prison populations to see whether the new statutes and overall trend toward detention rather than alternate sentences had any impact on the numbers of locked up children. The figures are astonishing: First, the number of children in confinement between 1993 and 1998 almost doubled. The statistics also differ based on gender. The number of incarceration sentences for male juveniles more than doubled, while the number of female offenders came close to tripling. In March of 2000, the number of children in prison was 1,708.[15]

Conditions within the juvenile detention centers across Great Britain are substandard when compared with international guidelines. A number of government and independent studies were conducted in the past few years, and while each study urged the need for reform, little has changed. A prison inspector reported about a juvenile facility in Werrington that the misery of the children was appalling, but what was even worse was that national authorities were not making any changes.[16] In 2000, prison inspectors released a report about Feltham, the largest juvenile jail in Western Europe. The facility "was described as: 'rotten to the core' and 'unacceptable in a civilized country. The report referred to the 'disgraceful and appalling conditions' that the 922 children and young people had to endure."[17] Inspectors learned of greater abuses in juvenile detention facilities than in the adult prisons. In regard to imprisonment in the United Kingdom, Amnesty International's response to their investigation was that the situation for juveniles amounted to a violation of international and domestic policy on the standards of decency for treating human beings.[18]

The issues found by Amnesty International are quite serious, and carry a risk that children in detention are in danger. For instance, overcrowding has been a major concern at Feltham. A deputy governor of the institution resigned in August 2001 after an inmate was returned to the jail following a suicide attempt. The youth was severely injured from his wounds, and remained in intensive medical care for days before his transfer back to Feltham. Prior to his resignation, the deputy governor had made repeated complaints to the prison service and asked them to stop sending inmates to the jail. He said that the worst problem at Feltham was overcrowding, and that from the lack of space an assortment of other issues arose. For instance, because there was nowhere else to place them, juvenile offenders were given housing in isolation centers, and were kept enclosed for twenty-two hours per day. Other children were integrated into the adult population.[19]

Children already in confinement should not be further abused by remaining in solitary confinement for days on end. The deviations from standards on treatment of detained juveniles are not unique to Feltham. The U.S. State Department investigated another British institution, the Portland Young Offenders Institute, and learned that wardens were finally suspended from the jobs after a fourteen-year history of alleged abuse against inmates.[20]

The reported conditions of juvenile detention centers are in violation of both international standards and the stated goals of national juvenile justice legislation. In February 2001, the government of the United Kingdom reported to the European Committee for the Prevention of Torture and Inhuman or Degrading Punishment. In regard to juvenile detention centers, authorities outlined their expectations for juvenile detention centers. Overall, the environment should be positive, and have good ventilation and lighting to provide a healthy atmosphere. Children should look at the center as a home rather than a place of punishment, and should be allowed to keep personal belongings. Their space should be adequately furnished and appropriately decorated.[21] But, both independent officials and government staff have found on numerous occasions that juvenile detention centers have not lived up to their stated objectives.

Finally, like the United States, juvenile offenders in the United Kingdom are also subjected to racial inequalities in sentencing. The Children's Society found that young black children are six times more likely to be sentenced to prison, and that in 1999, 31.6 percent of the population in Feltham was black.[22] The combination of a trend toward punishment measures rather than rehabilitation as the underlying ideal of juvenile justice with the substandard conditions in the nation's juvenile detention facilities has left juvenile offenders at risk. Children are abused, left in confinement for days, and are not provided with necessary care. The methods of punishment in the United Kingdom need to be overhauled.

IRELAND

Ireland enacted the Convention on the Rights of the Child in 1992 with the hope of safeguarding children from abuse and mistreatment. "Regarding the definition of the child, the [Irish] delegation explained that the age of majority is eighteen and the age of criminal responsibility is presently seven."[23] There are, however, further requirements to prosecute children at the age of seven. At the time of the original meeting with the Committee, the Children's Act of 1908 was the law that guided the treatment of young Irish offenders and delinquents. This statute lists the age of criminal responsibility at seven; to prosecute such a young offender the government has the additional burden of proving that the child understands that his or her actions were wrong. "Children between the ages of 7 and 14, to be convicted, must be proved by the prosecution to have known what they did was wrong."[24]

Ireland began to reform their statutes based on criticism from the United Nations. The Children's Bill was debated in Parliament from 1996 through 1999 and intended to raise the age of criminal responsibility to ten. While the years passed with significant debate but little change, the age of criminal responsibility was finally altered at the start of the new millennium. The latest alterations to juvenile law passed the Irish Parliament as the Children's Act of 2001, and exceeded the expectations of justice reformers. At present, the age of criminal responsibility for Irish minors is set at twelve years.[25]

In regard to the maximum age at which a youth offender can be processed through the juvenile justice system, Irish law allows only for children through age sixteen to remain within the youth courts. All offenders over the age of seventeen are prosecuted as adults. But like the United Kingdom, other factors impact whether a child is considered an adult under law. Alternative issues that are considered include both the seriousness of the offense and whether a juvenile acted with a legal adult in the commission of the crime. If either of these requirements is met, juveniles are transferred out of the youth courts and sent to the Crown Courts. While seriousness of offense can be a flexible issue with multiple factors like violence and victimization playing a role, it is an unbendable requirement that if a person under the age of seventeen is charged with murder, his or her case must be moved out of the youth court.[26]

Ireland only recently altered its juvenile court laws. In 1996, the Parliament amended Regulation 3 of the Juvenile Court and Assessors for County Courts Regulation of 1979. The new regulation states that: "(1) A juvenile court shall be constituted for each petty sessions district in Northern Ireland and . . . (2) Where a juvenile court is sitting for the purpose of exercising any jurisdiction conferred by or under the Children Order of 1995 it shall have jurisdiction throughout the county court division in which it is situated."[27] This act allows for a juvenile court to exist within each of the district courts that sentence adults and hear civil cases. It is similar to the American system in that it has different courtrooms within a building to allow for a juvenile judge to operate in one room, while the traffic court can operate down the hall. The formation of juvenile courts within the same realm as the adult penal courts is not a violation of United Nations prerequisites.

The Children's Court, located in Dublin, is the only court in Ireland exclusively meant to deal with juvenile issues. However, other courts can handle juvenile cases as well as other matters. For instance, the jurisdiction of the District Court is different than the Children's Court: "The District Court in Ireland, which is the equivalent in England with the Magistrates' Court but with professional judges, has jurisdiction to deal summarily with all indictable offenses regarding children, except homicides. . . . Children's proceedings in the District Courts are held at a different time and a different place to adults."[28] District Courts have been allocated the same jurisdiction as the Dublin Children's Court so that juvenile offenders are subjected to the same type of proceedings without having to travel to the capital.

Ireland, like the United Kingdom, grants the police force vast discretion in dealing with juvenile offenders. The police are the first point of contact that a juvenile has with the justice system. These powers are allocated under a Juvenile Liaison Scheme, expressly meant to allow police alternate responses to juvenile offenses rather than handing the child to the courts. The options available to the police are to take no further action, to issue an informal warning and advice, to administer a formal caution, which will remain on the offender's criminal record, and to prosecute the offender in court.[29] The alternatives to court proceedings allow for the police to form a relationship with offenders without a blemish on the record to occur. The police are specifically trained in this practice, entitled "diversion," and it is integral to the juvenile court system because it provides a proficient way to rehabilitate young offenders without subjecting them to the traumas of drawn-out court proceedings.

Irish law differs on whether parents have the right to court involvement in judicial proceedings. Beginning with first police contact, authorities are supposed to immediately contact the appropriate parental figure. However, while the adult is generally allowed to accompany the offender at all stages of judicial contact, it is not a legal right.[30]

But, a 1996 report to the United Nations explains that the denial of parental involvement with police switches to a required involvement once the process of charging a youth with a crime becomes official: "Where an arrested person is under seventeen years, a parent or guardian must be informed of the arrest, the reason for the arrest, and the right to consult a solicitor. The parent or guardian is also required to attend at the Garda station without delay."[31] Although emotional support and guidance are expected from the parent, Ireland does not require that a parent or guardian bear any responsibility for the crimes of their children. While their involvement is needed, the juvenile still faces sole responsibility for all criminal action.

In regard to the right to representation, like the United Kingdom, Ireland guarantees legal aid to both children and adults alike. The Irish parliament has legislated that any offender unable to afford counsel will have it provided by the state. Other factors apply to the assignment of counsel. First, the offenders must prove that they are financially unable to bear the cost of an attorney. Second, the court considers whether the charge is serious enough to merit the need for legal assistance for the duration of their defense.[32] Children in conflict with the law are generally always considered to have "special circumstances," so they will always have legal services provided when they and/or their family cannot afford it.

Finally, Ireland is interesting in that it does not make court proceedings permanently closed to the public. In the same United Nations report, Irish delegates stated that, "It is not the practice of the media to publish any information concerning criminal trials that could lead to the identification of children involved in those proceedings."[33] But, it is not legally mandated that courts remain closed to the public. Thus, while the media may not publish the name of an offender or the circumstances regarding his or her case and crime, anyone who sits in on the proceedings can discuss what occurs inside.

Ireland does not fully consider the social exclusion that might occur in a community that learns of a juvenile's offenses. The entire purpose of the privacy protection as afforded to juveniles and not adults is that it is assumed that children have committed minor offenses and that they have a greater capacity for rehabilitation than their adult counterparts. If a neighborhood learns of a child's indiscretions, they might blame the youth for any problems in the area. Although Ireland blocks media involvement in youth court proceedings, many of the surrounding nations take the right to privacy further by closing the court to all parties without justifiable reason for involvement in the trial.

Judges in Ireland have a variety of options that they can utilize when sentencing a juvenile. They can dismiss the charge, allow the offender to leave with only a warning, issue a sentence of probation that includes appropriate, order noncustodial supervision, impose a fine for damages inflicted from the criminal action, remand the youth to an industrial school, order detention in either a juvenile facility or a prison, and they have the option of making the parent fully responsible for any further criminal actions of the offender. The option that courts use most often is a custodial sentence, both for adult and juvenile offenders alike.[34]

In recent years, the number of juvenile detention centers has fluctuated at various times because of renovations and closures. Nonetheless, a report to the Committee on the Rights of the Child gives an overview of the types of centers that can be found in the nation, and the government division that bears responsibility for detained youths. Males below sixteen years and females below seventeen years are the responsibility of the Department of Education. There is a further dichotomy for these youths in where they may be remanded. Children under fourteen years are sent to industrial schools, while older youth offenders are detained in reformatory schools. In the mid-1990s, there were five detention centers for youths in Ireland.[35]

Irish law further splits all offenders over age sixteen through an investigation of their criminal histories. Offenders over age sixteen are supervised by the Department of Education, unless the severity of the crime calls for administration with the Department of Justice. This policy allows for rehabilitation to apply to first-time offenders. For example, first-time thieves will be rehabilitated but a child convicted of assault with a deadly weapon will be punished. The only way children under sixteen can attend institutions run by the Department of Justice is through a specific court order.[36]

The government representatives continued their United Nations report by claiming that children are offered a wide range of rehabilitative services, including drug programs, counselors, psychologists, and physicians. However, independent researchers found that children in Irish detention facilities are not receiving the necessary social services to aid them in rehabilitation. The Human Rights Commission found that, "Mental health services for children in custody are 'seriously inadequate' with a 'potential to endanger children's health and put lives at risk.' Children are not getting the level of health and educational services to which they are entitled."[37] In another report on juvenile detention, representatives from the media described a much different picture. Shanganagh is a male detention center for offenders ages seventeen to twenty-one. The *Irish Times* found that an overwhelming majority of the youths were in school, including general education, artistic, exercise, technology, and vocational skills classes.[38] Thus, there is some conflict among sources as to whether youths are afforded their right to education, even when incarcerated.

Detention centers in Ireland have additional problems regarding their locations. The government admits these problems, but has done little to alter them. First, the few juvenile justice centers in Ireland are all located in the same region. All three establishments are located in Eastern Ireland, so offenders from different regions have limited contact with their families. The issue of class is important in this respect; unless the family is fortunate enough to own a car, the child will suffer detachment.[39]

Like many other nations, the lower number of female juvenile offenders leads to discrepancies in treatment of offenders based on sex, because the system is simply more prepared to deal with male offenders. For example, Irish law requires that detention facilities and prisons for older juvenile offenders exist separately from facilities that are more like reform schools. The continuous effort to rehabilitate the younger and less delinquent offenders includes the option of keeping this group separate from older offenders at all costs. While this practice works well for male offenders, there is no separate juvenile prison for female juvenile delinquents.

Irish authorities admitted to the United Nations that females of all ages are sent to prison. Girls over age seventeen are remanded to adult facilities because there is no comparable institution for the "in-between" group. This policy affects younger females as well. Girls under seventeen years of age who have been ordered by the Court into the supervision of the Department of Justice because their behavior has deemed them too unruly for the Department of Education facilities are also sent to prisons. These prisons lack the capacity to offer any separate program for the youths, although authorities claim there is an effort to keep youngsters away from adult inmates during recreation periods.[40]

The issue of juvenile integration into adult prison populations is not specifically reserved for females. The Irish government states that they cannot guarantee that children will be kept out of adult jails, although they will do their best to do so. If the choice for a young male offender who has been remanded to an adult institution is between integrating him into the population or keeping him in solitary confinement, the authorities believe it is in the best interest of the youth to come into contact with adults. The authorities state that they hope this decision is unnecessary, but admit that they cannot make guarantees.[41]

FRANCE

The Centre for Europe's Children report, "Ages at Which Children Are Legally Entitled to Carry Out a Series of Acts in Council of Europe Member Countries," noted various ages in which children are allowed to complete a number of activities, including marriage, hold a right to property, and assert independence from their guardians. According to an investigation of France, the age of criminal responsibility is thirteen. Comparing this number with required ages for other legal entitlements is somewhat disheartening. While children can be prosecuted in a court of law and punished for their crimes at the brink of puberty, they cannot marry until the age of eighteen and are not legally entitled to work full time until age sixteen.[42] France believes that a child is mature enough at thirteen to understand his offense and pay the penalty for any criminal action, but does not believe that French youths are mature enough to make decisions about marital relationships and employment.

The United Nations held a meeting regarding France and the rights of children under the French legal system on April 11, 1994. The committee mentions the age at which offenders are still considered juveniles, when children are still prosecuted under the juvenile court regulations: "For persons aged from thirteen to eighteen years, criminal liability was deemed diminished; even in cases of very serious offences a court could issue a reasoned decision as to the reduction of liability."[43] France is somewhat more in line with United Nations regulations in defining juveniles responsible for criminal actions as offenders aged eighteen and under. The national penal code has included a clause in their criminal statutes that allows for children to remain in the juvenile justice system, even for severe and violent crimes.

Like the United Kingdom and America, France instituted a separate court for minors charged with criminal offenses in the twentieth century. France's system is unique in that it employs a two-step process. When a juvenile offender is brought to court, "the examining magistrate or the children's judge carry out the preliminary investigation of the case. Then either the delinquent is judged at the court of Assizes for minors whose derailment and sanctions are different from the major court of Assizes [It is in charge of minors between sixteen and eighteen years old] or he is judged at the juvenile court that is in charge of minors who are less than sixteen years old."[44]

Thus, depending on the age of the offender, the youth will either stand before a stricter juvenile court for older children or a more moderate juvenile court for younger children. Age is not the only factor that decides which court has jurisdiction over an individual case. If the crime is of serious and grave nature, the age definitions are overlooked in an effort to hold the minor to a higher standard of liability. The separation of courts reflects French understanding that there is a vast difference in the mental capacities of twelve-year-old children and seventeen-year-old young adults who commit crime.

The major difference between the lower and upper courts is their supporting ideologies. At the minor court of Assizes, the approach is more punishment oriented, but at the juvenile court level, the approach is more of a social-welfare approach. Both juvenile courts employ educational objectives. They are "also authorized with regard to so-called civil or protective measures, i.e. imposing measures for the protection of the education circumstances on minors."[45] In addition, a specialized private service provides the French court with information regarding the social and psychological circumstances of the offending youth, which the court is expected to take into consideration when making any decision.

France has additional measures that other countries lack to implement juvenile justice differently from adults. In the 1997 report to the United Nations, the nation describes the "urban recovery pact," which includes the goals of hastening the process of children through the judicial system to limit any emotional damage, instituting alternate measures that are more rehabilitative, and allocating more time and funds to the deterrence of youth crime.[46] France has followed the guidelines set forth by international organizations regarding the treatment of offenders in conflict with the law. Not only does France employ a separate juvenile court system, but it also has implemented policies to hasten the process of juvenile cases so that any emotional impact on the child will be short lived.

France also employs policies requiring parent or guardian involvement when a child stands before a court of law. Like Irish statutes, French law requires that police contact parents whenever a minor is held in custody, either formally or informally. French delegates reported to the Committee on the Rights of the Child that, "Parents were immediately informed and were allowed access to the minor."[47] The judicial power of the children's court likes to gather as much information as possible about the offender. In theory, the judge of the child convenes the minor, his parents or his tutor, the person to whom or the service to which the child is entrusted, and any other person that it wishes to hear.[48] But, there is no regulation requiring parental involvement once court proceedings begin. The information from police is the first contact that a parent has with the juvenile justice system, but their involvement as proceedings advance is solely up to their discretion.

In regard to the right to representation, French law has supported legal aid for anyone accused of crimes since the era of the French revolution. The role of the French *avocat* is somewhat different than the role performed in neighboring nations, because the French system is less of an adversarial process and more of a fact-finding endeavor with court actors working together to achieve a common goal. Regardless of the differentiation in role, France, like its neighbors, guarantees a right to legal aid in criminal court. "In the law of the revolutionary period (*le droit intermédiare*), the inquisitorial system was retained, though much reformed; *instruction* was made public, and the right to the assistance of a lawyer was introduced."[49] In addition, to eradicate any unfairness due to wealth, France guarantees that persons unable to afford an attorney will have an *avocat* provided for them. As of 1982, the government bears the cost of attorneys, but they assign them to an offender rather than allowing one of their own choosing.[50]

The proceedings of the youth court are private, including only the presence of individuals who have reasonable involvement with the offender.[51] In addition, the youth courts in France reserve the option to seal the records of juvenile proceedings from the public and expunge them once a child reaches the age of criminal liability. "A young person could make a request to have his details expunged from the records after three years—although that possibility did not apply to cases heard in the assize courts . . . some judges automatically expunged details from the record after three years if the minor had not reoffended."[52] The additional precautions allow for protection of the reputation of juvenile offenders while they are rehabilitated from a criminal life. If the child does not commit further illegal action, the court additionally rewards him by taking already private records and expunging them.

The policy of French law regarding punishment of juveniles is matched in practice. France makes every effort to rehabilitate youth offenders without detaining them, and keeping them involved in the social welfare system rather than imprisoned. In a meeting with the United Nations Committee on the Rights of the Child, the French representative Mr. Fonrojet stated that children should be kept out of detention unless the circumstances were so extreme that authorities were left with no other option. For instance, "With regard to sentencing, no custodial sentence could be passed on a minor under thirteen years of age; educational measures might only be ordered. In the case of minors over thirteen, a children's court was not empowered to pass a custodial sentence or a suspended custodial sentence without giving adequate grounds for such action."[53] In regard to custodial sentences, guidelines state that children must receive lesser sentences than adults for the same crimes, unless exceptional circumstances apply. For every similar crime committed by adults and juveniles, the juvenile can only be subject to a sentence less than half of what their adult counterpart could face.[54]

French law also expresses a desire to incorporate a sense of remorse in the offender, and for juveniles, this is considered a part of rehabilitation. The victims and their families are often incorporated into any sentence. The purpose of such sanctions is both for the offender to take responsibility for his actions and allow him to learn of the impact of his crime through bringing him together with the victim. If the victim is unwilling, the offender can alternately be sanctioned with community service. The available alternatives to detention prove that the French are more concerned with instructive measures than confinement and punishment.[55]

Other rehabilitative measures utilized in France as an alternative to custodial sentencing include a variety of social services. The children's court understands that many children involved in criminal offending come from households that are not supportive. Thus, part of the rehabilitative process is the decision of the courts as to whether the offenders should remain in their present living situation or whether they should be placed in more suitable homes. The judge retains the option of sending social workers into the juvenile's home to monitor them and provide services for a whole family unit. Judicial options also include sending a youth to a rehabilitative school, but one in which the youth is allowed to return home at night. Finally, a judge can make the decision as part of sentencing that a youth can no longer remain in the home environment if it is providing bad influences. The child must reside with relatives or any other suitable guardian.[56]

Even when detention is utilized, the ideals of rehabilitation are expected to continue to play a role in the sentence. Like the noncustodial measures, offenders are expected to learn the impacts of their actions. Thus, detention includes regular schooling, exercise, and the learning of new skills.[57] But, like many other European nations, the downfall of French juvenile justice is the conditions of detention. The entire penal system in France has been scrutinized for abusive and illegal conditions. Amnesty International's findings included rampant overcrowding as a result of longer and overused sentences of custody. Again, overfilled facilities are directly correlated with a higher risk to the personal safety of youths, leaving the staff unable to protect the children from one another. In addition, there were reports of physical abuse by guards.[58]

While these assertions are horrendous, one factor that separates France from many other nations is that it refuses to allow minors in detention to be integrated into adult prison populations:

> According to the terms of article 11 of the ordinance of 2 February 1945, "in all cases minors shall be held in special quarters or failing that in special premises. They shall as far as possible remain isolated at night." Every effort is made to limit the duration and the most harmful effects of imprisonment. In order to improve the conditions of imprisonment for minors, the Government has selected fifty-two establishments [that] offer the possibility of maintaining family relations and avoid family relations being isolated in unsuitable quarters.[59]

Overall, France has made great strides in rehabilitating youth offenders but remains in need of improvements of their entire prison system, for both juveniles and adults.

GERMANY

Germany has a long-standing history of human rights abuses, yet is presently the nation that provides children with the most protection when involved in criminal proceedings. The "Ages at Which Children are Legally Entitled to Carry Out Certain Acts" lists the age of penal majority between eighteen and twenty-one years of age, depending on the child's maturity. The actual age of criminal responsibility at which children can be held criminally liable for their actions is fourteen.[60] While criminal liability begins at the age of fourteen, Germany continues to define offenders as juveniles until the age of eighteen. An offender is then defined as a young adult for the ages eighteen to twenty-one, and the legal system will take mitigating circumstances into consideration for the possibility that youths in that age group will be prosecuted by the juvenile court rather than face adult charges.[61]

Unlike France, German law uses age eighteen as adulthood not only for criminal liability, but also for the ability to contract, to own a residence, to marry, and for emancipation from guardians. The national law recognizes that juveniles who commit crimes are not more mature than youngsters planning to marry or sign contracts; instead, Germany has a relatively uniform system in which a juvenile becomes an adult in a variety of capacities.

German law also includes flexibility regarding the severity of offense. But, unlike most nations that allow criminal responsibility to increase when the crime is more severe, Germany decreases the liability of a youth offender when the crime is less severe. For instance, the Youth Criminal Law has held since 1953 that:

> Children below the age of fourteen years are under the age of criminal responsibility, they are incapable of crime. . . . It's all the same even if it is a serious act. . . . Teenagers can be guilty of an offense if they are matured enough in their moral and mental development to appreciate the tort of the act and to act in accordance with the appreciation. In the case of some offenses or in the case that the teenager has special personal characteristics it is possible, that he is incapable of crime, although he is already older than fourteen years of age. Adolescents principally can be guilty of an offense, except if they are in diminished responsibility or incapable of appreciating the tort of the act or acting in accordance with such appreciation due to a pathological emotional disorder, profound consciousness disorder, mental defect or any other serious emotional abnormality.[62]

Germany combines the notions of psychological and emotional factors that lead to the diminishment of criminal liability with a much higher age at which offenders can continue to be prosecuted by the Youth Court. While other nations use severity and gravity of the offense to relocate young offenders into adult criminal courts, placing juveniles next to hardened adult criminals, Germany seems increasingly more concerned with the impact of mental stability on the youthful commission of crimes. More than any other country included in this study, Germany goes to great lengths to protect its child citizens.

Germany has a specific juvenile court, as well as an entire set of laws regulating their jurisdiction, titled *Jugendgerichtsgesetz*. Under this body of law, it is the responsibility of the prosecutor and the court "to prove and find out whether the juvenile offender has the so-called *stafrechtliche Reife*. This means that the juvenile offender is mature enough in his moral and mental development to appreciate the tort of his crime and act in accordance with his appreciation."[63] The court is required to commence this investigation in addition to the strict age requirements that decide which youth offenders are processed by the juvenile system. The prosecutor and court must prove that the child has both moral and mental development on the biological level as well as on the psychological level.

Like France, multiple courts in Germany have jurisdiction over juvenile offenders. The local court is the Juvenile Court, which has either one juvenile judge to oversee proceedings, or a *Jugendschoffengericht*, which is a three-person panel consisting of the juvenile judge, one female juvenile juror, and one male juvenile juror. The local courts have jurisdiction only over cases that have punishment measures of education, discipline, and imprisonment up to one year. The local court is comparable to the misdemeanor court in the American system that separates less serious crimes from felony offenses. More serious crimes in Germany are decided in the District Courts, either in the small Criminal Chamber or the great Criminal Chamber. Each chamber has a panel of three judges, but in the small Criminal Chamber, only one member is a jurist; the others are one male and one female juror. In the great Criminal Chamber, every member of the deciding panel is a jurist. In addition, cases in all courts require a prosecutor specially trained in juvenile matters that have experience in educational reform. Further specialized prosecutors are required in crimes of death that are not a result of manslaughter and/or negligence.[64]

In addition to the regular court fixtures of judge and state representation, German juvenile law also requires that the Juvenile Court Assistance (JCA) be involved in all court proceedings. JCA workers are concurrently trained in social welfare as well as in the legal rights of minors, and it is their job to get as much information about the circumstances of the offense and the life of the juvenile. "The main task of the Juvenile Court Assistance is to bring the educational, social and welfare points into the Criminal Procedure. For this reason the social worker should explore the personality, the development and the social environment of the juvenile offender. . . . This takes place by conversations with the juvenile offender himself, with his parents and, as necessary, with the teachers in the school and the instructors in the training place."[65] German juvenile courts rely heavily on the information from the JCA, taking into consideration all of the factors in the life of the juvenile, rather than merely the crime itself.

The processes of diversion in Ireland and the United Kingdom are also practiced in Germany, but instead of police discretion, the prosecutor makes the decisions. The practice of diversion was legalized in the 1990 "First Change Law" amendment to the juvenile law. This defines diversion as the possibility to avoid formal procedure for an educational reason, in an effort to avoid the negative influences of running a child through formal proceedings. If the prosecutor feels that an alternative educational measure can be imposed, either before or during juvenile proceedings, they have the power to suspend the charges and allow the offender out of court without a blemish on his or her criminal record.[66]

It is important to note, however, that while the prosecutor makes the original intention to suspend charges, the full diversion process cannot be carried out without the agreement of the children's judge or judges. The juveniles also reserve the right to refuse the alternate diversion process if they would rather continue their case in front of the court.[67] Germany has gone beyond international expectations in establishing a specialized system for juvenile offenders. A variety of officers of the court are involved in juvenile criminal proceedings, all of whom take a number of factors into account in the hope that rehabilitation rather than penal measures will help to reintegrate the youth back into society.

Germany requires parental involvement in all phases of court proceedings for juveniles in conflict with the law. At the earliest point of investigation into a criminal incident, the JCA will begin their investigation into the social life of the juvenile. The social worker employed by the JCA is required to not only converse with the offender, but also with his or her parents. When official court proceedings begin, the presence of the parents or guardians is required unless it is deemed detrimental to the offender. The reasoning behind the requirement is that the judiciary feels that parents can be helpful in learning more about the youth and the reasons why he committed the crime. In addition, they hold a separate right to appeal any judicial decisions, so they are also mandated to appear for their own legal benefit. The only time that parents can be excluded is if the Court finds that they are detrimental to the offender. These policies apply to all offenders under the age of eighteen.[68]

Thus, in regard to parental involvement, German juvenile law holds that the involvement of adults in court processes must only occur if they are in the best interest of the offender. While parents have rights when their children are charged with any criminal offense, their rights are limited if they will not aid both the court and the child on the path to rehabilitation. Similarly to the case-by-case process in which parents and guardians are excluded or allowed in court, the public can be excluded depending on the circumstances of the case. According to German statutes, "In the procedure against juvenile offenders the court sitting in principle is not public. . . . But if there is only an adolescent, the sitting on a case is public."[69] To reiterate, juveniles in Germany are distinguished as teenagers and adolescents. While adolescents are above the age of eighteen, they continue to hold a diminished capacity for understanding their crimes until the age of twenty-one. For all offenders under the age of eighteen, the Court protects their right to privacy from public knowledge of their offenses.

Finally, Germany also provides all defendants regardless of age with the right to legal aid. "Everybody has a right to defense. For those who cannot afford a lawyer, the court will appoint counsel. The defendant does not have to pay for this counsel. If he chooses a lawyer for himself and this lawyer is not appointed by the court, he may pay for legal aid."[70] However, while juveniles are given access to an attorney, it is also notable that the German Juvenile Court is not viewed as an adversarial setting. A lawyer may be obtained to represent a child charged with a crime, but other actors in the court are constantly present and working with the juvenile's attorney and the Court to decide what is in the best interest of the child. The social workers of the Juvenile Court Assistance, the special juvenile prosecutors, and at times, parents, are all considered to have a role in informal representation of the juvenile offender.

German law is committed to a goal of rehabilitation for juvenile offenders, and the underlying ideal makes a distinction between adult and juvenile criminals. The adult system is committed to punishing the offense, with less regard for the circumstances and needs of the offender. Youth offenders, on the other hand, are the center of all decisions regarding them. A juvenile can be legally accountable for his actions, but the goals of the system continue to incorporate the need for education and therapy within acceptance of responsibility.[71]

Like France, German juvenile jurists have a wide range of options in sentencing, including education, disciplinary measures, and youth imprisonment. The system of sentencing is tiered, and each harsher penalty can only be instituted if it is found that the less severe disposal has failed. Each grouping of measures contains a variety of options that can constitute a punishment. Educational measures include a range of possibilities, including a period of community service, involvement in some conciliation between the offender and the victim, special vocational training or social training, and probation with supervision by a social worker. Regardless of the sentence, the objective of each of these options is to resocialize the offender into a law-abiding citizen.[72] The education measures, *Erziehungsmaßregeln*, have a fixed length for which they may be implemented. They are not considered a sentence, but rather referred to as a direction. These measures cannot be put in force for over two years. If the juvenile disobeys some requirement of his direction, instead of lengthening the time frame, the judge can order a youth detained for a period no greater than four weeks.[73]

Disciplinary measures differ slightly in that they include many of the same provisions, but require that a record is made of all punishment. For the more serious youth offender, short-term detention can be ordered, but must take place in separate and secure youth facilities. In addition, all offenders subjected to short-term detention must be kept away from youths sentenced to imprisonment. These measures are an attempt to protect the youth from the influences of more serious offenders and to continue the rehabilitative process. Usually, such detention will occur in an educational facility, which is considered different from the juvenile detention center. The only way that this form of sentence can be implemented is if all other methods of rehabilitation have been exhausted. Any detention must have the purpose of continuing the resocialization process. Confinement can occur in a state education facility, or in a "therapeutic apartment."[74] Both types of locales provide a secure setting for juveniles in need of rehabilitation but are less imposing than confinement facilities.

The disciplinary measures also include both a formal reprimand by the court and the requirement of reparations for the victim. Like France, Germany includes a measure that teaches remorse for the victim of the crime, believing that understanding the impact of actions on other individuals is integral in the rehabilitation of an offender. In regard to the payment of damages, the offender can either provide restitution directly to the victim or to some comparable public institution. Regardless, the youth can only be ordered to use financial resources as a sanction if the funds are solely the juvenile's, and not from either a parent or friend.[75] The requirement that a juvenile utilize his own resources to make reparations for the offense furthers rehabilitation by forcing the youth to take responsibility for his actions.

Youth imprisonment is the final option that a judge can pursue when sentencing a juvenile, and it can only occur if all other options have been exhausted or the seriousness of the crime requires more severe measures. Juveniles can be sentenced to a prison term of no less than six months and no more than five years. The reasoning behind the relatively long minimum sentence is to ensure that the goals of reeducation have an opportunity to be met.[76] Thus, even when youths have committed heinous crimes and other less severe measures have failed, the punishment of detention requires an element of education and rehabilitation so that the offender will refrain from further criminal activity.

Imprisonment can only be ordered in very exceptional circumstances, and the order of this sentence requires certain findings by the court, or the conclusion of so-called "*schädliche Neigungen.*" This term means that the juvenile has been found to have a propensity for dangerous behavior, and that he or she is defective in his or her personality. Such a finding can only occur if a youth is also found to be likely to commit further criminal actions.[77] Basically, youths must have a long history of criminal tendencies and the Court must find social and psychological disorders to order imprisonment. German law employs a balancing system in this matter; while the rights of the offender are highly valued, those who are extremely violent and pose a threat to society must be confined. But, this confinement will still include education and rehabilitation.

SWEDEN

While Sweden is not as advanced in juvenile safeguards as Germany, it also has a much better record than other Western European nations. In Sweden, "the age of criminal responsibility is fifteen. But, special rules in regards to sanctioning apply until the age of twenty-one. For example, only if there are exceptional grounds may an offender below the age of eighteen be sentenced to imprisonment."[78] Like Germany, Sweden includes a clause that allows offenders to be treated as juveniles until the age of twenty-one. The severity of the crime only becomes a factor in which a juvenile may be treated as an adult once the offender has reached the age of eighteen.

A representative from Sweden, Mr. Hakansson, further explained the rules surrounding the age of criminal responsibility at a United Nations meeting held on July 7, 1993. Hakansson claimed that children cannot be responsible for their crimes unless they have reached the age of fifteen, regardless of any extenuating factors. He further discussed the impact of law on offenders who have attained the age of eighteen: "Custodial sentences could not be handed down before the age of eighteen except for very grave reasons. Moreover, a person aged under eighteen might not be arrested if it felt that a supervision measure was sufficient."[79] Like Germany, Sweden chooses to use the impact of severity of the crime on whether the offender is treated as an adult or juvenile only after the child has reached the age of eighteen. Sweden has the highest age of criminal responsibility in the world. Compared with Ireland and some American jurisdictions, Sweden's age of criminal responsibility is more than double the age range.

Sweden, one of the more liberal nations in regard to juvenile justice codes, surprisingly did not have a separate court for juvenile proceedings until very recently. Hakansson further informed the United Nations Committee on the Rights of the Child that "a government commission on young offenders was at present contemplating the possibility of setting up a permanent court to deal with suspected young offenders."[80] Cases involving juvenile crime are tried by the same courts as meant for adult criminals, in the lower courts, or in the Supreme Court on appeal. But, while the adult and juvenile courts are not fully separated, the justice system employs different policies when youths are involved. In the lower courts three noncourt-oriented assessors, who are specifically trained in juvenile issues, aid the judge. In addition, larger cities have sitting judges that deal solely with juvenile offenses.[81]

In response to concerns stated by the United Nations and other international rights organizations in regard to the lack of juvenile courts, Sweden quickly altered its justice system. The Care of Young Persons act was amended and established in 1995, making many changes to the juvenile justice system in Sweden. While a separate court was not implemented, other factors surrounding juvenile proceedings were updated. Swedish representatives presented the modifications in a 1996 report to the Committee on the Rights of the Child. First, the amendments include specific provisions to achieve a more rapid and qualitative procedure for juveniles in conflict with the law. When a juvenile is suspected of a crime, the prosecutor and police work together to ascertain both the facts of the case as well as the specific circumstances in the offender's life. Both police and prosecutors are specifically trained in juvenile matters. Police are required to attend a program titled "Juveniles," which covers police involvement in relation to juvenile criminal and social policy, as well as young offender psychology. In addition, the police and prosecutor leading the initial investigation are required to inform local social welfare organizations to involve them as early as possible in the proceedings.

The prosecutor can decide whether to prosecute the case, but in addition to the actual offense, he must consider whether the juvenile is already under the care of the social welfare system, whether the crime was committed because of mischief and rashness, and also whether the child showed any remorse to the investigators about the crime.[82] From these decisions, the prosecutor has the right to implement an alternative to involvement by the court. This can only occur with the agreement of the social welfare agencies, and applies to less serious offenses. Often the alternative is not a rehabilitative measure but instead a fine or monetary imposition on the offender.[83]

It is also important to note that while other nations have a set juvenile justice system, one of the main factors in Sweden's decision not to do so is the extremely low level of juvenile crime. In the international scene as a whole, juvenile crime is on the rise, but the situation in Sweden is an anomaly. The national population is almost nine million people, yet in 1999, only fifteen thousand youths between the ages of fifteen and seventeen were convicted of crimes.[84] Economically, the decision to implement an entire juvenile justice system where there is simply not that much juvenile crime would be senseless. Instead, Sweden has utilized alternative codes and measures to protect juveniles during criminal proceedings, and has effectively ensured that the goal of justice for youth offenders is not purely punitive.

Swedish delegates reported to the United Nations and "confirmed that a lawyer must be appointed as a matter of course to a person under the age of eighteen who is liable to a penalty other than a fine. If a minor under the age of eighteen was liable only to a fine, he could nevertheless request the court to appoint a lawyer for him. If the court refused, he himself would have to pay for a lawyer of his choice; the same applied if he decided to retain a lawyer other than the one appointed by the court."[85] It is interesting that Swedish law specifically allocates the right to an attorney although they continue to prosecute youth offenders in adult court. The guarantee to legal aid for any offense other than those punished with a fine is a reflection of the nation's attempt to provide troubled youths with protections even though Sweden does not employ a separate juvenile court. Furthermore, according to "For the Record: 1997," the guarantee of defense aid is not guaranteed to adults in the same way: "Juveniles have greater chances than adults of obtaining a public defense counsel under a special provision."[86]

Swedish parents also play a role in the criminal proceedings of their children from a very early stage. At first contact with police, the parents or other appropriate guardians are beckoned to the station and expected to remain with the youth through all interrogation.[87] Because juvenile court proceedings are not held separate from adult criminal trials, the provisions regarding special rights of juveniles are limited. While the Swedish police are required to inform parents, their involvement in all other judicial meetings is a right but not a requirement. After initial knowledge of the issue, it is up to the adult and the minor they hold responsible to determine their involvement.

The right to privacy from public knowledge of criminal behavior is another special provision afforded to juveniles in conflict with the law. "When a person under twenty-one is prosecuted, hearings may be held behind closed doors if attention is manifestly detrimental to the young person."[88] The right to privacy is not guaranteed as in many other nations, but again, Swedish circumstances are somewhat unique. The relatively low number of juvenile offenses has not led to the mandate of a separate court for offenses. Thus, all provisions are reserved for the few cases in which a juvenile is charged with a crime. While privacy from public knowledge is not a guarantee, the court is required to take into consideration the detrimental effects of releasing information about the juvenile to the public. It seems that if open hearings and records have the possibility of badly impacting a juvenile's rehabilitation, the court chooses to close proceedings.

In regard to the sanctions available to punish delinquent youth, Sweden continues to be somewhat of an anomaly because of their incredibly low rates of juvenile crime. This differentiation explains many of the choices government authorities have made regarding juvenile justice. For instance, while separation between adults and juveniles in a prison setting is a requirement of international standards for children, Sweden does not adhere to this policy. While at first this seems shocking, Swedish authorities have explained that it simply does not make sense to build separate juvenile facilities when there are so few juveniles in need of confinement. Mrs. Gynna-Oguz, a representative from Sweden to the United Nations, claimed, "at present approximately 4,000 children aged between fifteen and eighteen were the responsibility of the social welfare committees within or outside specialized institutions and that only ten or so young persons under eighteen were at present in local prisons where adults who had committed serious offences were not detained. If a special prison to house those ten young offenders were to be built, it would make contacts between them and their families very difficult."[89]

In fact, various laws in Sweden discourage imprisonment and prohibit a number of sanctions for minors. Both capital punishment and corporal punishment are outlawed; it is illegal for parents to physically discipline their children as well. Offenders cannot be sentenced to life imprisonment unless they were over twenty-one at the time of the crime. The law also requires that detention is used only as a last resort. Instead, youth offenders should be placed on probation or given community service. Care through social service institutions that do not require custody is also an option.[90]

In the very rare instance that youths must be sentenced and remanded to a prison, the authorities do their best to keep youths away from adult offenders within the facility and to continue the education of the minor. The few existing youth prisoners are placed in establishments as close to their family homes as possible. The objective of this preference is that the family will play a role in rehabilitation, particularly in the difficult transition period from incarceration to liberty. In regard to youth offenders specifically, the justice system takes into consideration the youth's circumstances by providing both education and additional training skills.[91]

Alternatives to criminal sentences in Sweden include an array of options. First, youths can be forced to pay a fine or reparations for their actions. More importantly, juveniles are commonly put into contact with any number of social welfare organizations that will aid in rehabilitation. The underlying ideals of Swedish juvenile justice are inherently more concerned with why a youth committed the criminal action and to help him become a lawful citizen, than in penalizing the child. Instead of taking a youth and throwing him into a prison system that carries the possibility of teaching him further criminal skills, Sweden is genuinely concerned with the education and betterment of the youth.

Finally, Swedish law allows for the containment of children, particularly those with substance abuse problems. This provision applies to both delinquents and nonoffenders. The Care of Young Person's Act permits for the creation of specialized schools for children that are a risk to themselves, such as youths with severe substance addictions. The youths are confined primarily because of their behavior, criminal or not, which opens the possibility for self-harm. The longest time youths can be kept against their will without a formal prison sentence is two months.[92] While this form of hospitalization uses forced captivity, it is different than imprisonment because it is led by a team of mental health experts, and it is meant solely for the benefit of the offender rather than having any punishment implications.

NOTES

1. Walgrave, Lode and Jill Mehlbye (eds.) *Confronting Youth in Europe: Juvenile Crime and Juvenile Justice.* Institute of Local Government Studies: Aug. 1998. [Online]. 26 Nov. 2002. Available: http://www.afk.dk/eng98/juvenile.htm

2. "Citizenship." *The Guardian, 15 October 2002.* Available: http://www.learn. co.uk/citizenship/onlinelessons/crime/activity3.asp.

3. Goldson, Barry, and Eleanor Peters. *Tough Justice: Responding to Children in Trouble.* London: The Children's Society—Edward Rudolph's House, 2001.

4. Goldson and Peters, 2.

5. ASEM Resource Centre, Child Welfare Initiative. "Trial. "*United Kingdom: Criminal Justice System Overview.* [Online]. Available: http://www.asm.org/documents/unitedkingdom/criminaljustice/2/.htm.

6. Walgrave and Mehlbye, 4.

7. Walgrave and Mehlbye, 5.

8. Walgrave and Mehlbye, 5.

9. Walgrave and Mehlbye, 6.

10. "Trial," Part D.

11. United Nations Committee on the Rights of the Child. "Initial Reports of State Parties Due in 1994: United Kingdom of Great Britain and Northern Ireland." 8 May 1998. [Online]. Available: http://www.hri.ca/fortherecord1999/documentation/tbodies/crc-c-11-add19.htm.

12. Winterdyk, John, (ed.) *Juvenile Justice Systems: International Perspectives.* Toronto: Canadian Scholar's Press, 1997, 79.

13. Winterdyk, 90.

14. Winterdyk, 91.

15. Goldson and Peters, 2.

16. Goldson and Peters, 2.

17. Goldson and Peters, 2.

18. Amnesty International "United Kingdom: Failing Children and Young People in Detention—Concerns Regarding Young Offenders Institutions." 1 Jun. 2002. [Online]. Available: http://web.amnesty.org/library/Index/engeur450042002.

19. "United Kingdom: Failing Children and Young People in Detention—Concerns Regarding Young Offenders Institutions."

20. "United Kingdom: Country Reports on Human Rights Practices." U.S. Department of State: Bureau of Democracy, Human Rights, and Labor. [Online]. Available: 23 Feb. 2001. http://www.state.gov/g/drl/rls/hrrpt/2000/eur/856.htm.

21. "Report to the Government of the United Kingdom." Council of Europe: European Committee for the Prevention of Torture and Inhuman or Degrading Treatment. [Online]. Available: http://www.cpt.coe.int/documents/gbr/2002-06-inf-eng.htm.

22. Goldson and Peters, 5.

23. Defence for Children International. "CRC Reports—Ireland." DCI Newsletter, vol. 4 no. 1 (April 1998). [Online]. 27 Oct. 2002. Available: http://www.defence-for-children.org/ong/DciHome.nsf/385f8d7c2ba5b2420025.

24. Burke, Olwyn. "Children, Young People and Crime in Britain and Ireland: From Exclusion to Inclusion—1998." *Scottish Executive.* [Online]. Available: http://www.scotland.gov.uk/cru/kd01/crime-25.htm.

25. "Children Act 2001." Irish Legal Transformation Initiative. University College, Cork. No. 24 of 2001, 8 Jul. 2001. [Online]. Available: http://www.uce.ie/law/irlii/statutes/2001_24.htm#z8.

26. "Northern Ireland: Criminal Responsibility." *Tigerchild: Parent's Magazine on the Web.* [Online]. Available: http://www.tigerchild.co.uk/pages/1438.asp.

27. "Judicature, Northern Ireland: Juvenile Courts." Statutory Rules of Northern Ireland. 1996. [Online]. Available: http://www.hmso.gov/uk/sr/sr1996/Nisr_19960302_en_1.htm.

28. Burke, 3.

29. "Northern Ireland," 1.

30. "Northern Ireland," 12.

31. "Initial Reports of State Parties Due in 1994," 540.

32. "Initial Reports of State Parties Due in 1994," 541.

33. "Initial Reports of State Parties Due in 1994," 547.

34. Burke, 5.

35. "Initial Reports of State Parties Due in 1994," 558.

36. "Initial Reports of State Parties due in 1994," 559.

37. "Report Highlights Children's Rights." *BBC News.* 7 Mar. 2002. [Online]. Available: http://news/bbc.co.uk/1/hi/northern_ireland/1858875.stm.

38. Healy, Yvonne. "IRT Education & Living: Making the Most of their Time—Some Young Offenders are Putting in the Effort to Gain Some Qualifications So That They Will Have Benefited from Their Stay in Prison." *Irish Times.* 25 May 1999.

39. Northern Ireland Human Rights Commission. "Northern Ireland Human Rights Commission Response to Future of the Juvenile Justice Centre Estate Review." 2000. [Online]. Available: http//www.nihrc.org/documents/land/43.doc. Accessed March 24, 2004.

40. "Initial Reports of State Parties Due in 1994," 564–565.

41. "Initial Reports of State Parties Due in 1994," 567.

42. Centre for Europe's Children, Council of Europe. "Ages at Which Children Are Legally Entitled to Carry Out a Series of Acts." [Online]. 27 Oct. 2002. Available: http://www.eurochild.gla.ac.uk.Documents/CoE/Reports/eacts.Eactes_5.htm.

43. United Nations. "Committee on the Rights of the Child, Sixth Session: Summary Record of the 140th Meeting: France" 11 Apr. 1994. [Online]. Available: http://eurochild.gla.ac.uk/Documents/UN/StatePartyReports/SummaryRecord/FranceSR140.htm.

44. Gabet, Gwénaël, Emmanuelle Gervier, and Pascal Weill. "Synthese d'Anglais." [Online]. Available: http://www.ac=-bordeaux.fr/Establissement/SudMedoc/comenius2/anglais.htm.

45. Walgrave and Mehlbye, 5.

46. United Nations Human Rights System. "For the Record 1997: France." 1997. [Online]. Available: http://www.hri.ca/fortherecord1997/vol6/france.htm.

47. "For the Record 1997: France."

48. "The Judge of the Children and the Juvenile Court." [Online]. Available: http://cdad54.repie.com/AcFinfJE.html.

49. West, Andrew, Yvon Desdevises, Alain Fenet, Dominique Gaurier, Marie-Clet Heussaff, and Bruno Levy. *The French Legal System.* London: Butterworths, 1998.

50. West et al., 111.

51. West et al., 83.

52. For the Record 1997: France."

53. "Committee on the Rights of the Child, Sixth Session."

54. "Committee on the Rights of the Child, Sixth Session."

55. "Committee on the Rights of the Child, Sixth Session."

56. "Committee on the Rights of the Child, Sixth Session."

57. Gabet, Gervier, and Weill.

58. Amnesty International. "Annual Report 2000: France." 2000. [Online]. Available: http://www.web.amnesty.org/web/ar2000web.nsf/countries/dd0509 c219703ee2802568f200552922?OpenDocument.

59. "For the Record 1997: France."

60. The Clearinghouse on International Developments in Child, Youth and Family Policy. "Ages at Which Children are Entitled to Carry Out Certain Acts: Germany." Colombia University. [Online]. Available: http://www.childpolicy intl.org/countries/germany.pdf.

61. Aronowitz, Alexis A. "Germany." *World Factbook of Criminal Statistics.* U.S. Department of Justice. 5. [Online]. Available: http://www.ojp.usdoj.gov/bjs /pub.ascii/wfbcjger.txt.

62. Freudenberg, Dagmar. "Youth Criminal Law in Germany." [Online]. Available: http://www.iap.nl.com/regconference/reg5.html.

63. Freudenberg, 4.

64. Freudenberg, 9.

65. Freudenberg, 7.

66. Freudenberg, 11.

67. Walgrave and Mehlbye, 5.

68. Freudenberg, Sec. B–2.

69. Freudenberg, Sec. B–2.

70. "Right to Defence and Fair Legal Procedures in the Member States and the Candidate Countries: Germany." 24 Feb. 2002. [Online]. Available: www.jura .uni-tuebingen.de/rux/pub/egpl.pdf.

71. Winterdyk, 238.

72. Winterdyk, 253–254.

73. Freudenberg.

74. Freudenberg.

75. Freudenberg.

76. Winterdyk, 255.

77. Freudenberg.

78. Wilkstrom, Per-Olof H., and Lars Dolmen. "Sweden." *World Factbook of Criminal Justice Statistics.* U.S. Department of Justice. 5. [Online]. Available: http://www.ojp.usdoj.gov/bjs/pub/ascii/wfbcjswe.txt.

79. United Nations High Commissioner for Human Rights. "Committee on the Rights of the Child, Third Session: Summary Record of the 57th Meeting." Geneva, 18 January 1993. [Online]. Available: http://eurochild.gla.ac.uk/Documents/UN/StatePartyReports/SummaryRecord/SwedenSR57.htm.

80. United Nations Committee on the Rights of the Child. "Third Session: Summary Record of the 57th Meeting: Sweden." 18 Jan. 1993. [Online] Available: http://www.eurochild.gla.ac.uk/Document/UN/StatePartyReports/SummaryRecord/SwedenSR57.htm.

81. "Third Session: Summary Record of the 57th Meeting." Pt. 36.

82. United Nations Commission on Human Rights. "Question of the Human Rights of All Persons Subjected to Any Form of Detention and Imprisonment." Fifty-Third Session. 14 Dec. 1996. [Online]. Available: http://www.hri.ca/forthe record1997/documentation/commission/e-cn4-1997-26.htm.

83. Wikstrom and Dolmen, 6.

84. Global March. "Worst Forms of Child Labour Data: Sweden." 2000. [Online]. Available: http://www.globalmarch.org/worstformreport/world/sweden.html.

85. "Third Session: Summary Record of the 57th Meeting."

86. United Nations Economic and Social Council: Commission on Human Rights." Question of the Human Rights of All Persons Subjected to Any Form of Detention or Imprisonment: Children and Juveniles in Detention." 18 Dec. 1996. [Online]. Available: http://www.hri.ca/fortherecord1997/documentation/commission/e-cn4-1997-26.htm#germany.

87. "Question of the Human Rights of All Persons Subjected to Any Detention or Imprisonment."

88. "Question of the Human Rights of All Persons Subjected to Any Detention or Imprisonment."

89. "Committee on the Rights of the Child: Summary of the 57th Meeting."

90. "Question on the Rights of All Persons Subjected to Any Detention or Imprisonment."

91. United Nations Committee on the Rights of the Child."Initial Reports of State Parties Due in 1992: Sweden." 23 Sept. 1992. [Online]. Available: http://www.un-hchr.ch/tbs/doc.nsf/385c2add1632f4a8c12565a9004dc311/6f8648e4f542ceac412561510039d4d0?OpenDocument&Highlight=0,CRC%2FC%2F3%2FAdd.1.

92. "Initial Reports of State Parties Due in 1992: Sweden."

5

Eastern Europe

I n examining the definition of a child in Eastern Europe, it is important to note that until the fall of the Soviet Union in 1990, a number of the countries in the region were subject to Soviet rule. Each functioned under the same form of laws, installed throughout the empire. After the fall of the Berlin Wall, many of the newly formed independent nations adopted new Constitutions and passed a body of new laws. These changes only occurred within the past twenty years. The Centre for Europe's Children published a report entitled "Juvenile Justice and Juvenile Delinquency in Eastern and Central Europe" and noted that, "for a number of countries the legacy of the Soviet legal and criminal justice systems has left behind a common history."[1]

In particular, Eastern Europe has a problem with the implementation of a juvenile court system. The Centre for Europe's Children released a comparative review of juvenile justice systems in Eastern Europe and in regard to the formation of juvenile courts claims:

> In general, it appears throughout Central and Eastern Europe, with notable exceptions, that there are few countries [that] have a dedicated juvenile court . . . for the majority of countries reporting, there is no special juvenile court but rather a modified form of court proceedings as they apply to adults presided over by a judge, more often than assisted by what are referred to as lay assessors or lay jurors—usually from the professional ranks of social workers, teachers, or pedagogues or at the very least from those who have some expertise with children or experience parenting.[2]

In an overall comparison with their western counterparts, the nations of Eastern Europe are lagging behind in the international quest to differentiate juvenile court proceedings from adult criminal trials.

There a quite a few similarities in juvenile justice systems among the nations examined in this chapter. For instance, the Eastern European countries have set the "age of criminal responsibility much higher. . . . The significance of this rests on the fact that whereas there seems to be little support for lowering the age of criminal responsibility [in Eastern Europe] . . . there seems to be considerable support in some Western European countries for raising it."[3] While legal policy across all of Europe is moving toward a higher age of criminal responsibility, Russia, Romania, and Poland appear to be circumventing the legal definition of a child by using alternative measures to prosecute and punish children who are legally not considered liable for their actions or to have the capacity to understand the crimes that they are charged with committing.

RUSSIA

Turning first to Russia, we note that the nation defines juveniles as young people between the ages of fourteen and eighteen, but also lists the age of criminal responsibility as sixteen, although it may be lowered to fourteen. While this may seem contradictory, it is interpreted to mean that age is not the foremost factor when determining a child's liability for an offense. The lowering of criminal responsibility is dependent on the type of offense and the severity of the crime. "Persons over fourteen years old will bear responsibility only for murder, major bodily injury, rape, kidnapping, larceny, robbery, burglary, stealing of firearms and drugs, malicious hooliganism, and train catastrophe."[4] The Soviet Union originally joined the United Nations in 1948, but reinstated their membership under their conversion to the Russian Federation in 1990. In reference to the age of criminal responsibility, Russia presented an original report to the United Nations Convention on the Rights of the Child in 1992. They restated that the age of criminal liability is somewhere between the ages of fourteen and sixteen, and also added that the court and prosecutor may agree to take the age of offender into account when deciding whether to press charges. Offenders under eighteen are afforded additional leniency, if the offender has "committed an act prima facie constituting a crime but representing no great social danger, and refer the matter to a commission on minors if the circumstances . . . are such that correction is possible without resorting to criminal justice."[5]

While Russia claims to use alternative measures such as commissions rather than criminal punishment for offenders and lists the age of criminal responsibility at its lowest at fourteen, youths even younger are sent to corrective institutions for offenses. Russia responded to questions posed by the International League for Human Rights in 1997, stating, "On the basis of a decision by the Commission for minors, 1,165 children between the ages of eleven to thirteen (1,241 in 1997) were sent to special closed correctional institutions . . . [but in the future] the decision to send children and teenagers to special correctional institutions as well as their release from these institutions can only be made by the court."[6]

There is a divergence from legal policy with actual implementation in regard to the age of criminal responsibility in the Russian Federation. If children cannot ever be held liable for their crimes under the age of fourteen, and that is specifically reserved for the most serious of crimes, then it should not be possible that alternative commissions hold the power of committing children to closed institutions for their offenses. The International League for Human Rights further comments on this issue: "[M]any of the positive articles of the law are likely to remain on paper only."[7]

In 1968, the Union of Soviet Socialist Republics implemented the first major guidelines for a juvenile justice system. They formed the Committee on Juvenile Affairs and enacted the Principles on the Committee of Juvenile Affairs. The Committee was, at this point, the only system that handled juvenile crime. They considered the cases of offenders up to the age of sixteen who had committed a dangerous act. The Committee also held jurisdiction over criminal delinquency cases for offenders up to the age of eighteen, as long as the crime was not considered violent or serious. When the Soviet Republic dissolved and the Russian Federation was formed, the new government outlawed the Committee on Juvenile Affairs, claiming that anyone charged with a crime must be tried in an actual court of law.[8]

The new democratic system is much more preventative than the Soviet process, and even in comparison to other nations. First, a department in the Ministry of Internal Affairs studies and predicts juvenile offenses based on a number of sociological factors. The department registers homeless youths, children with unacceptable home environments, and children who have had any previous connection to an offense in an attempt to thwart juvenile delinquency. The staff members at the department usually have educational or psychology backgrounds.

The government utilizes preemptive measures before a delinquent reaches the court phase by keeping regular contact with youths who have the potential to be in conflict with the law. But, when a juvenile is charged with a crime, the procedure immediately becomes more formal and involves multiple court actors. Judges, who must have at least five years' legal experience, hold initial proceedings to determine the age of the offender through proof of official documentation, as well as the juvenile's emotional maturity, character, and living conditions.[9]

The first step in the formal investigation also includes discussions with the teachers of the offender. The purpose of the initial inquiry is to insure that the trier of fact receives all the relevant circumstances regarding the juvenile. The work of the alternate investigators sometimes transfers to later proceedings through the Commission of Juvenile Offenders and Protecting Their Rights. This is an administrative body that is similar to the original Committee on Juvenile Affairs under Soviet rule. Their job is to define state and public response to juvenile crimes, and they can make appeals to the courts when a juvenile is charged with an offense.[10]

But, while juveniles are afforded limited special treatment in the eyes of the law, there is no distinct juvenile court: "All juvenile cases are heard in a general court of law."[11] Russia's attempts to employ preventive measures to limit juvenile offenses and to involve more circumstances in juvenile investigation have not lessened international scrutiny for the lack of a juvenile court. Amnesty International reported the United Nation's dissatisfaction with Russia's refusal to create a formal justice system for juveniles. The 1999 public statement claims, "The Russian Federation was also harshly criticized for not implementing the 1993 Committee's recommendations to establish a separate juvenile justice system, with separate juvenile courts and trained and qualified judicial and other justice officials."[12]

Thus, juveniles in Russia are only given extra protections until the formal trial begins. At the start of a trial, the same judges and jurors who hear adult cases try the juveniles in a general adversarial court setting with the same forms of evidence from both sides. Although an investigation shows that the defendant is a juvenile, the juvenile remains subjected to the adult court system that has more of a punitive outlook. The overriding purpose of the juvenile court is the understanding that a youth is much easier to rehabilitate than his adult counterpart, and that a distinctive court system, separate from adult proceedings, is formed to focus on those goals. Without divergent proceedings for adults and juveniles, the purpose of making a distinction between them is lost.

Interestingly, the Russian Federation combines the representation of a juvenile offender with the right of parental involvement. At the earliest stage of justice system contact, both a lawyer and a parent have a right to be present. If a parent is unable to attend, a teacher can take on the role as an alternate guardian.[13] Both the parents or legal guardian and the representative of the minor also aid in the defense of the charges to the court. In a 1992 United Nations report, delegates presented information about amendments to the Criminal Code that were under consideration by the *Duma*, or Russian Parliament. The amendments allowed for legal assistance from the moment of police contact, and desired the presence of an attorney, particularly in all forms of interrogation. In any case with a juvenile defendant, an interpreter will be provided if necessary, and at the cost of the state. The attorney and guardians of all youths charged with crimes are afforded the right to any information that the state has, to challenge the government in a court, have access to all documents in the proceedings, and can present evidence.[14]

These rights, along with a number of other alterations to the criminal code, finally became law in the summer of 2002. "January's shift to jury trials—limited to cases such as murder, rape and treason—is part of a process that began in July when the Russian parliament adopted 3,500 changes to the criminal code. The law, now being phased in, is modeled on the Western doctrine that the best chance for a fair verdict is an adversarial process."[15] These changes also allowed the right of representation from the moment of arrest to no longer be a provision specifically reserved for juveniles in conflict with the law; this is now accorded to all Russian citizens. "It establishes a defendant's right to an attorney upon arrest."[16]

While parental involvement is considered as important as the right of representation in the stages of interrogation and police contact, the judge overseeing the hearing can determine whether parents should play a role once formal court proceedings begin. "The investigator retains the right to prohibit the involvement in the case of a child's legal guardian if there are grounds for supposing that this might harm the child's interests."[17] The investigator, the social worker responsible for investigating the social and emotional welfare of the juvenile offender and making recommendations to the prosecutor, helps make this decision through her initial reports and inquiries. If it is recommended that parents and guardians have some involvement, then the court often places responsibility for the child on the parents during court proceedings. During the preliminary phases of court proceedings, "there are special provisions that allow the minor to be placed under the guardianship of his or her parent(s), or a relative or suitable guardian as recognized by the court. . . . The guardian must state in writing (in arbitrary form) that they recognize their responsibility to supervise the minor and to bring the youth to court as required."[18]

While rights recognized by most nations for juvenile offenders are also recognized in Russian law, Russia is somewhat of an anomaly in regard to the need for closed proceedings:

> All juvenile cases are heard in general court of law and require the participation of the youth and his or her lawyer. Unless it is felt that the case could have a negative impact on the youth, *all juvenile cases are heard in open court*. In addition the court has a right to remove the minor from court when evidence, which according to the defense or crown, could have a negative effect on the minor [emphasis original].[19]

Without regard to the social welfare of the juvenile, the court allows the public to attend all proceedings. Many nations choose to close hearings so that youths can avoid social repercussions of being known as a delinquent, in an attempt to further rehabilitation. The irony of the Russian regulations are that they will allow members of the public without any standing in the case to participate in hearings, while reserving the right to deny the defendant's participation. One of the fundamental principles of justice systems based on due process is the right to hear any evidence against an individual and the option to refute those statements. If the juvenile is barred from the open courtroom during a hearing that primarily regards his actions, the right to know what occurs in the proceedings is denied.

The underlying objective in the sentencing of Russian juveniles in conflict with the law is more punitive than rehabilitative. In deciding how a juvenile may be punished, a judge takes into account the danger that a youth poses to society rather than the youth's needs. In making this decision, a judge will consider the personality of the youth and also estimate the threat the youth poses to society. The purpose of the punishment decision is mainly that the youth accepts blame for his criminal activities.[20] Instead of considering the root of the problem by examining what led the youth to a deviant lifestyle, judges in Russia are expected to pay more attention to the youth taking responsibility for his action.

Options for punishment are listed in the Russian Criminal Code. They include a prison sentence, community service without custody, a monetary fine, mediation with the victim so that the offender accepts the impact that his action had on a fellow citizen, loss of property, and dismissal without sanctions.[21] Capital punishment remains legal for juvenile offenders, but can only be used in the most heinous offenses. While Russian law includes the death penalty, it is actually considered an abolitionist de facto nation, or a country that continues to list the death penalty as a penal option, but has not actually executed anyone for over ten years.[22] Interestingly, while independent researchers hold that juveniles are still legally allowed to be executed, even if it is never practiced, Russia denies such legislation to the United Nations. In their Initial Report to the Committee on the Rights of the Child, Russian authorities stated that the death penalty was not an option for any offender under the age of eighteen.[23]

While juvenile imprisonment was once incredibly popular in the Soviet Union, a recent trend in Russia has begun to use alternatives to sentencing. The substitute institutions still require confinement, but not without rehabilitative and educational materials. Russian judges have only recently begun to implement these alternate establishments as a sentence. The correctional institution is required to educate offenders so that they can become successful members of the work force. However, such facilities are reserved for youths who are not considered dangerous and if the youths are found to have the capacity to alter themselves into law-abiding citizens. Most importantly, Russian law does not recognize the correctional institution as punitive, and placement in one does not require a formal conviction.[24]

National authorities informed the United Nations as to what each of these "labour and educational colonies" must include. There must be an area for housing minors during their stay, with specific centers for learning. Each center should have an area dedicated to education. The teaching units should include classes of normal education, and in addition, vocational and technological skills. Other areas include less restrictive environments in which youths are meant to begin a transition for a return to the free world. Finally, the institutions are expected to provide counseling to the children, including both regular mental health services and guidance for jobs.[25]

But, a number of investigations have shown that the actual conditions of youth detention facilities are nothing like the "educational colonies" that the government claimed to have. And, the government itself has finally admitted that juvenile detention facilities are plagued with problems. In a report to the International League for Human Rights, representatives held, "In 1998 alone, the prosecutor's offices' inspections of these institutions revealed 2,139 violations of the law and 108 unlawful legal acts. In connection with these violations, criminal cases were launched against more than 200 officials."[26] The abuse and lack of educational measures in such facilities has led to the conclusion that Russian facilities actually will lead to more juvenile crime. While the use of correctional institutions that do not include formal conviction is notable, unless the institutions live up to their goals of rehabilitation, the offender will quickly return to an illegal lifestyle upon release.[27]

A recent media investigation focused on the Kursk pretrial detention center for minors, discussing both the reasons that the children committed offenses and the condition of their confinement. The article opens by claiming that it is a combination of the failure of the welfare system with poverty that has lead youths to illegal activities. The reporter interviewed a juvenile judge who held that many of the children in conflict with the law are from deprived backgrounds. They have no food and steal to eat, and while the law punishes them for their acts, many young offenders have not purposefully committed criminal acts.[28]

The conditions within this prison are appalling. Rampant disease and infection present a serious risk for juveniles in detention. A majority of the youths enter the institution with HIV, hepatitis, and tuberculosis. Overcrowding of cells quickly leads to the spread of such infections. Juveniles account for the majority of the HIV prison cases, and one out of every ten prisoners has tuberculosis.[29] As if the severity of forced removal from a home situation is not traumatic enough for detained youth offenders, Russia places them at risk for acquisition of incurable and deadly diseases.

Instead of rehabilitating youth offenders, the education colonies are instead feeding grounds leading to the adult prisons. For instance, over half of the released juveniles quickly recidivate, and are then sent directly to adult facilities. Those who are not released by the time they reach eighteen years of age are immediately transferred into adult prisons.[30] These statistics prove that the goal of rehabilitation in juvenile institutions is not being met. Either children are held for so long that they are forced into adult facilities, or if they are lucky enough to be released, the lack of resocialization within the institution leads them directly back to criminal activity. Finally, gender disparity in juvenile detention has a detrimental impact on female offenders in Russia. Of all of the colonies and youth prisons, only three are specified for female offenders. Many are kept far from their families and cannot contact relatives.

While the penal system in Russia for juveniles is in obvious need of improvement, a lot of the problems are not from lack of caring on the part of officials. Unlike wealthier European nations plagued by allegations of abuse, minors in Russia are generally cared for and fed, but the economic status of the nation makes it difficult for the offenders to receive effective rehabilitative care. At the Lokniskaya penal colony, for instance, the staff wages a daily battle for supplies. The staff grow their own produce and make the children's clothing. Personnel often supplement the funds of the institution with their own resources. Sadly, very few of the children forced into impoverished conditions have been found guilty of violent crimes.[31]

The staff at Lokniskaya make every effort to provide for these children, both with material goods and emotional support, but there simply is not enough funding to effectively complete their goals. In addition, if the crime of the youth is not serious, instead of forcing youths to live in destitute circumstances, wouldn't it make more sense for children to receive noncustodial care so that they may remain in the comfort of their families? While it has been noted that many institutionalized youths are already used to poverty, children in need would be better off with their families than in an impoverished institution.

POLAND

Poland has a higher age of criminal responsibility than Russia, yet it also reserves the right to hold a minor criminally responsible for his actions in the commission of certain crimes. According to Poland's Assessment by the Separated Children in Europe Programme, "Pursuant to the Penal Code, a person under the age of seventeen cannot be held responsible for having committed a prohibited act. . . . But, a juvenile who was at least fifteen at the time of committing the offense, shall be held responsible in case of committing the most serious crimes, such as murder, rape and kidnapping."[32]

The ages that Poland attributes to criminal liability exist mostly as paper policy. If a minor is under fifteen, regardless of the crime, he or she is not supposed to be prosecuted under criminal law because the age of criminal responsibility is synonymous with liability. However, youths well under that age can be found in national corrections establishments. In 1996, the European Committee for the Prevention of Torture or Inhuman and Degrading Treatment visited a number of juvenile detention centers throughout the nation. According to the report:

> The Correctional establishment and Home for juveniles in Swidnica occupied two separate buildings dating back to the late nineteenth century. Although essentially managed as one establishment, the two institutions performed distinctly different functions. The Home was designed for short-term stays (of up to six months) of boys aged between thirteen and sixteen, after which they would either be released or assigned to a correctional establishment. . . . As regards the correctional establishment, it catered for boys aged between fifteen and twenty-one years.[33]

While there appears to be a differentiation in youth establishments based on the age of criminal responsibility, Poland is faced with the same question as Russia. If children cannot be liable for their acts, how is it possible to detain them under the auspices of the title "home"?

Poland is one of the notable exceptions to the trend of Eastern European nations' refusal to institute separate juvenile courts. Poland entitles its juvenile court system the "Family Court." It has jurisdiction over juveniles that commit criminal offenses based on the Act on Proceedings Concerning Juveniles, which states: "A young person, who is engaged in criminal activity but cannot be held penally responsible pursuant to the Penal Code because of age or lack of maturity, may however be subject to a penalty on the basis of the Act on Proceedings Concerning Juveniles."[34] The main aim of the use of the Family Court instead of criminal adult courts is an attempt to rehabilitate the youth and also protect him from any demoralization that could occur in a criminal proceeding. But, there is also a separation in the kinds of proceedings that are held within the Polish courts. The Family Court can either meet under "educational" (more rehabilitative) proceedings or correctional (punitive) proceedings, depending on the severity of the crime and the age of the offender.[35]

In the Polish Family Court, a family judge who listens to all testimony from witnesses and lawyers makes all actions. The court is also obligated to provide an offender above thirteen years old with copies of all the decisions made by the judge.[36] While the Polish system is not as defined or complicated as some of the other nations in the world, juveniles in conflict with the law are given special protections in compliance with international standards regarding juvenile courts. The nation is substantially more dedicated to juvenile legal rights than other Eastern European countries, but Poland would benefit from the use of additional psychologists and teachers, to determine the extenuating circumstances that lead the youth to crime.

Poland only recently began to require representation in court for anyone under the age of criminal majority. Previously, the right to legal aid was considered optional, but could be assigned by the court. But, along with many other changes, the right of access to a lawyer for all juveniles recently became mandatory. "The court is also obliged to appoint a defense counsel where the accused is a minor (under 17 years old). When the defense counsel is appointed *ex officio*, he shall be under obligation to act in the proceedings until they are validly concluded."[37]

However, the manner in which attorneys are appointed to represent both adult and juvenile offenders alike is interesting. There is no separate body of criminal defense lawyers; instead, all practicing attorneys are kept on an updated list that is rotated. Once an attorney has been named as legal aid, he is required to defend his client. In a manner somewhat more just than other legal systems wracked by social differentiations, Polish law fixes minimal rates for legal assistance fees. In addition, the court determines the lawyer's fee based on the complexity of the case and the amount of work involved in defense. The fees for attorneys appointed by the court instead of chosen by the client are paid for out of the court's budget.[38]

Like attorneys, parents of offenders are integrally involved in court proceedings. They have as many rights as the juvenile himself. First, "court is obliged to provide not only the parents or a guardian of a juvenile but also a juvenile above thirteen years of age himself/herself with copies of all decisions taken in these proceedings. . . . The parents or guardian and the juvenile himself/herself may appeal the court's decision on the application of educational or reformatory measures to a higher court."[39] Parents are encouraged to remain involved in the court. If the parent feels that the offender has not been treated justly, they reserve their own right to appeal, separate from the child and his attorney. They are also notified of court proceedings from the first stage of contact.

On an interesting side note: When children are considered under the age of criminal responsibility, Polish law can require parents to bear the costs of their crimes. In February 2000, three males under the age of ten were linked to a bomb threat at a hospital. The *Polish News Bulletin* reported that, "The boys were identified within hours, but considering their age will not be held responsible for the incident. Their parents will probably be forced to cover the evacuation costs, which amount to zl 10,000."[40] While minors that are considered criminally responsible are liable for their own actions, for children considered by law incapable of understanding their offense, the parent or guardian assumes responsibility.

Finally, while Polish law originally required that juvenile courts remain closed to the public, recent amendments to the criminal code allow the victims of juvenile crime to participate in court proceedings. "The harmed person will now be allowed to participate in the proceedings, which thus far was not possible. They will also be notified of instituting legal proceedings and the final decision of the court."[41] Thus, the court remains closed to most of the public, but the rise in juvenile offenses in recent years has led Polish legislators to take the rights of the victim into account. Still, the youth court remains essentially closed to the rest of the public.

The sentencing experiences of juveniles in Poland are much like the experiences of children in Germany. There is a graduated system of possible sentences that may be administered depending on the seriousness of the crime and the failure of previously attempted rehabilitative measures. According to the Polish Penal Code, the Family Court sentences a young person who cannot be fully liable for his or her actions. Judicial bodies have a variety of available options for sanctioning a young offender. They can order probation under a social welfare worker or an officer, require the youth to pay for the damages caused by the criminal action, attend a specified educational institution, and/or remain separate from certain individuals that have been found to be a bad influence. Each of these options is meant to be invoked in the interest of rehabilitation and in the best interest of the juvenile. The only actual punishment listed by the act is remand to a reformatory, and that can only occur if the educational measures have been exhausted.[42]

During the last decade, the Polish government slowly made advances in lowering the number of juveniles in detention by providing alternative sentences. In a report to the United Nations, authorities noted that between 1992 and 1994, the total number of youths sentenced to correctional facilities has gone down, while the number of juveniles in the overall justice system has risen.[43] While it is distressing that more juveniles have become involved in criminal activity, it is heartening that smaller numbers of juveniles are mandated to detention facilities while greater numbers of youths are given sentences such as probation.

According to government authorities, children sent to correctional centers are afforded educational and rehabilitative measures. These facilities are not barred like prisons, and instead remain open so that the children do not feel restricted. In addition, the required work that is part of rehabilitation is completed outside of the institution, which reminds the juvenile of possibilities after release. Education and vocational training can also occur outside of the institution. For instance, youth offenders might be allowed to attend a normal public institution during their sentence. Classes also are extended beyond general requirements and include exercise, sports, arts, and culture. To retain a sense of family environment, detainees are not required to wear uniforms and are allowed to keep personal effects. Finally, the rules regarding visitors are liberal.[44] The independence given to youth distinguishes the experience of adult prisoners whose lives are determined at the whim of guards and other officials.

In the 1990s, however, independent researchers twice found that conditions of detention for Polish youths were nothing like the government's ideals of education. Initial inspections occurred across the nation from 1990 to 1992, and researchers found children with shaved heads that were constantly impeded by both physical and mental constraints. Staff physically, emotionally, and verbally abused children. For instance, a popular punishment was to force the youth to remain in their pajamas throughout the day. This penalty is both degrading and unsanitary. In direct opposition to the claims of open facilities where youth continue to have contact with the outside world, inspectors spoke with children who had not left the institution in months. This does not apply to leaving the grounds; many of the youths had not ventured outdoors in weeks. Unfortunately, later investigations found that the problems still existed. The 1997 to 1998 inspections found continued use of physical punishment and abuse. Worse, children remained unaware of their right to complain about their circumstances. Finally, the penalty of remaining in one's pajamas throughout the day was still widely utilized.[45]

On the other hand, the research delegation was pleased with the material conditions in the detention facilities and the educational opportunities they offered children. Inspectors noted that the facilities looked renovated, and were appropriately furnished and of a good size. In regard to education, the Correctional Establishment in Swidnica had both a school for primary classes and an area for vocational training. The vocational classes included work with metals and wood. Classes take up six days of the week, evenly split between general education and skills learning.[46] Overall, while Poland has some issues with detention conditions and overuse of it as a sentence, it appears that the government has made advances in improving prison establishments and providing alternative sentences for youths. While the juvenile justice system cannot at present be defined as purely rehabilitative, it is well on its way.

ROMANIA

Romania denotes the age of criminal responsibility with the exact same year as Poland. Under the newly adopted 1991 Constitution, "The Penal Code stipulates the age of criminal responsibility. The child under fourteen is presumed not to have the capacity to infringe the penal law while the minor between fourteen and sixteen years old will be responsible only if there are proves [*sic*] that he was aware of his act."[47] Unfortunately, little is known about what policies are instituted for children under the age of fourteen because there are no national laws regarding the issue.[48]

The lack of penal codes applying to younger offenders has allowed Romania to circumvent the policy on criminal liability and definition of a child. Like the Russian Federation, Romania has detained children as young as ten years of age for offenses but has labeled the punishment "reeducation." According to one United Nations report, "It was not clear from the information provided whether there was a clear distinction between the special reeducation schools for children below the age of ten whose conduct contributed to the spread of vice and the special schools that existed under criminal law provisions. Placement of children in reeducation schools was likely to be regarded by the children concerned as a punishment rather than as a means of reeducation."[49] Detainment for the purpose of "reeducation" based on offenses committed by children under the age of criminal responsibility, again, does not seem different from penal institutions for juveniles over the age of fourteen other than in name.

Like Russia, Romania does not employ a separate juvenile court system. But while Russia utilizes other methods to protect youth offenders, juveniles in Romania are afforded very few additional protections. Not only are juvenile offenders faced with the same criminal proceedings that adult delinquents confront, they also have more limited rights than the older criminals. In its initial report to the Committee on the Rights of the Child, Romania stated the following:

> In the event of criminal proceedings, where a minor more than fourteen years old has committed and is charged with an offence, the proceedings take place in his presence, in a separate private session. The parents, the guardian or curator, the tutelary authority and the counsel for the parties may attend, with the approval of the court. If the court considers that the proceedings may have an adverse effect on a defendant who is a minor less than sixteen years old, it may have him removed from the courtroom, but not before he has been heard.[50]

Romania's notion of protection of juveniles in the justice system should shift to allow children to be seen by alternate courts rather than decide that for their protection, the proceedings can continue without their presence. While this seems somewhat surprising for a nation that has recently begun to reinvent its penal codes, it is important to note that, like Sweden, Romania has an extremely high age of criminal responsibility. Technically, juveniles are not supposed to be held liable for any crimes committed under the age of fourteen. In addition, the law refers to any citizen over sixteen as of age to have adult liability for their actions. The need for a juvenile court might have been overlooked because the short time period in which children are considered juveniles by the law does not economically justify a need for a separate juvenile court.

But, even if Romania holds children liable in the same courts with the same trier of fact as adult proceedings, there are additional measures that juveniles could be afforded. For instance, juveniles should be guaranteed that a rehabilitative ideology reinforces their encounter with the legal system. In addition, instead of banishing young offenders from the courtroom during proceedings that regard them, the Romanian criminal courts should include social welfare workers to insure that judges take all the circumstances of the youth offender's life into account. The United Nations reprimanded the Romanian delegation in regard to these issues during a Committee on the Rights of the Child meeting. A Committee representative claimed, "With regard to general principles, there was still a problem of incompatibility between Romanian legislation and the provisions of the Convention, especially with regard to refugees, juvenile justice and child labour."[51]

According to the most recent amendments to the Romanian Criminal Procedure Code, all hearings in juvenile court must be kept closed to the public: "Art. 485: The session involving the judgment of the juvenile criminal takes place separately from the other sessions. The session is not public. . . . When the juvenile is under sixteen, the court, after the hearing, can request his removal from the session, if the court considers that the judicial investigation and the debates could have a negative impact on the minor."[52] While the juvenile is considered criminally responsible for his actions, he has a limited role in the court proceedings if the judge declares that his presence is unnecessary. Thus, while the statute seems somewhat in violation of international standards for juvenile rights, the reasoning behind exclusion is intended for the best interest of the child.

Romania, like many of its Eastern European neighbors, requires parental involvement in all phases of court proceedings. At the point of initial contact with criminal investigators, parents are summoned to participate. But, if for whatever reason a guardian declines the invitation to participate, the investigator still retains the right to charge the juvenile. After initial contact with the police, a social investigator is employed to research issues regarding the emotional, psychological, and physical circumstances of the offender's life. During this phase, parental involvement is considered integral. Once formal court proceedings commence, the parental role is similar to the investigatory phase. Parents are summoned and expected to give insight to the judge, but if they elect to abstain from the hearings, the court can nonetheless issue a decision.[53]

Finally, Romanian law is in compliance with international standards on the administration of juvenile justice in regard to the right for legal aid. In a 2000 report to the Convention on the Rights of the Child, the nation stated that police and any judicial worker are required to inform the child of the charges against him. It is also the responsibility of the authorities to ensure that legal assistance is obtained and present at appropriate times. The process of formal charging can only occur in the presence of an attorney.[54] In addition, if the youth cannot afford a lawyer, the court will appoint one. The right to defense continues throughout all phases of judicial contact: "Legal counseling by lawyers is obligatory for minors in all of the phases of a penal trial and is a guarantee for the exercise and respect of procedural rights. . . . In the absence of a chosen lawyer one has to be provided. . . . Legal counseling being mandatory, the investigator will make sure that the lawyer is present when the defendant is being heard. The arrested defendant has the right to contact his/her defense counsel."[55]

Romanian law dramatically changed with the introduction of the 1978 amendments to the Penal Code. In regard to the punishment of minors in conflict with the law, the modifications greatly lowered the number of children serving sentences in prisons. While juveniles were still confined, they instead were sent to reform institutions rather than to prisons. The new Romanian Penal Code is less punitive. It lowered the total number of crimes that citizens could be charged with, and implemented guidelines for less harsh sentences. All offenders, particularly juveniles, are treated more leniently by the court than under previous penal codes. Most importantly, previous mandates of prison were replaced by recommendations for rehabilitative sentences.[56] Prior to the changes, juveniles were sent to prison and were legally supposed to be remanded to correctional homes called "special training institutes" when found guilty of criminal action. If a correctional home proved to be insufficient for rehabilitation, then a minor could face imprisonment, but must be kept segregated from all adult criminals.

Romanian authorities told the United Nations that juvenile detention would only be utilized as a last resort, and that judicial bodies were given a wide variety of alternative sentences to choose from instead. Judges are required to take a number of factors into consideration, including balancing into the equation what would be best for the minor. The factors include the harm to society caused by the crime, the physical condition of the youth, and the life circumstances of the offender, including his relationship with his family and the physical conditions in the home. In addition, the judge is required to note the maturity of the youth as perceived through his intellect and morality.[57]

While considering these factors, judges have the option of a variety of sanctions that can be considered educational. Youths can be sentenced to supervised liberty, in which a guardian or other relative adult will be responsible for their activities. If the youth is afforded the moderate sentence, there are other requirements for rehabilitation. If the minor is sentenced to supervised liberty, which entails the responsibility for the youth falling under the discipline of the guardian or another competent adult, the youth is required to perform community service in his or her spare time. The purpose of this penalty is to help the youth learn that he is both connected to and responsible for what occurs within his community. On a psychological level, the youth can foster a sense of self-worth and cultivate a law-abiding mindset.[58]

If a judge has exhausted other options, a minor may be imprisoned or detained in a correctional facility. The lack of juvenile prisons usually means that children are held in adult penitentiaries, but should be separated from adult criminals and given special treatment. The Romanian government claimed that areas in prisons specifically reserved for minors do in fact exist. In addition, laws require that imprisoned youths are educated regardless of their circumstances. They are taught general classes such as reading and math, and are also given vocational training to provide them with a marketable skill upon release. Juveniles are differentiated from adults in that they can only be forced to work while imprisoned if they are over fifteen and have a physician's consent. They are also granted greater access to visits so that they can remain in contact with their families, and are provided with more opportunities for recreation. Finally, prisons are prohibited from placing juvenile offenders into isolation.[59]

But, investigative sources have shown that Romania does not follow its own policy. First, alternative sentences like probation are not considered during sentencing. Even worse, juvenile offenders are consistently integrated into adult prison populations, a move that puts the physical life, mental health, and rehabilitative process of the younger offender at risk. Independent organizations are already working toward remedying this situation. Tiffin University has forged a partnership with American organizations in an attempt to alter the Romanian juvenile justice system. The overriding goal of this partnership is to highlight the usefulness of probation, which Romanian judges had a penchant to overlook. The alliance hopes that greater use of probation will limit the overuse of imprisonment for nonviolent youths that presently permeate the adult offender population.[60]

The U.S. government reported other problems with detention of Romanian juveniles in their human rights investigation. Three detention centers reserved specifically for juveniles have finally been constructed, but the problem of youths in adult prisons remains. The report notes that even with a large increase in budget, conditions within the prisons continue to be harsh. Social welfare workers remained concerned with both the overcrowding of prisons on the whole and the vast number of juvenile offenders integrated into these populations. In 2001, for instance, prisons across the nation "exceeded their total capacity by almost 15,000 people."[61] If Romania would consider alternate penalties that allowed minors to remain in their homes, the problem of overcrowding would quickly die away.

The United Nations lodged an additional complaint about children in detention. International representatives believe that children are subjected to physical punishment, and that understaffing and disorganization in these centers forges a system that lacks appropriate complaint procedures for a child. Basically, even if a child knows that he is being mistreated, there is no set procedure for him to follow to correct the situation. First, no domestic organization has taken a serious initiative to monitor the use of physical punishment in institutions, and concurrently, children who are experiencing abuse do not know whom to contact.[62] Without intervention, the cycle of abuse for children in institutions will continue. It appears that the Romanian government needs to invest more, both financially and legislatively, in the protection of children who have been convicted of criminal activity.

HUNGARY

Hungary follows the national policies of other Eastern European in regard to minors that commit offenses. Like its neighbors, the age of criminal responsibility in Hungary is fourteen years of age. In addition, a juvenile is defined as a child above fourteen but under eighteen years of age. Age of the offender also relates to punishment measures in the Penal Code. "If the juvenile has completed his sixteenth year when committing the crime it [the punishment] may be fifteen years, in case of a crime also punishable by life imprisonment, and ten years, in case of a crime punishable with imprisonment exceeding ten years."[63]

According to a report submitted to the United Nations, Hungary allows age to affect the definition of a child in regard to punishment in an effort to further safeguard the rights of juvenile offenders, but with different limits than suggested in the above-mentioned document. "The longest term of imprisonment that may be imposed on a minor who was not yet 16 when the crime was committed is five years. . . . A number of provisions in the Hungarian Criminal Code were amended in 1993 to ensure that the punishment of deprivation of liberty is inflicted only in the most necessary instances, and for the shortest possible term."[64] Regardless of how much punishment is limited based on the status of the juveniles it is commendable that Hungary has followed the legal policy of its Penal Code. Children under the age of fourteen are not held liable for their actions.

Hungary, like Poland, has specific provisions for juvenile court proceedings. The Criminal Procedure Code defines the three courts in Hungary as local courts, county courts, and the Supreme Court. Local courts have the original jurisdiction over any case, civil and criminal. County courts, in special cases, also have original jurisdiction, but more often are utilized on appeals from the lower courts. Finally, the Supreme Court only has appellate jurisdiction, to which either the defense or the prosecution can appeal. In each of the three courts there is a division for juveniles. A professional jurist is assigned by the Minister of Justice to sit for juvenile cases. In less serious cases, the judge hears the case alone, but it is required that for more serious juvenile delinquents and in the county courts that the judge is aided by two additional jurors. It is additionally required that one of the lay-assessors be a teacher. There is also a difference in the investigators who are the original contact for the juvenile with court proceedings. In local court jurisdiction, regular police officers who do not specialize in juvenile issues are assigned to the case, while in the county court, all juvenile offenses must be investigated by the Youth Department of Police Headquarters.[65]

In addition to police involvement, like Ireland, the prosecutor retains the right to suspend the charges against a juvenile offender. While the process is not called diversion, it is very similar. The juveniles have their charges suspended but remain under the supervision of court authorities. If the offender effectively reforms over the time frame, then the indictment is erased. "Since 1995, an amendment to the rules of criminal procedure introduced the possibility to postpone the indictment. If the conditions of indictment exist and the minor has committed a crime punishable with not more than five years of deprivation of liberty, the prosecutor may postpone the indictment for a period of one to two years."[66] In what is generally considered the correct method of implementing diversion in a variety of nations, Hungary further reserves the right for juveniles to decide that they would rather follow through with the indictment than allow the prosecutor to suspend charges.

The principles that support the use of a juvenile court require the separation of youth offenders from their adult counterparts. Criminal proceedings involving a juvenile do not revolve only around the facts and circumstances of the case. Instead, all court actors have an interest in deducing the social and mental capacities of the youth. The police are expected to study the living conditions and home of the offender. In addition, the court acquires a report from the school or work supervisor of the juvenile.[67] The judge and the assistants utilize all of the information to take into consideration the offender's life situation when making decisions for or against the youth.

While the written policy of juvenile justice in Hungary is both more advanced than many of its European neighbors and in conformity with international standards, the reality of the juvenile courts is not particularly advantageous for youth offenders. First, "there is often no real connection between the social protection system and the investigators, and the procedures officers use during the investigation. . . . The police have no vested interest in giving the juvenile suspect any opportunity to prove their innocence."[68] In addition, while judges are purposely named to the bench to supervise juvenile proceedings, they receive no training, either before their service or during it. The additional reports required by the court as necessary to make a fully informed decision about the offender have backfired in juvenile courts. "Owing to the excessive burdens on police and courts, the investigation and trial of cases are highly prolonged. It is not infrequent for two or three years to elapse between the delinquency and the court ruling."[69] The intentions of the Hungarian penal codes have yet to be met by the actual evolution of an effective juvenile justice system.

Hungary also safeguards the rights of juveniles by mandating that all young offenders be provided with legal counsel from the moment of arrest.[70] And, in line with international standards on the administration of justice, if the child and his family are unable to afford legal aid, it is the responsibility of the government to provide counsel. "If the juvenile delinquent has no defence attorney the police are obligated to call in one and ensure that the defence attorney be present at the first hearing."[71]

In addition, parents or alternate guardians bear the responsibility of acting as an additional legal representative for the minor throughout all contact with authorities. They are expected to attend all formal proceedings with the court, and are also contacted at the time of arrest and invited to be present at the initial police interview. The Hungarian Penal Code, as there is no separate law for juvenile criminal procedure, outlines the role of the guardian throughout all contact with the offender. First, "the juvenile delinquent's guardian should be summoned as a witness so that the character, the level of intellectual development, and general background of the juvenile [can] be better revealed."[72] While the guardian originally participates as a witness for court actors to help them understand the offender's criminal action, once formal proceedings commence the guardian becomes more like another legal representative.

However, the judicial body retains the right to prohibit parental participation if it decides that it will be detrimental to the child. If the parent is excluded, the court appoints another suitable adult to act as the guardian during the duration of the hearing: "During the procedure the juvenile's legal representative (usually the parent) has the right to speak on behalf of the youth. In case the legal representative is impeached or excluded, the investigative authority should appoint a case guardian through the local guardianship authority."[73] Interestingly, the automatic right to counsel differs from that of adult offenders. "For adult defendants, the amendment maintains the previous rule according to which the authorities have to inform the suspect that in case he should fail to retain a lawyer to act for him within three days of the communication of the charge the authorities appoint a defense counsel *ex officio*."[74]

Finally, in an effort to protect the reputation of the offender, proceedings are held in private and the records are not released. The decision to close hearings is made on a case-by-case basis, and it is only done when the judge declares it to be in the best interest of the offender. In a reaction to a rise in juvenile crime, change has been made in the policy to keep the offender's identity a secret: "it is the discretion of the police to allow a criminal case to be published during the phase of preliminary investigation. As the number of juvenile crimes rises, and the offenders have become more and more cruel, there is an intense public and media interest in criminal cases."[75] A review of the Hungarian justice system has shown that open cases happen more often than not. Schools are informed of criminal activity and instead of helping the youth, educators immediately force the child out of school. Some of the schools have even suspended a child under mere suspicion, rather than waiting for the legal body to announce a judgment. In these cases, the child is socially ostracized regardless of his or her guilt or innocence.[76]

There are other divergences in the Hungarian juvenile justice system with what national law has guaranteed. While the right to defense and guardian involvement is present in legal doctrine, the implementation and protection of this right is often denied by authorities. "Unfortunately, police investigations very often do not observe the rules relating to notification and presence of the legal representative or the guardian or the involvement of a defense attorney. . . . Although no data prevail, on the basis of the social and cultural background of the perpetrators, we can say that the defense attorney plays only a marginal role in protecting the rights of suspected offenders. A defense attorney is called in only when the family cannot provide their own attorney."[77] This description differs greatly from the expectations of both the Hungarian Penal Code and international guidelines regarding juvenile justice. The right to defense, to protection from the public, and other special provisions are offered to young offenders specifically to aid in their rehabilitation. When the basic principles of justice are denied, repercussions include the violation of international treaties, but, more importantly, harm to the juvenile's capacity to reintegrate into society as a reformed citizen.

The goals of juvenile sanctions in Hungary are meant to be rehabilitative rather than punitive. The nation has incorporated the Convention on the Rights of the Child into their national law, and has added the goal of prevention in sentencing. The purpose of sanctions is to protect society and the offender equally, and also to help the juvenile become a law-abiding citizen. Finally, Hungarian law holds that detention can only be used if all other options have failed.[78] Like many nations, Hungary employs a tiered system of penal sanctions in the hope that imprisonment will only be used in exceptional circumstances and as a last resort.

Juvenile punishment in Hungary is not fully separated from adult sentencing because both are determined by the same penal code. However, in a comparison of options for sentences, juveniles are afforded milder sanctions for the same crimes as adults. For crimes that an adult would receive life imprisonment, a similarly situated juvenile may only be sanctioned for fifteen years or fewer. For all other crimes, juveniles cannot be imprisoned for longer than ten years.[79] In addition, the use of capital punishment is outlawed for adult and juvenile offenders alike, and juveniles, regardless of crime, cannot be sentenced to life imprisonment. Only youths aged twenty and over at the time of the commission of criminal action can be sentenced to life imprisonment.

The penal code may frame the sentences for both adults and juvenile offenders together, but all detention facilities in Hungary are separated by age. All juvenile imprisonment must occur in establishments specifically reserved for young offenders, and in theory, should only be utilized when all other alternative sentences have proven ineffective. Substitutes for detention include probation, a fine if the juvenile has his own funds to pay the costs, or a reformatory institution. The reform establishment is different from imprisonment because its objectives are rehabilitation. Also, the term of remand to a reformatory cannot be greater than three years.[80] If imprisonment is utilized, the prison facility must be separate from adult penal institutions. The only crimes that a juvenile may receive a prison sentence for include those that carry a minimum of two years for a serious felony, or is the juvenile has a one year or longer sentence and is also a known recidivist.[81] All other sentences of confinement must occur in reformatory institutions.

The opinions of independent researchers who have visited prisons in Hungary diverge on whether the conditions and life of the juvenile offender will benefit from confinement. First, "By international standards, the average length of incarceration could be considered severe. With confinements averaging one-and-a-half years, their educational value is questionable. Contacts with the local social system are arbitrary and lack professional protocol. Juvenile delinquents in state custody are often 'forgotten' by the earlier protection institution and the county Child and Juvenile Protection Institute. For them rehabilitation is almost hopeless, as most of them have nowhere to go and their family ties are uncertain or nonexistent."[82] In addition, there are only three detention centers, all located in or around Budapest. Thus, even those children who have a supportive family are often too far away to remain in close contact with their relatives.

But, the Council on Prevention of Torture and Inhuman or Degrading Punishment (CPT) found that while detention centers are not by any means pleasant, there was little violation of the rights of minors, and the staff tried to make the experience of children both educational and rehabilitative. Most importantly, the delegation did not document any instances of physical abuse by staff either through interviews or personal inferences. There were a small number of reports of verbal cruelty, but inspectors found that staff-inmate relationships appeared satisfactory.[83] Like Russia, Hungary benefits from dedicated citizens who are committed to the future of young offenders, but their effectiveness in achieving their goal is hindered by national financial situations.

In addition, material circumstances and educational opportunities were deemed acceptable. The only major complaint was that solitary confinement cells in the facility used for discipline were not well lit, the toilets were not working, and the rooms were poorly ventilated. The CPT delegation was pleased to note that in 1999, a number of children in detention were schooled by outside teachers. Other inmates participated in vocational training courses and skill workshops. In addition, some of the juveniles were provided with paying jobs during their incarceration.[84] Juvenile prisons in Hungary are by no means an enjoyable experience for minors, and although there are specific issues that the nation has committed to mending, overall, juveniles are not horribly mistreated while incarcerated.

NOTES

1. Centre for Europe's Children. "Juvenile Justice and Delinquency in Central and Eastern Europe: A Review." [Online]: 15 Oct. 2002. Available: http://eurochild .gla.ac.uk/documents/coe/reports/juvenile_justice/jj&jd.

2. "Juvenile Justice and Delinquency in Central and Eastern Europe" 5.

3. "Juvenile Justice and Delinquency in Central and Eastern Europe," 5.

4. Nikiforov, Ilya V. "Russia." *World Factbook of Criminal Justice Systems*. U.S. Department of Justice. [Online]. Available: http://www.ojp.usdoj.gov/ bjs/pub/ascii/wfbcjrus.txt.

5. United Nations Convention on the Rights of the Child. "Committee on the Rights of the Child—Consideration of Reports Submitted by State Parties Under Article 44 of the Convention: Russian Federation." 22 Oct. 1992. [Online]. Available: http://www.hri.ca/fortherecord1997/documentation/tbodies/crc-c-3-add5.htm.

6. Altshuler, Borris. "Implementation of the Convention on the Rights of the Child: League Reports—Russia. International League for Human Rights. 1997. [Online]. Available: http://www.ilhr.org/ilhr/reports/children/html.

7. Altshuler, Borris, 5.

8. Winterkdyk, John (ed.) *Juvenile Justice Systems: International Perspectives.* Toronto: Canadian Scholar's Press, 1997, 214.

9. Winterdyk, 223.

10. Filamer, Mikhail and Rustem Maksudov. "Three and a Half Years of Restorative Justice in Russia." Centre for Social Justice and Legal Reform, 5. [Online]. 30 Oct. 2002. Available: http://www.sprc.ru/3hyears.html.

11. Winterdyk, 226.

12. Amnesty International. "Public Statement: Russian Federation." 8 Oct. 1999. [Online]. Available: http://www.pili.org/lists/piln/archives/msg00468.html.

13. "Committee on the Rights of the Child: Russian Federation."

14. "Committee on the Rights of the Child: Russian Federation."

15. LaFraniere, Sharon. "Russian Courts Give Power to the People: Revival of Jury Trials Marks Shift from Soviet-Style Justice System." *The Washington Post.* 22 Dec. 2002, A24. [Online]. Available: http://www.washingtonpost.com/wp-dyn/articles/A23767-2002Dec21.html, (accessed March 24, 2004).

16. LaFrainere.

17. "Committee on the Rights of the Child: Russian Federation."

18. Winterdyk, 225.

19. Winterdyk, 226.

20. Winterdyk, 227.

21. Winterdyk, 228.

22. Death Penalty Information Center. "Abolitionist and Retention Countries." Aug. 2002. [Online]. Available: http://www.deathpenaltyinfo.org/article.php?scid=30&did=140#Ordinary%20crimes.

23. United Nations Committee on the Rights of the Child. "Initial Reports of State Parties Due in 1992: Russia."

24. Winterdyk. 228.

25. "Initial Reports of State Parties Due in 1992: Russia."

26. Altshuler, 6.

27. Altshuler, 8.

28. Ward, Olivia. "In Russia, A Criminal is a Criminal, Whether he is 14 or 44." *The Toronto Star,* 11 Feb. 2001.

29. Ward, 1.

30. Ward, 2.

31. Ward, 3.

32. Separated Children in Europe Programme. "Poland—Country Assessment: Respondent—Warsaw University Legal Clinic." Oct. 2000–Feb. 2001. [Online]. Available: http://www.sce.gla.ac.uk/global/documents/eng.repliesquestionnaires/poland_engq.htm.

33. European Committee for the Prevention of Torture and Inhuman or Degrading Treatment. "Report to the Polish Government on the Visit to Poland." 30 June–12 July 1996. [Online]. Available: http://www.cpt.coe.int/en/reports/inf1998-13en.htm.

34. "Poland—Country Assessment," Part 5.

35. "Juvenile Justice and Delinquency in Central and Eastern Europe," 5.

36. United Nations, Committee on the Rights of the Child. "Initial Reports of State Parties Due in 1993: Poland." Geneva: 11 Jan. 1994. [Online]. Available: http://www.eurochild.gla.ac.uk/documents/un/statepartyreports/initialreport/polandir.htm.

37. Hermelinski, Wojciech. "Access to Legal Aid for Indigent Criminal Defendants in Central + Eastern Europe, Country Report: Poland." *Parker School Journal of East European Law* vol. 5, nos. 1–2. 1998. [Online]. Available: http://www.pili.org/library/access/jeel1998/poland.htm. Accessed March 24, 2004.

38. Hermelinski, 4.

39. "Initial Reports of States Parties Due in 1993: Poland."

40. "Economy, In Brief." *Polish News Bulletin of the British and American Embassies,* 8 Feb. 2000.

41. "New Rules for Handling Juvenile Cases." *Polish News Bulletin of the British and American Embassies,* 30 Jan 2001.

42. "Poland—Country Assessment

43. United Nations International Covenant on Civil and Political Rights. "Fourth Periodic Reports of State Parties Due in 1994: Poland." 14 Mar. 1997. [Online]. Available: http://www.unhchr.ch/tbs/doc.nsf/(Symbol)/CCPR.C.95. Add.8.En.

44. "Fourth Periodic Reports of State Parties Due in 1994: Poland."

45. The Helinski Foundation for Human Rights. "Some Remarks on Human Rights Protections in Poland (in Connection with the Fourth Periodic Report of Republic of Poland on Implementation of the International Covenant on Civil and Political Rights.)" [Online]. Available: http://www.hfhrpol.waw.pl/en/index.htm.

46. "Report to the Polish Government on the Visit to Poland."

47. The National Authority for Child Protection and Adoption. "Legislation in the Field of Child Protection in Romania. 2001." [Online]. 27 Oct. 2002. Available: http://www.mcrnet.ro/legis_romania.htm.

48. East East: Focus on Children. "Children in Conflict with the Law in the Central and Eastern European Region." 20 Apr. 2001. [Online]. Available: http://www.mcrnet.ro/newsletter.htm.

49. United Nations High Commissioner on Human Rights. "Committee on the Rights of the Child–Summary Record of the 122nd Meeting: Romania." 21 March 1995. [Online]. Available: http://eurochild.gla.ac.uk/Documents/UN/StateParty Reports/SummaryRecord/RomaniaSR122.htm.

50. United Nations Committee on the Rights of the Child. "Initial State Party Reports Due in 1992: Romania." 14 Apr. 1993. [Online]. Available: http://www.bayefsky.com/reports/romania_crc_c_3_add.16_1993.php.

51. United Nations Committee on the Rights of the Child. "Summary Record of the 119th Meeting" Geneva: 20 Jan. 1994. [Online]. Available: http://eurochild.gla.ac.uk/Documents/UN/StatePartyReports/SummaryRecord/RomaniaSR119.htm.

52. "Romania—Criminal Procedure Code: The Basic Rules and Actions in a Criminal Trial." Provided by Corpus Juris. [Online]. Available: http://www.era.int/domains/corpus-juris/public_pdf/romania_criminal_procedure_code.pdf.

53. "Romania—Criminal Procedure Code."

54. United Nations Convention on the Rights of the Child. "Committee on the Rights of the Child—Consideration of Reports Submitted by States Parties Under Article 44 of the Convention: Periodic Reports of State Parties Due in 1997: Romania." 18 Jan. 2000. [Online]. Available: http://193.194.138.190/tbs/doc.nsf/385c2add1632f4a8c12565a9004dc311/0e4c1b3d04f3091ec1256c5a0035d136/$FILE/G0243077.pdf.

55. "Periodic Reports of State Parties Due in 1997: Romania."

56. "Romania: Penal Code." July 1989. [Online]. Available: http://www.1up-info.com/country-guide-study/romania/romania230.html.

57. "Periodic Reports of State Parties Due in 1997: Romania."

58. "Periodic Reports of State Parties Due in 1997: Romania."

59. "Periodic Reports of State Parties Due in 1997: Romania."

60. Romanian-American Suitable Partnerships. "Promoting Juvenile Justice Reform: A Partnership between Tiffin University and the Humanitarian Association of Sts. Peter and Paul." RASPNEWS. 4 Oct. 2001. [Online]. Available: http://www.worldlearning.org/pidt/romaniagrants/news_pjjr.html.

61. "Romania: Country Reports on Human Rights Practices 2001." United States Department of State: Bureau of Democracy, Human Rights, and Labor." 4 Mar. 2002. [Online] Available: http://www.state.gov/g/drl/rls/hrrpt/2001/eur/8327.htm.

62. United Nations Convention on the Rights of the Child. "Summary Record of the 119th Meeting (Closed): Nambia, Romania." January 25, 2001. CRC/C/SR.119. (Summary Record of the 19th Meeting (Closed)." Palais de Nations, Geneva. 1994. [Online]. Available: http:www.unhchr.ch/tbs/doc.nsf/0/16a450df0b5fl5534125615100579175 2Opendocument. Accessed March 24, 2004.

63. Rahói, Maria. Prosecutor at Budapest. "Juvenile Justice System in Hungary." [Online]. Nov. 2002. Available: http://www.iap.nl.com/regconference/reg6.html.

64. United Nations High Commissioner on Human Rights. "Committee on the Rights of the Child—Consideration of Reports Submitted by States Parties Under Article 44 of the Convention: Hungary." 24 Sept. 1996. [Online]. Available: http://www.eurochild.glas.ac.uk/Documents/UN/StatePartyReports/Initial Report/HungaryIR.htm.

65. Rahói, sec. 2.

66. "Consideration of Reports Submitted by States Parties Under Article 44 of the Convention: Hungary."

67. Rahói, 3.

60. Winterdyk, 317.

60. Winterdyk, 319.

70. Rahói, 5.

71. Winterdyk, 315.

72. Winterdyk, 314.

73. Winterdyk, 315.

74. "Country Report: Hungary." Access to Legal Aid for Indigent Criminal Defendants in Central and Eastern Europe. *Parker School Journal of East European Law.* Vol. 5, nos. 1–2: 1998. [Online]. Available: http://www.pili.org/library/access/jeel1998/hungary.htm.

75. Rahói, 6.

76. Winterdyk, 317.
77. Winterdyk, 317.
78. Rahói, 9.
79. Winterdyk, 307.
80. Winterdyk, 308.
81. Rahói, 11.
82. Winterdyk, 321.
83. European Committee for the Prevention of Torture and Degrading or Inhuman Punishment. "Report to the Hungarian Government on the Visit to Hungary." 5–16 Dec. 1999. [Online]. Available: http://www.unhcr.ch/tbs/doc.nsf/385c2add1632f4a8c12565a9004dc3311/8f6194bb2d23a586802564bf004d53a2?OpenDocument&Highlight=0,Hungary.
84. "Report to the Hungarian Government on the Visit to Hungary."

6

✛

The Middle East

In addition to conflict because of political and religious differences among the various nations in the Middle East, there is also a good deal of diversity in the application of juvenile justice systems. Among the Muslim countries, Iran is unique for choosing to utilize fundamental Islamic laws as the basis of its penal codes. Israel, on the other hand, is a Jewish state. Thus, while other regions in the world have a sense of uniformity in their treatment of juvenile offenders, the Middle East is a region where each nation applies its own individual rules to minors that commit crimes.

ISRAEL

Unlike the other nations in the region, Israel is a secular state with Jewish tenets interspersed in family law. The nation was formed in 1948 with land that had previously been a protectorate of Britain. Criminal law was largely adopted from the British system, with Israel introducing various alterations. Still, many similarities in the age of criminal responsibility can be connected to the United Kingdom's laws. The minimum age of criminal responsibility developed as follows:

> Under the British mandatory government law of 1937 a person less than nine years old is not legally responsible for his or her acts. Children aged nine to twelve could be held legally responsible, but the prosecution had to prove that the child could know that he or she should not have behaved as she or he did. Under the new Israeli law this situation changed, and the minimum age of criminal responsibility was raised to fourteen, and then lowered again to twelve.[1]

First, it is interesting that in a protectorate, the British laws were used as a basis to create a lower age of criminal responsibility than was enacted on the United Kingdom mainland. Second, although the age of criminal responsibility is higher than the United Kingdom's present statute, it remains lower than in most Western European countries. Israel is considered to have one of the most technologically advanced societies in the world. Nevertheless, countries across Eastern Europe that have only recently forged laws have much higher ages of criminal liability for their child citizens.

When referring to the age at which an offender can no longer be prosecuted as a juvenile, the British-Israeli comparison is as follows: "Under the British mandatory government law a person was considered a minor until the age sixteen. Under Israeli law the upper bound was raised to eighteen, first for females, and later on for males as well."[2] Again, Britain upheld a lower age of criminal responsibility in its protectorate than on the mainland. The United Kingdom only allows offenders to remain within the juvenile justice system until eighteen unless extenuating factors come into play. Israel, on the other hand, has reached the standards of international rights organizations, requiring that offenders under the age of eighteen be kept within the more lenient and rehabilitative juvenile justice system. Israel has also attempted to keep responsibility for crime the same regardless of gender. Instead of affording additional protections to young female offenders, Israel altered their laws and applied the same maximum age for juvenile protections to males as well.

Like Colombia, Israel's unique status in the Middle East combined with its history of attacks has led the nation to circumvent basic age requirements in an effort to limit terrorism. During the ongoing *Intifada* that began in September 2001, a rash of suicide bombings has led the government to install a different set of laws for Palestinian juveniles. "Recent cases of . . . Israeli detention include Palestinians held for reasons of security, including some as young as sixteen years old. Military Order 132 allows for the arrest and detention of Palestinian children aged from twelve to fourteen years old."[3]

The Israeli juvenile court system lists education and rehabilitation as its objectives, but it also endeavors to keep the interest of the community in mind when making decisions regarding offenders. The court of peace is primarily responsible for handling juvenile offenses. "As a court of peace it may deal with most offense categories, including offenses that are ordinarily within the jurisdiction of the district court (the most important exceptions are murder, state security offenses, and drug offenses)."[4] The court of peace operates as both magistrate courts and district courts.

Concerning who is appointed as a juvenile judge, either an individual is only appointed for a set time period or he or she has a permanent appointment to the juvenile court. Israel has attempted to separate the juvenile court from the location of the adult proceedings as much as possible: "In principle, the juvenile court has to be located, as far as possible, in a location that is not used for the sessions of other courts. However, a separate building is not usually available, and the juvenile court may have to satisfy itself with separate halls in the court building."[5]

The actual proceedings of the court are divided similarly to the American juvenile justice system. The first part involves the determination of fact while the latter half involves the disposition decision. The determination of facts portion of the proceedings requires that a probation officer submit a report about the psychological and emotional state of the offender if the judge has already issued a finding of guilt. The probation officer is a representative from the Juvenile Probation Service, under the Ministry of Welfare. Probation officers are required to investigate and write the report at the time of arrest, but depending on the outcome of the determination of facts, may not be asked to submit their information. Interestingly, even if a juvenile is found guilty of a crime, the judge is not required to institute any form of punishment or alternative treatment; the offender may be simply released.[6]

Although Israeli Arabs only make up 20 percent of the general population, they are greatly overrepresented in the juvenile court. According to a study that Haj-Yahia, Rahav, and Teichman completed in 1978, the reasons that the minority population makes up a larger percentage of youth offenders in juvenile courts might not be "necessarily due to discrimination by the Jewish officers of the justice system. The major finding, in that study, seemed to be the differential recommendations made by probation officers to the police and the juvenile court."[7] The power of the probation officers is important not only because it treats Israeli minorities different than Jewish citizens, but also because it reflects the overall large influence that the probation officer has over the court. Although the Juvenile Probation Service is supposed to be a separate body from the court, probation officers effect dispositions, probably more than intended. But if the probation officer is fair and correctly reports all of the circumstances that led the juvenile to commit an offense, then their power should work in favor of the offender.

Again, Israeli criminal laws were adapted from British codes at the time of independence, and therefore reflect many of the same guarantees to juveniles that the laws of the United Kingdom promise. But, in a divergence from most democratic nations, the right to legal defense is allowed, but legal aid is not mandatory. "A minor has a right to legal representation. If the defendant does not have a lawyer, and the charge is serious, and whenever the court deems it necessary for the juvenile's interest, the court must appoint a defense attorney. When the juvenile is not represented by a lawyer, it is the court's duty to explain the charges to the defendant."[8] While the right to employ an attorney is respected, the legal system forges a class-oriented approach to justice that leaves the children in poor economic situations with no legal aid. It is obvious that an offender from a wealthy family will automatically hire a defense attorney. And, with additional help, a juvenile increases his chance of acquittal or of receiving a lesser sentence. The child of lesser means who commits a minor offense will be disadvantaged in court as compared to his peers.

On the other hand, the Israeli juvenile court attempts to provide the defendant with legal aid by walking him through all court processes. In any case where there is no legal counsel, "the court should help the juvenile in the interrogation of witnesses. This is done by allowing the defendant to present his (or her) version of the case and asking the questions implied by this version. The court may interfere with legal discussion and ask questions in order to clarify issues."[9] These safeguards appear to reverse the impact of lack of counsel by providing help, but in reality, there are a number of problems with this scenario.

First, it is a conflict of interest if the court acts both as a finder of fact while also taking responsibility for providing the minor with legal guidance. The very nature of the trier of fact occupation is to remain detached from the adversarial parties so they will make a fair decision. Second, the chances that a scared juvenile offender will be as effective as a trained attorney at asking questions and making important points are slim. While the State of Israel offers the right of attorney, in actuality, it is a right only respected for those who can afford it.

Alternatively, Israeli law respects the right of privacy for the juvenile offender and recognizes that hiding facts about the case from the public is imperative to the process of rehabilitation. Even at the initial phase of investigation, the authorities are required to keep all information off record. "The JOS [Juvenile Offender Section] often utilizes a special interrogation process, which does not lead to the formation of an official police record. . . . Presumably, these unique procedures may prevent the process of escalating involvement in crime."[10]

The protection of the minor's right to privacy continues through formal court proceedings. "Juvenile court sessions are typically closed, although the judge may allow other, nonpartisan individuals, to be present. This permit is usually granted to individuals who have a direct involvement with the accused, or who may be involved in the rehabilitation process—members of the family, teachers, probation officers and social workers. As a rule, the identity of the accused and the witnesses should not be publicized if they are under sixteen years old."[11] Unlike the right to defense, Israeli law effectively protects all juveniles from public scrutiny and stigmatization, regardless of the social class of the offender.

Finally, parent involvement in Israeli juvenile justice is based somewhat on the age of the offender, and somewhat on arbitrary decisions made by the authorities in an individual case. A 1993 report to the United Nations states that the police rules include provisions that the parent or guardian must be present at any interview with a youth under the age of fourteen. However, police are given the discretion to decide whether the presence of the parent could either be harmful to the youth or impede the investigation. In addition, when the youth is fourteen years or older, parents are not given the right of presence at questioning, but again, the police retain the option to decide otherwise. Often, when a parent of an older youth requests to be present, the police follow an informal policy of allowing them as long as there is no reason not to.[12] While the law allows police to bar parents from interrogation of children over the age of fourteen, authorities often allow the presence of parents in the hope of learning more about the life and situation of the child. As previously noted, judges often allow parental involvement once formal court procedure begins, as long as the parents are acting in the child's best interest. If they are detrimental to the rehabilitation process and the basic determination of fact, the court reserves the right to exclude them.

The underlying rationale of the sentencing phase of the Israeli juvenile justice system is rehabilitative rather than punitive. In a report to the United Nations, government representatives stated that the Youth Law of 1971 was rehabilitative. The legislation also outlines the sanctions that can be implemented for a convicted minor, either treatment or punishment.[13] If the offender is found guilty of his crime, the court has three options that it can employ in sentencing. The court can convict and sentence the youth, can order treatment for the minor without entering an actual conviction, and, finally, can instead discharge the minor with a warning but with no sanctions or alternate treatment. The decision to rehabilitate youth offenders instead of penalizing them is supported by members at all stages of juvenile justice intervention. The juvenile judge historically makes decisions with the minor's interests in mind. However, mirroring other nations, Israeli authorities have recently begun to question whether the rehabilitative approach is effective in limiting the recidivism of youth crimes, and whether taking the interest of society into consideration would have a greater impact in lowering youth crime.[14]

In particular, the use of the conviction and punishment option involves a sentence of one of the following: actual imprisonment, a suspended prison sentence, placement under the surveillance of a probation officer, a fine, compensation, or public works. In addition, there are alternatives exclusive to minors, such as placement in a closed residence instead of imprisonment.[15] Many of the modes of treatment are similar, and include provisions of supervision, probation, reparations to the victim of the action, and psychological or substance abuse treatment.

The juvenile detention centers in Israel are meant to uphold the aims of treatment. In *(Minor) v. State of Israel*, the Supreme Court issued a decision that declared, "The conditions of detention and prison, even without the characteristics of such places, are liable to cause severe emotional shock and trauma. More often than not, a minor is liable to encounter a world of drugs and serious crime. The court must become a 'father to minors', and preserve them—whenever possible—from this experience."[16] Again, detention can be used for both punishment and treatment, and the government distinguishes between these options. Offenders can either be sentenced to custodial treatment or custodial punishment. Punishment is only used when the minor has committed a serious felony, and must accompany a formal conviction so that the youth comprehends the seriousness of his or her actions.[17] These centers require that children are well cared for and provided with education, rehabilitation, recreation, and medical care during their stay. They cannot be placed in solitary confinement, unless it is in self-defense and for the safety of the staff and other residents.

Very few juveniles are actually sanctioned with imprisonment, but for those who are, the nation has responded with a well-run juvenile detention system. The Israeli government adopted their laws from a combination of sources, but had to create a prison system basically from scratch. In the process, authorities built a prison specifically for male juveniles. *Hasharom* is reserved for youths aged fourteen to eighteen years, but also allows young adults through their twenties to remain instead of transferring to an adult facility. The government is working toward making the facility drug free.[18] Male offenders risk the possibility of integration into the adult prison population, but female youth offenders must be placed with adult criminals. There is one female prison in the nation, *Neve Tizra*, and it is the custodial house for women of all ages, integrated regardless of offense or past criminal history.[19]

The recent increase in youth crime led to the construction of a new juvenile facility in 2001. The prison service had dedicated itself to the goal of forming a humane institution for youth offenders that will work to resocialize them into law-abiding citizens. The result of this objective was the opening of Ofek Juvenile Prison in May 2001. This is a totally separate facility completely reserved for youths under the age of eighteen. There are 124 units, separated into four wings that help further segregate offenders based on their criminal pasts. While one wing has only minimal security, another is closed and is reserved to punish infractions and to withdraw more serious offenders from the general population.[20]

Ofek Juvenile Prison has many of the same rehabilitative goals that are found in Israel's juvenile reform institutions. The establishment is meant to be both educational and restorative. The facility is meant to be safe and fulfill the needs of young adults. The overriding objective of the institution is for youths to gain proper skills that will help them exist as law-abiding citizens.[21] Overall, Israel attempts to keep youths out of prison unless there are exceptional circumstances. All of the possible sanctions for juveniles convicted of crime have a rehabilitative basis, from compensation for the victim to actual imprisonment.

But, Palestinian children in conflict with the law are not treated in the same way. During the first *Intifada*, Israeli officials constructed a military prison for youths charged with engaging in all forms of rebellious activity. At this time, neither the prisons nor the military had a method to handle Palestinian children under the age of sixteen. As a result, a juvenile detention camp was created in 1987, and at one point, housed over one hundred youths.[22] In less violent times, the military worked out a new system that allowed for Palestinian parents to pay a fee for their child's crime and buy the child's freedom.

The most recent phase of violence has returned to periods of detainment for Palestinian youths that are often divergent from the rehabilitative experience of incarcerated Israeli juveniles. The Human Rights Watch found that vast numbers of Palestinians of all ages were arrested and detained in 2001. Allegations of abuse, including physical violence, inhumane conditions, refusal to provide sustenance, and torture were noted. In January 2003, the number of Palestinians held without formal charges exceeded five thousand.[23] Detention without formal charges, torture, and violence are far from the promises of rehabilitation of the Israeli government for minors in conflict with the law. While terrorism and ongoing violence have led both Palestinians and Israelis to desperate measures, there is no excuse for differential treatment of child offenders based on ethnicity.

EGYPT

In 2001, Egypt reported to the United Nations that they have legislated the age of criminal responsibility at seven.[24] In 1997, Egypt elaborated their rules regarding age attainment for criminal liability to the same committee. The Penal Code of 1883, which is partially still in effect, states, "children aged under seven years are not criminally responsible, and sets forth specific measures for dealing with delinquents aged over seven but under fifteen. . . . By virtue of Act No. 31 of 1974, juvenile justice is dealt with in a separate code that anticipates the Convention on the Rights of the Child in setting the age of majority at eighteen years."[25]

Severity of the crime also has an impact on the age of liability for juveniles. Offenders are not to be treated in a similar fashion as adults unless they are eighteen years of age. For instance, homosexual activity is considered illegal and immoral under Egyptian law. In May 2001, Egypt arrested a number of individuals on suspicion of such activity. One of the arrested offenders was a juvenile, but instead of lumping him with the adults rounded up in the same crackdown, the government prosecuted the sixteen-year-old as a juvenile.[26] Thus, while Egypt tends to have a much lower age of criminal liability, the age at which an offender is no longer considered a juvenile is high enough that children are afforded protection under the law. In addition, keeping youths under the age of eighteen in the juvenile courts is a policy that appears to be adhered to.

Egypt also has a separate juvenile court. According to a report to the Committee on the Rights of the Child, "the juvenile court has exclusive jurisdiction over any offence committed by a child, whether it be a serious or lesser offence, except for serious offenses committed by a child aged over fifteen with an adult accomplice, in which case the minor and adult are tried by the criminal courts."[27] This system is somewhat different from other nations that generally give jurisdiction to adult criminal courts when the crime is severe. Egypt explicitly refuses to allow any juvenile out of the jurisdiction of the juvenile justice system, even if the crime is murder, unless it is a crime that was committed with an adult. While other nations set up a specific place and location for any legal proceedings, Egyptian law allows for hearings to be conducted at social welfare centers, particularly if the child has been placed there. This is an alternative way to reassure the offenders and separate their legal experience from that of adult criminal proceedings. Without a courtroom, a child is less likely to feel intimidated and fearful.

The trier of fact panel is made up of three judges and two experts. The judges are considered legal experts that undergo intensive training to earn the responsibility that comes with juvenile justice. They are hand-picked from the top-scoring graduates in law schools, and then can become magistrates. But, there are three further requirements to become a juvenile judge: "The president of a juvenile court must have more experience than an ordinary judge, and hold at least the rank of court president; the judge must be of the personality that fits him to work with children . . . the judge must successfully have followed specialist courses in the problems of facing juveniles,"[28] which are coordinated by a national judicial center.

The experts are equally important in the case. Egyptian law requires that one of the court aides must be a woman. The experts, like the Israeli probation officers, have the responsibility of investigating and writing a report about the mental, emotional, and physical capacities of the offender. In addition to the court aides, social workers' involvement is required, and they are responsible for reporting the roots of the delinquent acts and recommending a number of possible court responses. The judge, however, reserves the power of having any of the court actors as well as the juvenile removed from court if he sees fit. When juveniles are dissatisfied with the outcome of a hearing, they have the right to appeal to a Juvenile Court of Appeals that is set up in the same fashion as the lower court. Appeal proceedings also include three judges and the assistance of two experts, one of whom must be female.[29]

Egypt requires that all children in conflict with the law must have representation before the juvenile judge. In a report to the Committee on the Rights of the Child, the nation recounted its policy toward juvenile legal aid: "In criminal cases the child must be defended by a lawyer. If the child does not select defense counsel, the public procurator or the court shall assign one in accordance with the rules laid down in the Code of Criminal Procedure. If a child charged with a lesser offence is aged fifteen or over and has no lawyer, the court can appoint one for it."[30] Nevertheless, Egyptian authorities do not consistently follow their own legal creeds. A 2001 Amnesty International press release discusses the case of a sixteen-year-old Egyptian male tried and sentenced to prison for his sexual orientation. The international organization found that, "During the initial two weeks of detention he was denied the fundamental right to meet his family or be seen by a lawyer. Confessions extracted from Mahmud during that period were used as evidence in a trial leading to his conviction."[31] It is notable that while a defense attorney is guaranteed for minors during formal court proceedings, it is not legally mandated that children have access to legal aid during custody. Based on the abuse of Mahmud, who was not charged with a violent crime, Egypt should extend their unquestionable right to defense during all phases of juvenile contact with authorities.

Interestingly, Egypt is one of the few countries outside the North American region that not only requires parental involvement in court proceedings, but will hold parents or guardians responsible for their child's offenses. Whenever a child has committed an offense or has been deemed by authorities at risk for becoming delinquent, a formal warning is issued to parents. A number of factors, like begging, late night carousing, truancy, and being found in the company of delinquents can suffice as evidence for the initial warning. "A written warning issued to the person exercising parental authority over the child, to see that the child behaves itself properly in the future; in the case of a repeat offence, the child's guardian will be held criminally liable."[32]

Children are removed from the care of their parents who are also held liable for crimes they did not commit, in violation of international standards on legal accountability. In a way, this has the capacity of further detriment to the juvenile offender. They are forcibly separated from their guardian and might be scarred with the knowledge that their actions caused punishment for their guardians. For children who commit crime as a cry for help, the criminal liability of their parents will not aid in rehabilitation. Egyptian criminal procedure and the offender would benefit from less punitive measures, such as the provision of therapy for the family and the aid of social workers in helping parents learn to forge a relationship of respect with their child.

Finally, Egyptian law guarantees that all cases are heard in private. National authorities reported to the United Nations, "Hearings in juvenile court are attended only by the juvenile defendant's immediate family, the witnesses, the lawyers, the social workers assigned to the case and other persons duly authorized by decisions of the court. The judges are empowered to have the child removed from the courtroom after hearing it, or to have any of the above-mentioned persons removed if they consider it necessary."[33] It is ironic that a court of law can give juveniles liability (albeit limited) for their criminal actions and punish them for any offense, yet, at the same time, find them too immature to participate in formal proceedings. It is a violation of the right to know the charges and hear witnesses against them generally provided to adults all over the world. Egyptian law allows for juvenile imprisonment, so youth offenders should at least be afforded the right of full participation in all hearings.

Egyptian law regarding the sentencing of minors convicted of criminal action is supposedly more rehabilitative than punitive. The age of criminal responsibility remains listed at seven, so national law has outlined the sentences for minor above seven and under fifteen as follows: The court can issue a warning as a sentence without any further sanction, can return a youth to the supervision of the parents, require vocational training, probation, or mandatory tasks that are, in effect, community service. Custodial sanctions include placement in either a welfare institution or a specialized hospital.[34] Capital punishment continues to be a possible sanction for crime in Egypt, but cannot apply to minors. Instead, alternative sentences are implemented. For instance, if a minor aged fifteen commits a crime that normally would warrant the death penalty, he is instead subject to life imprisonment. If the same minor committed a crime that would normally receive detention, the minor is instead placed on probation. Children aged sixteen to eighteen cannot be executed or sanctioned with forced labor, and instead are sentenced to detention.

When an Egyptian minor is sentenced to detention, he must be sent to a specialized institution that is separate from adult prisons and administrated in a joint venture with the Minister of Social Affairs and the Minister of the Interior. When a juvenile is sentenced to detention, laws require that a number of authorities remain in contact with the offender and periodically arrive to inspect the conditions of his confinement. The law holds that the judicial body or relevant expert must visit the custodial setting every three months to ascertain that conditions are acceptable. Social workers are also expected to remain in touch with the juvenile in a more individualized manner, by providing guidance for the youth and supervising his conduct.[35]

There are also limitations on the length of sanctions that include confinement. First, the longest sentence a child may serve is ten years, and that is reserved only for serious offenses, with five years as the maximum for a less serious offense, and three for any other delinquency. All social welfare institutions are required to provide either education or vocational training or a combination of both. Interestingly, Egypt willingly admits that the policy of the nation for juvenile justice is not matched in implementation. Authorities stated to the United Nations: "On paper the system looks exemplary, but that does not mean that it is good in practice. There are many problems, but far from concealing them, Egypt is striving to tackle them head-on."[36]

One of the biggest problems facing the juvenile justice system is the lack of funds for proper institutions. The government states that facilities do not have adequately trained staff or equipment, but they are diligently working to change that. On the other hand, independent researchers have recorded incidences of violence against juveniles without proper court involvement. One Amnesty International appeal reports the arrest and torture of twenty-nine individuals, including three youths, alleged to have connections with an Islamic militant group. The organization found that the suspects were beaten and mercilessly tortured. One description included the use of electric shock. All the suspects, including the youths, were held in this manner for some time, until an eventual transfer to adult prison facilities.[37] While this report could very likely be an anomaly of the treatment of juveniles in conflict with the law, it is evidence that Egypt is plagued with not only financial issues, but also with the implementation of illicit punishment without any intervention by the courts.

IRAN

Turning next to Iran, we note that the impact of Islamic law on the legal codes is recognized through the ages at which children can be held responsible for their crimes. Unlike other nations that set a definitive age of criminal responsibility, only youths who have not reached the age of puberty can be exempt from liability for their actions. "Note 1 of Article 1210 of the Iranian Civil Code, ratified by the Islamic Consultative Assembly in 1991, says a girl achieves puberty after 9 lunar years and a boy after completing 15 lunar years and that these groups of persons are considered adults mature and are permitted to execute all legal transactions."[38]

Interestingly, the law differentiates by over six years between the age in which a minor can become an adult for females and for males. The United Nations is dissatisfied with this differentiation. In the 2000 "Reports to Treaty Bodies," the Committee on Human Rights notes that: "The Committee also expressed concern at the fact that the definition of the child in the Civil Code and the Islamic Penal Law results in the arbitrary and disparate application of laws and discriminates between girls and boys with respect to legal capacity."[39] While age of criminal responsibility is merely one in the list of discrimination between males and females, the immense impact of the penal differentiation cannot be overlooked. "Legislation of the Islamic Penal Code according to which women's right to live is not protected as the right of a full human being and in which girls of nine years of age (but not boys) are considered of age of criminal responsibility."[40]

Iran has one of the lower ages for criminal responsibility in the Middle East. However, the Iranian judiciary does not explicitly follow the penal ages based on the lunar years. "Fortunately, Islamic jurisprudents are not united in their opinion about the age of maturity. Some jurisprudents believe that if the Islamic Code has set puberty age for girls at nine (lunar years) and that of boys at fifteen (lunar years), these years are set for praying obligations."[41]

In contrast to Egypt, which improves on the low age of criminal responsibility in their statutes by allowing juveniles to remain under protective juvenile court systems at least until the age of eighteen, Iran does not allow for a maximum age to be considered a juvenile. The Committee on the Rights of the Child has stated their concern regarding this issue: "provisions in law allowing persons under eighteen to be prosecuted for crimes in the same manner as adults, without any special procedures, and to be liable for the same penalties as adults."[42] There is no transition period in Iran during which juvenile offenders, upon reaching the age of criminal responsibility, have a limited liability for their actions by facing consequences presented by a juvenile court. Instead, young, first-time juvenile offenders can face the same penalties as much older and experienced criminals.

The lack of differential treatment directly results from the fact that Iran does not have a juvenile justice system. The Committee on the Rights of the Child listed the lack of juvenile courts or judges as one of the worst atrocities in the nation. The "Reports to Treaty Bodies" claims: "Concern was also expressed over: provisions in the law allowing for persons under eighteen to be prosecuted for crimes in the same manner as adults, without special procedures, and to be liable for the same penalties as adults; the failure to guarantee the right of juvenile delinquents to protective and rehabilitative measures."[43] There is actually a court located in Tehran named the Juvenile Court, but there are no explicit procedures in the Islamic Penal Codes that set out any differentiation in goals, objectives, or procedures that differ from the adult courts.

In their initial report to the Committee on the Rights of the Child, Iran claimed that they were in the process of forging separate justice divisions for youth offenders. National representatives stated, "Regarding juvenile courts, according to the directive of the judicial branch a special branch has been established with the follow-up of the Centre to investigate offences by children and juveniles on a full-time basis."[44] However, there has been no creation of juvenile courts, regardless of promises to the United Nations. A movement within the nation has also begun criticizing the Iranian government for their treatment of juvenile offenders. An article by an Iranian legal scholar quotes a reaction to the lack of specified guidelines for trials with child defendants: "It is the duty of the government and the judicial system to have the social worker and the lawyer accompany the child as soon as he/she is arrested and for the duration of the trial, until the execution of his/her sentence. Until realization of this task, most of our problems will persist."[45]

Part of the explanation for the lack of a separate juvenile justice system is the reliance of Iran for their penal procedures on the ancient Islamic *Sharia*. It is a code of religious laws that the more radical Islamic nations have begun to rely upon for criminal procedures. The rules include harsh punishments, no differentiation for juvenile and adult crimes, and no separate objectives for the rehabilitation of children in conflict with the law. Iran willingly joined the United Nations, but has explicitly refused to include any international standards within their codes that conflicted with Islamic law. "In 1993, the government of the Islamic Republic of Iran joined the Childs Rights Convention with a precondition that wherever the provisions of the Convention conflicted with Iranian civil and Islamic code, the I.R. of Iran will not be bound to comply to them."[46] Iran has continued to act under its promise to the United Nations even when Islamic codes call for extremely harsh measures against juvenile offenders. Without any form of juvenile court, the nation is in violation of international standards on the desirable procedures for handling children in conflict with the law.

In 2000, the Iranian Parliament was able to reinstate the right to have an attorney present in court proceedings, a right denied since the 1979 revolution. "MPs voted by a large majority to adopt the measure to allow those on trial the right to 'consult or call the services of a lawyer at all stages of an inquiry or trial' and to have defense present in the courtroom."[47] It can be assumed both from the lack of a separate juvenile court and the extremely low ages of criminal liability for males and females that this right applies to youth offenders as well. Girls under nine and boys under fifteen years of age are automatically tried in the adult court, and thus are afforded the recently reinstated adult right of legal assistance.

Since there is little formal separation between juvenile and adult offenses, it would seem that parents would have no required involvement in criminal proceedings. But, Iranian parents are minimally included when the offending child is under the age of criminal liability. Iranian authorities reported the following to the United Nations: "Article 49 of the Islamic Penalties Act stipulates that if a child commits a crime he/she will not be held liable. However, the education and disciplining of the child will be given to the guardian. If necessary, the court will instruct the house of correction to carry out this task."[48] It is somewhat contradictory to state that, although a child must be disciplined by his parents if he is too young to be held criminally liable, the house of correction can be called upon to administer discipline. If the child is too young to be criminally liable, the court should not have the power to instruct parents and guardians to punish their child or to require discipline by any public authority. Liability simply means that an offender can be held accountable for their actions and face punitive consequences for their actions. If there is no liability, there should be no "discipline."

In regard to whether trials of juveniles are held in public, in a similar fashion to the right to an attorney, whatever applies to adult offenders can be transferred to children. Since there is no separate juvenile justice system, affirmation or denial of rights to adults will also be guaranteed to children. International standards recognize a need for public trials for adults, but closed trials for juveniles. Adult courts are often kept open so that the public bears the responsibility of ensuring that justice is fair and impartial. If the court is closed, the judicial body can violate rights of participants, but the public will never have the knowledge to lodge a complaint. While juvenile courts are often closed, the involvement of interested parties allows for a justice watchdog.

Iran, to the dissatisfaction of Amnesty International, holds all court hearings in secret. In yearly press releases, the organization demands that Iran end this practice. For instance, when four students were sentenced to death in 1999 for demonstrating against the government, the trial was held in secret. The advocacy group stated, "The trial appears to have been conducted in complete secrecy and with no opportunity for a proper appeal procedure. We are calling for immediate commutation of the death sentences, urgent clarification of the names of those sentenced, fair retrials and the release of all those held for their peaceful participation in the demonstrations."[49] Again, trials held in secret deny the offender the right for the world to know of his judicial mistreatment. In this case, students were given a death sentence, which will be carried out without the consent of impartial jurors or public agreement.

Iranian law does not separate juvenile offenders from adult criminals, and the objectives of justice are generally much more punitive than rehabilitative. Without making any differentiation in regard to the age of the offender, Iran utilizes both corporal and capital punishment as criminal sanctions. In their report to the United Nations Convention on the Rights of the Child, government authorities stated that the range and type of corporal punishment can be necessary for the "education" of a juvenile. The punishment should be reasonable, and actual guidelines depend on the crime and are decided by the court.[50]

The use of corporal punishment for youth offenders is not limited to exceptional circumstances. Minors can be beaten for the crime of intermingling with the opposite sex. In July 2001, fourteen young males were publicly thrashed, receiving between twenty and seventy lashes, for approaching women and consuming alcohol. In the same month, fifty youths were flogged for attending a party where males and females illegally fraternized.[51] While these youths technically are not considered juveniles under international guidelines, under Iranian law, younger children accused of the same crime would be treated similarly because of the low age of criminal responsibility. In other nations, harassing males and consumption of alcohol are considered criminal offenses but of the least serious nature. It seems rather excessive that a nonviolent action, even if it is illegal, should be punished with physical brutality.

In regard to the death penalty, Iran executed two juveniles between 2000 and 2002.[52] In addition, the use of capital punishment is not reserved for the most severe offenses. Amnesty International reports, "In Iran, the death penalty continues to be widely used and is often imposed, Amnesty says, for vaguely worded offenses, including political offenses and those relating to freedom of belief. It says the sentences are frequently imposed after unfair trials. It says scores of executions—including some carried out in public—were reported in Iran, although Amnesty says the true figures may be much higher."[53] Unlike the United States and other nations that permit the death penalty for minors, but never actually execute criminals until they have attained eighteen years of age, Iran executed a seventeen-year-old male in 1999, leaving little time for appeal or proof of innocence.

In Iran, there is no distinction between the sentencing of adults and children, but actual conditions of detention allow youths to remain separate. If a child is found guilty, the Centre for Correction and Education takes over their care. Juveniles are separated from one another based on gender, age, and severity of offense. Iranian law divides juvenile establishments into three parts. One area of the institution is for youths who will be confined temporarily, one unit is for children in need of correction, and a final location is reserved for youths who have been sentenced to imprisonment. Within each center, youths are further divided by age, offense, and any criminal history. Female offenders are kept separate from the male population at all times.[54] The Centre requires involvement in both educational and vocational activities for all remanded minors, with the aim of enhancing the correct development of the youth based on Islamic teachings. Also, the Centre provides literacy programs, involvement in cultural affairs, and learning appreciation for art and music.

In Iranian juvenile detention facilities, much emphasis is placed on the psychological well being of the youth. Goals include individual and group therapy based on initial interviews with youth to ascertain any psychological disorder, the building of familial relationships, music therapy, and personality tests and enhancement. Interestingly, the Centre assigns disciplinary matters to the youth residents in an attempt to heighten their social awareness. The activities within the center all have a purpose of teaching youths responsibility for their actions. Thus, children are assigned to help staff make disciplinary decisions, and are expected to participate in councils that offer rewards and punishments to fellow detainees for their adherence or deviance from rules.[55] The use of peer evaluations is unique to the Iranian detention system.

The juvenile detention center in Iran is commendable considering that there is no separate juvenile justice system. However, the use of physical force and executions as legal sanctions are a violation of international standards on the rights of children and adults. In other nations, any physical contact with a youth offender is considered abuse, but Iran allows corporal punishment to discipline youth and adult offenders for their actions. In addition, while detention conditions seem better than in other countries, Iran would benefit from limiting the liability of child offenders by assigning less strict sentences for crimes that are similar to adult actions.

SYRIA

The age of criminal responsibility in Syria has similar requirements to many other countries; for instance, children responsible for offenses are still afforded less of a liability than if they were adults. In 1997, a summary of one of the Conventions on the Rights of the Child meetings was released in the "Defence for Children International" newsletter. Initially, the Committee was distraught at the lack of interest on the part of Syria to better the rights of their juvenile citizens. The report began by noting that, "The Higher Committee for Child Welfare, which is responsible for children's issues in Syria, was not present at the meeting. Instead, Syria was represented by a delegation from the permanent mission in Geneva, which is quite unusual."[56]

While the lack of Syrian involvement in the United Nations investigation might not have made a difference in the national ability to protect their children, it shows little interest in a desire to follow U.N. standards for the rights of juveniles. Based on the presentation by the Geneva delegation, the United Nations commented: "Another issue of concern was the low age of criminal responsibility, which stands at seven. Although children from the age seven to fifteen may not be sentenced, their cases are considered by the special courts. It is up to the judge to decide how to deal with them."[57]

The age of criminal responsibility is extremely young. Many children under the age of ten are incapable of reading simple sentences, yet Syria claims that these children can be held and punished for their crimes. In addition, while other nations with low ages of criminal responsibility at least allow offenders to remain within the juvenile system until the age of eighteen, Syria's penal codes deem anyone aged fifteen and over as completely liable for their actions. Syria has relatively low age requirements for other rights in which a juvenile becomes an adult. For instance, the age of consent to marry for males is fifteen; for females, it is thirteen.[58] Syria has a sense of uniformity in its understanding of maturity and the age in which youths can make cognizant decisions, in issues ranging from marriage to the choice to commit crimes. While international human rights organizations would prefer if the ages of legality for all activities were raised, at least the nation is not singling out youth offenders to accept adult responsibility over the rest of their peers.

Syria created a complex juvenile justice system with the objective of protecting and rehabilitating children in 1974. Article 31 of the Juvenile Delinquents Act No. 18 states:

> Juveniles shall be prosecuted before special courts, known as "juvenile courts," which shall take the following forms:
> (i) Full-time and part-time district courts competent to hear cases involving felonies or misdemeanours punishable by a term of more than one year's imprisonment.
> (ii) Summary courts, presided over by a justice of the peace, competent to adjudicate, in their capacity as juvenile courts, in cases involving other types of misdemeanours and contraventions.[59]

Juvenile judges are chosen based on their experience with juvenile affairs, rather than their seniority within the legal realm. In addition, the rehabilitative goals are distinguishable in the wide variance of people who hear juvenile cases. Not only is a jurist present from the office of the Minister of Justice, but other court actors include two civil servants representing the Ministry of Education, the Ministry of Social Affairs and Labour, and the Women's Federation, each of whom is required to serve a term of two years while handling juvenile criminal cases.[60]

The involvement of specialists in hearing juvenile matters is a reflection of the desire of the Syrian government to limit the criminality experienced by juveniles. The judge reserves the right to keep the offender out of the proceedings after he has been heard if the offender's presence will be detrimental. In addition, teachers at the offender's school and anyone who has had contact with the offender are brought into the proceedings to allow the judiciary panel to make a fully informed decision regarding the child. While the Syrian system is not fully formed in that each additional actor within the court does not have a set role, and the police and prosecutors are not juvenile specialists, it is much better than the Iranian system.

Syria, unlike Iran, has a long-standing and well-developed system of juvenile justice that works to protect juvenile rights. In their first report to the United Nations, Syrian representatives defined the implications and requirements of the Juvenile Act of 1974. First, all hearings are held open to any individuals with vested interest in the juvenile, but closed to the general public: "The Juvenile Delinquents Act stipulates that, contrary to the procedural rule under which trials must be held in public, juveniles (children) must be tried in camera in order to keep the child's identity secret and prevent his or her future from being endangered. This confidentiality also applies at the time of arrest and investigation."[61] Syria requires the juvenile the right to a shield from public scrutiny to take effect at the first instance of contact with authorities. Thus, police are not allowed to release names of children in custody and the press is given no information regarding the offender.

Not only are courts closed to the public, but all transcripts are sealed. "The Juvenile Delinquents Act prohibits publication of the transcript of the court hearings in order to protect the psychological and social integrity of the juvenile. It also prohibits any form of publication of a photograph of the juvenile, anyone who contravenes this provision being liable to prosecution."[62] Syria, both in keeping the trial closed and keeping all transcripts of the case away from public scrutiny, has made a serious dedication to the rights of juveniles in conflict with the law. The stated reason for such laws, including the psychological and social integrity of the child, and the protection against the endangerment of his future, reflects a desire for rehabilitation of the offender.

The Syrian government, in line with international standards, recognizes that when juveniles are not punished by social banishment for their mistakes, there is a greater chance of halting illegal action. The requirement banning publication of juvenile trials also extends to repeat offenders. For instance, a child convicted of a crime at thirteen and then arrested again at sixteen does not have an increased liability for his or her second offense because the judicial body knows nothing of it: "Judgments handed down against juveniles are not entered in the judicial register and, consequently, juveniles cannot be sentenced on the basis of their past record (repeated offenders), nor are they liable to ancillary or additional penalties."[63]

For both adults and juveniles, Syrian law allows a right to an attorney of their choice. "Defendants before these courts are entitled to the legal representation of their choice; the court appoints lawyers for indigents."[64] Syrian law takes class differentiations into account when requiring that all offenders be provided with an attorney, both those who can afford representation and those who cannot. Parents are also afforded a right of involvement in juvenile criminal procedure. In addition, if the judge requests their presence to learn more about the offender, they are required to oblige: "At any stage of the proceedings, the court may summon the juvenile's guardian or tutor, or the person in whose custody the juvenile is placed, or a representative of the body in the custody of which the juvenile is placed, together with a representative of the Social Service Office, if appropriate, or the probation officer and shall listen to the statements of these persons together with those of the juvenile."[65] The parents, unless they are found to be detrimental to the child, are asked to participate to aid the court in rehabilitating the offender.

Syrian law lists a number of alternatives to imprisonment for juveniles in conflict with the law. Their report to the United Nations lists the following as reform measures meant to rehabilitate the offender and implemented in their best interest: Juveniles can be placed under the guidance of parents or another appropriate family member. If the family setting proves inadequate, youths can instead be placed in an appropriate institution that will take on the parental role. Other options include placement in a reform establishment, or detention in a juvenile home. Finally, Syrian juveniles can be put on probation, and/or restricted from associating with certain individuals or participating in certain occupations.[66]

In addition to the wide variety of options that judges can utilize during sentencing, guidelines strictly control lengths of sentence for youth offenders, particularly any sanction that includes detention. All custodial measures must include vocational training. In a remand institution, juveniles must remain for at least six months, but are additionally afforded a guarantee of release by the time they are eighteen. Syrian law also outlines the purpose of the differences in forms of custodial sentences, particularly those that will not end at the attainment of eighteen years. Juveniles can be held in homes that operate as medical centers if the judge notes that their criminality is related to mental health disorders, and there is no specific length for this form of detention. Instead, they are hospitalized until treatment has concluded. Unlike other forms of juvenile sentencing, reaching the age of adulthood does not automatically end confinement. Probation is used at the tail end of the confinement sentence to help the offender assimilate back into the community.[67]

In total, there are four juvenile reform institutions and twelve juvenile remand centers in Syria. While both are under the administration of the Ministry of Social Affairs and Labour, the purpose of each type of institution differs. Remand centers are primarily for pretrial detention and allow a period of investigation into the psychological and social well being of the minor. After the period of observation, the staff at the remand center is expected to aid the court in proposing a sentence if the youth is found guilty of a criminal offense. Reform institutions, on the other hand, are for juveniles found guilty. They are theoretically supposed to provide vocational and educational training to youths, but the government has admitted that they are not living up to either their own or international standards of rehabilitation. The government further admits that lack of space and capacity to hold juveniles has limited the actual services that can be offered to juvenile offenders.[68]

Again, youths in Syria are considered minors until the age of fifteen; once an offender has reached that age he can be subjected to similar sanctions as his adult counterparts. However, Syria allows for the most serious punishments to be lessened for the seriously delinquent children. For crimes that adults could be executed for, youths can receive terms of labor between six and twelve years. For felonies usually punished by lifelong hard labor or life imprisonment, youths can receive a maximum of five to ten years of forced labor. Finally, when youths commit crimes that an adult would receive any length of imprisonment or labor, they can only receive a punishment of labor for one to five years.[69] While this practice is not technically considered combining youths and juveniles together because in this case those above fifteen have greater liability than younger juveniles, international standards look down upon any nation that allows anyone under eighteen years to reside in adult incarceration establishments.

Finally, although adult offenders can be sentenced to life imprisonment or execution, no offender can be subjected to either sanction until they have reached eighteen years of age. Like Egypt, however, the Syrian government has violated their own policy in regards to juvenile offenders when a youth is involved in an antigovernment activity or organization. The Human Rights Watch released a report regarding Syrian citizens that were imprisoned for years because of their suspected connections to militant Islamic groups. In April 1995, a Syrian lawyer reported the following:

> They are all from my neighborhood and they all were juveniles when they were arrested. They were taken from their tenth grade examination halls. Their only crime was that they had relatives in the Islamic groups. Some were tried and sentenced by the field court to six years, the maximum term for juveniles. But when their sentences expired, they were kept in prison for seven more years. They were held for over thirteen years. The lawyer emphasized the unfairness of the field court proceedings: "They were not really tried. No lawyers attended. The prisoners were blindfolded. They were informed of their crime, and then they were sentenced. These were not trials."[70]

Syria claims that the practices of juvenile sanctions are rehabilitative and in the best interest of the offender, but in certain instances, the government is in violation of its own policy regarding juvenile detention.

NOTES

1. Rahav, Giora. "The Epidemiology and Etiology of Crime in Israel." *Crime and Criminal Justice.* In Robert R. Friedman (ed), *Crime and Criminal Justice in Israel: Assessing the Knowledge Base toward the Twenty-First Century.* Albany: State University of New York Press, 1998.
2. Rahav, Giora, 80.
3. Giacomelli, Giorgio. "Torture, Prisons, Detention, and Juvenile Justice." Excerpted from *Mission Report on Israel's Violations of Human Rights in the Palestinian Territories since 1967.* United Nations, 21 March 2001. Available: http://electronicintifada.net/referencelibrary/hrdocs/doc_page41.shtml.
4. Rahav, 83.
5. Rahav, 83.
6. Rahav, 84.
7. Rahav, 94.
8. Rahav, 84.
9. Rahav, 84.
10. Rahav, 81.
11. Rahav, 83.
12. "Periodic Reports of States parties Due in 1993: Israel."
13. "Period Reports of State Parties Due in 1993: Israel."
14. "Periodic Reports of State Parties Due in 1993: Israel."
15. "Periodic Reports of State Parties Due in 1993: Israel."
16. "Periodic Reports of State Parties Due in 1993: Israel."
17. "Periodic Reports of State Parties Due in 1993: Israel."
18. Shavitt, Gavriel. "The Israeli Prison System: Historical Aspects." *Crime and Criminal Justice.* In Friedman, *Crime and Criminal Justice in Israel.*
19. Shavitt, 282.
20. Israeli Prison Service. "Ofek Prison (Juveniles)." 2001. [Online]. Available: http://www.ips.gov.il/ShabasEng/Prisons/prisons.asp?gush_id=56&org_id=87.
21. "Ofek Prison (Juveniles)."
22. Simon, Rita J., and Judith R. Simon. "Inside Israeli Prisons: An Eyewitness Report." Miami, FL: ELR Productions, 1992, 23.
23. Human Rights Watch "Briefing to the 59th Session of the United Nations Commission on Human Rights." 27 Feb. 2003. [Online]. Available: http://www.hrw.org/un/chr59/omnibus.htm#12.
24. United Nations. "Committee on the Rights of the Child—26th Session: Egypt." Geneva, 8–26 Jan. 2001. [Online]. Available: http://www.ishr.ch/about%20UN/Reports%20AND%20analysis/crc%20-%2026th%20session.htm.
25. United Nations Committee on the Rights of the Child. "Consideration of Reports Submitted by State Parties Under Article 44 of the Convention: Egypt." 11 Nov. 1999. [Online]. Available: http://www.hir.ca/fortherecord2001/documentation/tbodies/crc-c-65-add9.htm.

26. U.S. Department of State: Bureau of Democracy, Human Rights, and Labor. "Country Reports on Human Rights Practices: Egypt." 4 Mar. 2001. [Online]. Available: http://www.state.gov/g/drl/rls/hrrpt/2001/nea/8248.htm.

27. "Committee on the Rights of the Child—26th Session: Egypt," 3.

28. "Committee on the Rights of the Child—26th Session: Egypt," 5.

29. "Committee on the Rights of the Child—26th Session: Egypt," 4.

30. "Consideration of Reports Submitted by State Parties Under Article 44 of the Convention: Egypt."

31. Amnesty International. "Egypt: Release Child Imprisoned for Sexual Orientation." 29 Dec. 2001. [Online]. http://web.amnesty.org/ai.nsf/Index/MDE120292001?OpenDocument&of=COUNTRIES\EGYPT.

32. "Consideration of Reports Submitted by State Parties Under Article 44 of the Convention: Egypt."

33. "Consideration of Reports Submitted by State Parties Under Article 44 of the Convention: Egypt."

34. "Consideration of Reports Submitted by State Parties Under Article 44 of the Convention: Egypt."

35. "Consideration of Reports Submitted by State Parties Under Article 44 of the Convention: Egypt."

36. "Consideration of Reports Submitted by State Parties Under Article 44 of the Convention: Egypt."

37. "Egypt: Three Juvenile and Twenty-Six Others Detained and Reportedly Tortured. Amnesty International—Worldwide Appeal." Feb. 2000. [Online]. Available: http://web.amnesty.org/web/wwa.nsf/wwa/Egypt-02-2000.

38. Ebadi, Shirin. "Children Rights Convention and Child's Rights in Iran." *Azma: Cultural, Social & Political Magazine.* Nov. 1999,12–13. [Online]. Available: http:www.netiran.com/Htdocs/Clippings/Social/991125XXSO01.html.

39. "United Nations Reports to Treaty Bodies—For the Record: The United Nations Human Rights Systems. Iran (The Islamic Republic of)." 2000. [Online]. Available: http:///www.hri.ca/fortherecord2000/vol3/irantb.htm.

40. Kar, Mehrangiz. "Second Class: The Legal Status of Iranian Women." *The Iranian.* 18 Apr. 2000. [Online]. Available: http://www.Iranian.com.Opinion/2000/AprilWomen.

41. Ebadi, 13.

42. "United Nations Reports to Treaty Bodies," 4.

43. "United Nations Reports to Treaty Bodies, 3.

44. United Nations Committee on the Rights of the Child. "Initial Reports of States Parties Due in 1996: Iran." 23 Jul. 1998. [Online]. Available: http://www.hri.ca/fortherecord2000/vol3/irantb.htm.

45. Ebadi, Shirin. "Conviction of the Children Under the Laws Was Better 76 Years Ago." Iranian Children's Rights Society. 2002. [Online]. Available: http://www.iranianchildren.org/ebadiconviction.html.

46. "Children's Rights Convention and Child's Rights in Iran," 12.

47. "Iran's Parliament Gives Defendants Right to Lawyer in Court." *Agence France-Presse* 24 Oct. 2000. Westlaw. [Online]. Available: http://web2.westlaw.com/search/default.wl?Action=EditQuery&DB=MIDNEWS&EQ=search&

Method=TNC&Query=Iran+%26+Parliament+%26+Right+to+Lawyer&RLTDB=
CLID_DB23523&ToFrom=%2Fsearch%2Fresult.wl&RS=WLW2.83&VR=2.0&
SV=Split&FN=_top&MT=Westlaw&EditQuery=+Edit+Query+.

48. "Initial Reports of States Parties Due in 1996: Iran."

49. "Iran: Time for Judicial Reform to End Secret Trials." Amnesty International Public Statement. 16 Sept. 1999. [Online]. Available: http://web.amnesty.org/ai.nsf/Index/MDE130251999?OpenDocument&of=COUNTRIES\IRAN.

50. "Initial Reports of State Parties Due in 1996: Iran."

51. "History Repeats Itself." *Iran Report.* Vol. 4, no. 26, 16 Jul. 2001. [Online]. Available: http://www.rferl.org/iran-report/2001/07/26-160701.html.

52. Human Rights Watch "The Death Penalty and Juvenile Offenders." Briefing to the 59th Session of the UN Commission on Human Rights. 27 Feb, 2003 [Online]. Available: http://www.hrw.org/un/chr59/deathpenalty.htm.

53. Patridge, Ben. "World: Amnesty International Seeks to end Capital Punishment in 2000." *Radio Free Europe: Radio Liberty.* 17 Jun. 1999. [Online]. Available: http://www.rferl.org/nca/features/1999/06/F.RU.990617120043.html.

54. "Initial Reports of State Parties Due in 1996: Iran."

55. "Initial Reports of State Parties Due in 1996: Iran."

56. Defense for Children International. "CRC Report—Syria." *DCI Newsletter.* Apr. 1997. [Online]. Available: http://www.defense-for-children.org/ong/DciHome.nsf/e1104681a013ab90025.

57. "CRC Report—Syria," 2.

58. United Nations Committee on Economic, Social, and Cultural Rights. "For the Record 2001: The United Nations Human Rights System: Syrian Arab Republic." 2001. [Online]. Available: http://www.hri.ca.fortherecord2001/vol3/syriatb.htm.

59. United Nations: Committee on the Rights of the Child. "Initial Reports of States Parties Due in 1995: Syrian Arab Republic." 14 Feb. 1996. [Online]. Available: http://www.unhchr.ch/tbs/doc.nsf/385c2add1632f4a8c12565a9004dc311/d554747d746135efc125635d0052a760?OpenDocument&Highlight=0,Syria.

60. "Initial Reports of States Parties Due in 1995: Syrian Arab Republic," Parts 223–235.

61. "Initial Reports of States Parties Due in 1995: Syrian Arab Republic."

62. "Initial Reports of States Parties Due in 1995: Syrian Arab Republic."

63. "Initial Reports of States Parties Due in 1995: Syrian Arab Republic."

64. Department of State. "Country Reports on Human Rights Practices: Syria 2001." Washington, D.C., 2002. [Online]. Available: http://www.terrorismcentral.com/Library/Government/US/StateDepartment/DemocracyHumanRights/2001/NearEastNorthAfrica/Syria.html. Accessed March 24, 2004.

65. "Country Reports on Human Rights Practices: Syria."

66. "Initial Reports of States Parties Due in 1995: Syrian Arab Republic."

67. "Initial Reports of States Parties Due in 1995: Syrian Arab Republic."

68. "Initial Reports of States Parties Due in 1995: Syrian Arab Republic."

69. "Initial Reports of States Parties Due in 1995: Syrian Arab Republic."

70. Human Rights Watch. "Syria's Tadmor Prison: Dissent Still Hostage to a Legacy of Terror." Apr. 1996, vol. 8, no. 2. [Online]. Available: http://hrw.org/reports/1996/Syria2.htm.

7

Africa

Many countries in Africa have only recently become independent. After decades of Western invasion and colonial rule, a number of nations on the African continent are only beginning to write their own laws and constitutions. Areas that have a wide variety of ethnic diversity were indiscriminately thrown together when ruling governments drew new boundaries. The era of colonialism also had serious impacts on the formation of juvenile justice systems. In reference to juvenile courts, many of the African countries involved in this study were colonized by the United Kingdom and other European nations after the trend of juvenile courts swept through the western world. But, the need for juvenile justice systems was apparently not as important in the colonized nations when westerners invaded, and the trend in youth courts began only when these nations achieved independence.

In addition, much of Africa had indigenous tribal cultures that were suppressed during colonial rule. But, many tribal traits survived and have also had an impact on the formation of the new independent nations. Thus, the laws regarding juvenile offenders across Africa are often a mix of the influence of both European law and indigenous tribal values.

SOUTH AFRICA

South Africa, after years of colonial rule by the Dutch and the English that forged a legal differentiation between Africans and whites, finally ended apartheid in the early 1990s. In 2000, the United Nations released a report regarding South Africa's statements on the rights of children in conflict with the law. The report notes that South Africa has pending legislation that would increase the age of criminal responsibility to ten years. At the time of this writing, any child above the age of seven can be liable for any offense.[1] While ten is an improvement over seven, it is still well below international standards.

South Africa ratified the Convention of the Rights of the Child, and also passed their own Constitution in 1996 that defines a child as anyone under the age of eighteen. Yet, in March 2001, the nation charged and held six children between the ages of seven and thirteen with crimes,[2] ages at which criminal liability is supposed to be limited. It is in complete violation of international standards for children as young as seven to have been sentenced to detainment.

South African law also allows for a young age at which children can be treated within the adult system. At age fourteen, juvenile offenders who are charged with serious and violent offenses are liable for their actions and face criminal consequences. "A child between the ages of seven and fourteen is also presumed to have limited criminal responsibility; the onus is on the state to rebut this presumption of reasonable doubt."[3] This limited liability ends at the attainment of fourteen years. The U.S. Department of State conducted its own investigation in 2000 and noted, "juveniles between the ages of fourteen and eighteen accused of serious crimes, including murder or rape, are sometimes placed in pretrial detention in prisons with adult offenders."[4] Thus, the policy of treating youths over fourteen as adults is actually in practice, even though the government incorporated international standards into their own laws, and professed that all offenders under eighteen would be treated as minors. Basically, there is a conflict within South African laws about how to define a juvenile.

South Africa has spent considerable time and energy trying to implement a separate juvenile court, but their efforts have not been fully achieved. The Child Justice Bill was proposed in 2000, and included plans for a separate judicial system for youths in conflict with the law:

> The proposed system further aims to encourage a degree of specialization in child justice practice. In so doing, the Commission is giving effect to a long-standing call from service providers and nongovernmental organizations for a distinct and unique system of criminal justice that treats children differently, in a manner appropriate to their age and maturity, which develops mechanisms and processes designed to achieve that goal. For instance, a specialized child justice court at the district court level is proposed.[5]

While the court has not been created at this time, the government remains committed to forming juvenile justice institutions. In the summer of 2000, three delegates from South Africa came to the United States to learn more about the juvenile courts and its workings. "On June 11, 2000, three visitors from South Africa and a representative of the United States Department of State visited the National Council on Juvenile and Family Court Judges in Reno. The South African participants visited the United States on a twenty-one-day visitor program to study the administration of United States courts. . . . South African courts are beset by a combination of heavy case load and lack of resources, including continuing education."[6]

Other initiatives in the Child Justice Bill include a process of diversion utilized in other countries. The proposal also includes a required preliminary inquiry overseen by a district court magistrate.[7] The creation of the system has been much slower than advocates have desired. As of March 2003, the bill had been slightly amended and finally introduced into the South African Parliament. Presently, the bill remains subject to investigation by the Justice and Constitutional Affairs Portfolio Committee.[8] South Africa is making an informed and laborious attempt to revolutionize how juveniles are treated when in conflict with the law. Until the bill passes and implementation actually commences, it is too early to tell whether the intentions will meet with success.

South Africa affords the right to representation for all offenders, and provides legal aid for those who cannot afford it. In a report to the United Nations, South African representatives admitted that their recent change to a fully democratic state and the end of apartheid led to the review of many laws reflecting these changes. The Constitution of 1996 spells out the right to defense for offenders of all ages. The Constitution

> provides that every accused person has the right to be presumed innocent until proven guilty beyond all doubt. All accused persons, including children, must be informed of the charges against them and be allowed legal representation and/or (in the case of children) representation by parents or guardians. The Legal Aid Amendment Act (1996) provides for legal aid to indigent persons (in civil and criminal matters), and also (as contemplated in the Constitution) for legal representation at State expense in criminal matters where substantial injustice would otherwise result.[9]

The rights of parents are integrated into the right to representation. A child can have his own attorney, or choose to be represented by a parent or guardian, or, if he so elects, the involvement of both parties. The South African Congress also took notice of the major class divisions in the society by providing for legal assistance even when the offender cannot afford it. This is particularly important in eradicating the racist ramifications of apartheid.

South Africa succinctly defines the right to proceedings closed to the public. "During a trial, the identity of a child accused below the age of eighteen may not be revealed."[10] Again, it is important to recall that the Child Justice Bill has yet to pass, although it has been under consideration for a number of years. Thus, while public knowledge of a juvenile offender is considered illegal, the nation has yet to implement any enforcements and requirements in that regard. For instance, if a newspaper was able to ascertain the identity of a juvenile burglar and chose to print it in the next edition, it is considered an illegal act, but no actual consequences for such actions have been determined.

The expungement of records is an additional protection that the South African Law Commission presented in a 2000 report. They state, "A criminal record has serious implications. A convicted person is branded forever as an untrustworthy member of society; a conviction compromises job opportunities permanently, and convicts are often the subject of suspicion and mistrust. These consequences can be especially serious for young persons who have to attempt to enter the job market with the liability of a criminal record for an offence committed whilst still a child."[11] The Commission further discussed the models that could be used to expunge juvenile records. They recommend that either all offenders have their record expunged after five years as long as no additional offenses are found, or that juveniles are split into groups, including those who committed less and more serious offenses. For instance, children convicted of violent felonies and sentenced to detention would always have a criminal history, but youths convicted of theft would have their records erased.

From the initial stage of police contact, it is imperative that children understand that they have a right to have their parents notified and involved. Again, while this measure is proposed in the Child Justice Bill, the long-awaited final approval still has not occurred. The South African Law Commission's Juvenile Justice Report provides ample data for why a consolidated juvenile law is a necessity. For instance, in regard to parental involvement, the Commission found that when children were originally arrested, only 31 percent were told that their families could be contacted.[12]

One reason that the juvenile justice bill has not passed is the number of diverging opinions regarding proper administration. For instance, in regard to the involvement of parents, a public prosecutor from Richmond, Virginia, notes that parental involvement should not be a requirement because many youth offenders come from unstable homes. The Committee of the Welfare Department contends in response that any appropriate adult would be better than no involvement of guardians.[13] The issue of parental involvement, the requirements of such, at which point it must commence, and whether it is a valuable clause for juvenile justice, continues to be debated with little satisfactory conclusions.

The goals of punishment in South Africa can be considered correctional. The nation is committed to rehabilitation of the offender. But, the underlying ideals of all criminal punishment put the needs of protection of society over the well being of the youth. In a report to the United Nations, authorities explained that youths can be released with only a warning from the court. More formal sanctions for minors under the age of eighteen include probation under the regulation of an appropriate individual. Custodial penalties include detention in a reform school, which can be applicable to minors of all ages, although it is generally reserved for youths above the age of fourteen.[14] Instead of rehabilitative sentences like therapy, community service, or even some form of reparations to the victims, South African law is focused on containing the problem that the offender poses.

South Africa continued its report by discussing the forms of detention that are available for juvenile offenders and the rights guaranteed to children in confinement. First, authorities contend that detention is used only when all other possible measures have failed, and for short time periods. Interestingly, youths can be sentenced to life imprisonment if their actions warrant such measures. At present, four South African youths are serving out life sentences. In regard to the death penalty, the new Constitution ruled it illegal for both adults and juveniles.[15]

The decision to outlaw the death penalty for all citizens is commendable. Statements in the report regarding juvenile separation from adult prisoners and detention as a last resort are false. In the same report, the government admitted that the number of child offenders integrated into adult prisons was a serious problem. In fact, the situation was severe enough to require the formation of a separate division under the Department of Correctional Services to enforce the policy of separation of adult and juvenile offenders, because in practice, children under eighteen have often been placed in adult penitentiaries.[16]

Like many nations, there is a dichotomy made by the South African government between reform schools and detention centers. Technically, reform schools are meant to be places of rehabilitation where younger offenders accused of less serious offenses are sent. These schools are under the jurisdiction of the Department of Education. Detention centers, on the other hand, are virtual prisons, differentiating little from adult penitentiaries, with the exception of the age of the offender. Like adult facilities, juvenile detention centers are under the administration of the Department of Correctional Services.

An investigation by the deputy chief lecturer of the Correctional Services Management department in South Africa and Dr. William Luyt of the German-based research organization, Technikon SA, proved that many of the statements by the government to the Convention on the Rights of the Child were fabricated. In both reform schools and detention centers, researchers found serious violations of international standards on human rights and domestic legislation regarding the administration of juvenile justice. First, the health conditions in both realms were disgusting, mostly as a result of overcrowding. In the juvenile reform schools, the average number of children per cell was ten. The conditions of overcrowding in prisons were much worse. Approximately twenty-three individuals are housed in cells, with the maximum number documented at sixty. These cells, even those with sixty inmates, have one toilet for everyone to share. A lack of ventilation and sanitary conditions exacerbate the stench and are detrimental to hygiene. The problem of overcrowding seen in adult facilities is mirrored in juvenile detention establishments.[17] The goal that detention will only be utilized as a last resort is clearly not being met if the need for prisons is great enough that authorities cannot build detention centers fast enough to accommodate the growing youth criminal population.

South Africa also promised to separate juveniles from adults in any form of detention. While in Places of Safety (or reform schools) this goal was often met; in prisons, the integration of offenders of all ages remains a problem. A survey of youths placed in prisons rather than juvenile reform schools found that almost one-third of minors had numerous opportunities to fraternize with adult offenders. One explanation is that, although present law condemns the practice of juvenile and adult integration, many of the youths were sentenced under prior laws that permitted such contact.[18] The purpose of separating juveniles is for their physical safety from adult offenders and their emotional well being. Allowing opportunities for contact between offenders of all ages places the juvenile and society at risk, particularly because the youth can learn about the criminal habits of long-time offenders.

In addition, international standards and South African law have banned any form of corporal punishment or physical violence against children when in detention. The Constitution forbids any form of violence against South African citizens, including any cruel and inhuman punishment. Using this body of law, the South African Supreme Court deemed corporal punishment illegal.[19] Nonetheless, a policy of nonviolence was not the case when investigators visited juvenile detention facilities. Survey results showed that in reform schools and juvenile prisons, approximately 19 percent of children reported that they had been whipped, and 26.4 percent of inmates in juvenile prisons reported an incident in which they were smacked, compared to 33.8 percent of reform school children who reported a smacking incident. Abuse occurred more frequently in youth prisons, but in total, more than 50 percent of surveyed inmates in both types of institutions had witnessed some form of assault.[20]

Recent media reports confirm many of the abuses alleged in this investigation. Pollsmoor, a South African prison that houses both adults and juvenile offenders, is incredibly overcrowded. In violation of national law, juveniles are housed in adult prison cells with adult offenders because the juvenile cells are too full. Scabies, or body lice, was reported as rampant in the juvenile section due to the effects of overcrowding on personal hygiene. In 2002, authorities investigated allegations that an average of six sexual assaults on juvenile inmates by prison staff occurred on a daily basis. Interviews with youths inmates revealed that staff at youth facilities came to work intoxicated, and would either abuse youths in a drunken rage or in an attempt to penalize them for minor infractions.[21] The abuse and mistreatment of juveniles in detention is horrendous, and is an issue that needs attention and resolution by the government.

Finally, punishment in South Africa is racially biased. This is another reminder that the nation functioned for many years under a system of apartheid that basically continues to have influence. In reference to juvenile detention, citizens of African descent are still second class to those of European descent. The new democratic government readily admits the problem, but has taken little action to rectify it. Authorities stated that the mistreatment of youths because of skin color, and whether there is a difference in funding for the youth facilities because of a detainee's race, are under investigation. Race is considered a probable cause for differential treatment of the conditions in which children are held, the term of sentence, and the rehabilitative programs offered.[22] Either the system itself remains racist, or the implications for African citizens facing lack of education and poverty have led to the number of incarcerated black and colored juveniles to far exceed the number of white children in detention.

The demographic breakdown in South Africa is approximately 75.2 percent black, 13.6 percent white, 8.6 percent colored, and 2.6 percent Indian.[23] But, in 2001, the number of juveniles in detention centers visited by Technikon representatives was divided by race as follows: "Ethnicity shows that 74 percent of the population is black, 20.5 percent is coloured, 2.8 percent is white, and 2.7 percent is Asian. Compared to the general population, colored inmates are overrepresented by 8.5 percent and whites are under represented by 12.7 percent."[24] The racial discrepancy is large enough to question why so few white children are detained. It could be a reflection of the wealth distribution that aids white offenders in remaining out of prison, or it could reflect racism within the court system. Regardless, the issue of race is another factor that the South African government should attend to when reforming the juvenile justice system.

KENYA

In 2001, Kenya stated in their report to the United Nations that the legal age of criminal responsibility is eight years old.[25] But, for the ages between eight and eighteen, when a person legally becomes an adult according to international standards, there is a wide range of variation within Kenyan statutes for how liable a youth is for the crime with which he is charged. The recognition of age eighteen for adulthood is rather superficial. The Human Rights Watch released an independent investigation of the abuse of homeless children by the police and justice system. The document claimed, "Children under the age of fourteen are to be detained in juvenile remand homes, which are under the administration of the Children's Department. Fourteen- and fifteen-year-olds may be detained in either juvenile remand homes or remand prisons for adults if the court finds that the child 'is of so unruly a character that he cannot be safely remanded to the custody of a juvenile home.'"[26] In addition, only males over the age of fifteen can have a sentence alternative to prison or reform schools. Those young males are sent to *borstal* institutions, a place where offenders are taught vocational skills along with primary education but that are notorious for their hard labor requirements.[27]

Although children are often sentenced with adults, Kenya's Children and Young Person's Act officially recognizes all offenders under age eighteen as part of the juvenile justice system. The only exceptions to charging a juvenile otherwise are when a juvenile is concurrently charged with an adult, or when the offense is manslaughter or any crime punishable by death.[28] Kenya claims that all individuals under eighteen years of age are considered juveniles, but in reality the government does not follow their own legislation. The discrepancy is not in the legal statutes, but rather in the willingness of the courts to sentence young offenders to the same institutions that adult courts send offenders.

While Kenya has a legal system reserved specifically for juvenile issues, it has had excessive problems. Presently, "the legal framework supports Juvenile Courts, although such courts are not really 'separate'—Nairobi is the only place in Kenya where a completely separate court sits as a juvenile court at present."[29] Another detrimental component of Kenya's juvenile justice system is the refusal to differentiate between children in conflict with the law and children in need of protection that their guardians have not been providing. The Human Rights Watch reports:

> Children's cases are supposed to be heard in special juvenile courts, established under the Children and Young Persons Act. The jurisdiction of juvenile courts extends to both criminal matters and noncriminal protection or discipline matters, . . . [which include] children under the age of sixteen who are deserted, parentless, beggars, vagrants, "uncontrollable," or who fall into "bad associations."[30]

Children who through no fault of their own are homeless are relegated into the hands of juvenile courts, which often make little distinction about whether the child has committed any offense when they make their decisions. In addition, the Human Rights Watch investigators reported that "despite the requirement that children's cases be heard in special juvenile courts, we found that children's cases are often heard in regular courts along with adult cases, where children are tried without the special protections accorded to juveniles under Kenyan law."[31]

On paper, the juvenile courts in Kenya sound both complex and functioning, but the reality for a Kenyan child in trouble with the law is not satisfactory. According to the Children and Young Person's Act, the juvenile courts are under the jurisdiction of the lowest level court, the magistrate's court. While the only actual separate court building exists in the capital, the law requires that juvenile courts sit in a distinct building or on different times and days as the adult courts. The Human Rights Watch again found the Kenyan judiciary in gross violation of their statutes. "Despite the requirements that children's cases be heard in juvenile courts, sixteen out of forty children that we interviewed who were brought to court said their cases were heard in regular courts mixed with adult cases."[32]

The police are also given a large amount of power regarding juvenile cases, and have been known to base the decision on whether an offender should go to adult or juvenile court on the child's appearance, even though the law states that all cases involving offenders under eighteen are mandated to the juvenile court. In some ways, the legal code allows a limitation of rights when the person in question is a juvenile. An officer can apprehend a child and bring him or her to court without a warrant as long as they can believe that the child is in need of discipline. This privilege is not only allotted to police, but also practiced by children's officers, and if parents or private citizens feel the need to, they can request that police exercise their right to take any child to court.[33]

Regardless of the methods used to get a juvenile into the court system, those children allotted the privilege to stand before the judge are not afforded any special protections for their age. Kenyan law states, "The procedure of hearing juvenile cases [in juvenile courts] is the same as in other courts in that the criminal procedure and rule of evidence must be followed."[34] The only seemingly intelligent procedure followed by the Kenyan juvenile courts (when children are not taken to adult proceedings) is that the law requires that the children's officer, supposedly synonymous with a social worker, prepare a report to present to the magistrate that includes both the circumstances of the offense as well as any other mitigating factors in the offender's lifestyle.

Throughout the 1990s, independent commissions investigating juvenile justice in Kenya learned that the right to representation was constantly ignored. In a 1997 Human Rights Watch analysis, researchers found that,

"To our knowledge, none of the children we interviewed were ever represented by legal or other counsel in either juvenile or regular courts."[35] A separate report by Anne Skelton in 1999, requested by the Royal Netherlands Embassy in Nairobi, found that little had changed. Ms. Skelton also included in her study changes from the (then proposed) Children's Bill that finally passed in early 2001. She found little help from the new legislation in regard to the right to representation. Skelton writes, "Legal representation of children is rare, and there is currently no state-paid legal aid system. The new Children's Bill does seem to offer some assistance to children who cannot afford lawyers, although how extensive this will be and how it will be funded remains to be seen."[36]

Interestingly, the Kenyan statements to the United Nations directly counter all assertions made by independent investigators. In regard to the right to legal representation, national authorities held, "The Constitution and the Criminal Procedure Code (Cap. 63, Laws of Kenya) provide due process rights in respect of any individual accused of a criminal offence. These include . . . [right] to a legal representative of the accused's choice; in capital offences, the accused is entitled to legal representation at public expense."[37] It is shocking that the government openly contends a guarantee that two independent research commissions were never able to document.

In reference to parental involvement in judicial proceedings, guardians have a right to participate in formal court proceedings if "he or she can be found and resides at a reasonable distance."[38] Again, Skelton found evidence contrary to official government statements. Not only are parents not contacted, but the involvement of guardians end up becoming a detriment to children. Youth offenders are kept in custody longer if an authority attempts to locate their families.

> Rarely do police contact parents or guardians during the first forty-eight hours after the arrest to inform them about the first court appearance. Unnecessary delays occur because the court then postpones the matter for a few days, sending children back to the police cells, so that they can "point out" their parents.[39]

Another divide exists between what Kenyan authorities claim is the process for juvenile justice and what independent researchers have found in regard to the privacy of children. The laws regarding juvenile criminality hold that the only individuals allowed to remain in the room during juvenile proceedings are employees of the court, any witnesses to the crime, the attorneys (although, again, legal assistance is rarely involved), and anyone with a vested interest in the youth, such as a parent or guardian. In addition, the law forbids any publication of identifying information about the offender, including their name, home address, or place of education.[40] While protection of the child from public scrutiny is commendable, it would be much more effective if children were not routinely tried as adults, automatically denying them the additional protection of privacy.

The stated ideals of the Kenyan justice system in regard to available sanctions for delinquents are in line with theories of rehabilitation. According to national representatives, the word "sentence" should never be used in relation to any offender under eighteen. Instead, any sanction that involves detention is meant to provide better living conditions for youths. The measure, based on the type of words the law applies to youth, is not supposed to be punitive.[41]

The written policy of Kenya also supports the rehabilitative goals through the incorporation of the welfare of the minor. First, capital punishment is outlawed for any child under eighteen at the time of the commission of the crime. Children are not supposed to be imprisoned unless it is used as a last resort, and more than one judicial body must approve the sentence of imprisonment before it can commence. In essence, all other measures must have been tried and failed to effectively deter a youth from criminal action before he or she can be imprisoned. A prison sentence can only occur if it is approved by a higher level court on appeal. If a youth is imprisoned, he or she is supposed to be kept away from adult offenders at all costs, both in housing and recreation.[42]

The substitute sanctions that are available instead of prison for minors encompass a wide spectrum. The judicial body is given the option of sentencing youth to probation, corporal punishment, fines in which the minor is expected to pay for the damage of his or her actions, supervision by an appropriate adult or officer of the law, or detention in either a reform school or *borstal* institution.[43] The use of corporal punishment or any physical violence against minors as a form of judicial discipline has been commented upon and outlawed by the United Nations, but Kenya continues to use it as a measure against delinquent youth.

In regard to the other punitive measures, Kenya is similar to South Africa in that it differentiates between rehabilitative places of confinement and detention centers. Unlike other nations, however, Kenya allows for three options of detention. Reform schools are educationally based rehabilitation centers, while *borstal* institutions teach vocational skills. Both options are alternatives to imprisonment, but for the gravest crimes, particularly if the youth is older, a prison sentence can be conferred. On the other hand, juvenile judges in Kenya reserve the right to apply nonphysical or detention sentences to youths by allowing them to compensate the victim for their actions, or have appropriate adults take responsibility for their custody.

Interestingly, the Kenyan government recognizes the failings in their juvenile justice administration that multiple independent researchers have studied and commented upon. For example, authorities noted that one of the downfalls of Kenyan courts is that little differentiation is made between children who have committed a crime and children who simply have no home.[44] Again, the nation has a serious epidemic of poverty that has created an extensive homeless population. Youths with no homes are often mistaken for juvenile offenders, and are subjected to punishment by police and court systems. In fact, independent commissions found that more often than not, street children were accosted and victimized by the system, from police to judges, for the crime of vagrancy. Youths that cannot find work and are not cared for in their home environment are criminalized for a situation that is out of their control.[45]

In addition, the problem of overcrowding in youth facilities is terrible, making conditions unbearable and unhealthy. The problem plagues all three forms of detention for youths, from adult prisons to reform schools. First, investigators found children as young as fourteen within prisons. Children must sleep next to toilets because cells exceed maximum capacity, and there is no room for them elsewhere. Children alleged constant physical abuse by both adult prisoners and prison staff. Even guards who did not personally violate the children were unwilling to protect them from other detainees. Sexual assaults were also noted as a problem.[46] The vile instances of abuse could quickly end if the Kenyan government would willingly follow their own policies of separating youth inmates from adult criminals, and only sentencing children to imprisonment as a last resort.

Other independent investigations into Kenyan detention facilities corroborated the findings of excessive physical violence. When the International Child and Youth Care Network interviewed young Kenyan males who had been in detention, they heard horror stories of abuse. The young inmates allege constant thrashing at the hands of older inmates. The youths were held in cells so over their capacity that they slept on the floor. The floor, however, was disgusting, and covered in human waste. Sexual assault of younger and smaller prisoners is rampant, and refusal to comply results in more physical violence.[47] This statement, and the many more like it, illustrate that sentencing practices in Kenya for juvenile offenders is often corrupt and dangerous. Instead of using detention as a last resort, as international standards require, or incorporating tenets of rehabilitation into sanctions, Kenya seriously abuses its youth population.

The physical settings of the detention establishments worsen the problems stemming from overcrowding. The cells in which children survive have little ventilation, are crawling with insects and rodents, and have no water. There is no furniture, like bed or desks, at which children can find some semblance of a comfortable home. Children sleep on the floor and are not given any linens. Because youths are expected to remove the majority of their clothing before they can be detained, the detainees remain confined in various states of exposure.[48]

The situation of overcrowding and abuse is not limited to the prisons. Inadequate conditions are also found in the remand homes, the institutions that are meant to be rehabilitative. Mr. Osunsade, a government representative, admitted that the majority of problems for youths in juvenile centers come from the situation of dire poverty across the nation. Domestic social welfare organizations consistently report that lack of resources is both what forces children out of schools and into punitive institutions. There are few vocational classes, and food provisions are tiny, simply because the establishments do not have adequate funding.[49] The classes that are meant to teach juvenile offenders to learn to hold jobs and care for themselves are no longer available. Worse, older juveniles facing serious charges like murder and rape are placed into remand homes. This practice also violates Kenyan standards of juvenile justice, which hold that spaces in remand home are reserved for younger offenders.

There are eleven rehabilitation schools in Kenya in which juveniles can be sent after sentencing, and although they are supposed to be split between youths who have been charged with criminal offending and those without homes, little distinction is made in assigning a youth to a certain establishment. Unlike remand homes and adult prisons, inspectors found that rehabilitative schools are not generally overcrowded, except in the school for females. Physical conditions, however, remained in a state of disrepair. Buildings were both old and dilapidated; floors were unfinished, and windows were broken in some places. Children were not provided with mattresses, but instead slept on frames covered by burlap.[50]

Like adult prison settings, youths in approved schools are often subjected to serious physical violence. "Children were beaten with wooden sticks for such infractions as having unkempt uniforms, talking, and refusing to do class work. As if the thrashings were not demoralizing enough, teachers often incorporated kicking and slapping into their physical abuse."[51] Any use of physical violence against minors is bad, but in Kenya, the situation is unpardonable. First, the use of violence is an acceptable form of punishment. Worse, it is not as though teachers are responding to violence with aggression; instead, children are savagely battered for breaching minor rules.

Residents of *borstal* institutions assert similar problems of abuse, at times much worse than the conditions of children in rehabilitation schools. First, children are not separated based on the seriousness of their offenses, so more violent youths are integrated into facilities with less aggressive minors. Besides reports of limited food, investigators found that children live in horrendous physical conditions. For instance, hundreds of youths are expected to share one bucket for their water source. This lack of hygiene has led to further problems like outbreaks of scabies. All clothing and toiletries are provided by the family, and if not, youths simply make do without.[52] Children receive no education during their stay, and are forced to do agricultural and menial labor seven days a week.

Punishment and abuse in *borstal* institutions range from beatings to solitary confinement. For instance, one institution's process for solitary confinement is as follows: "You're stripped of you're clothing and put in the cell. They pour water on the floor, and give you only a half ration of food once a day, but they give you plenty of water to drink. There's a bucket for a toilet, and you sleep on the floor. You stay in there until the superintendent decides to let you out."[53]

Investigations into Kenya's justice systems have uncovered possible reasons for why all detention facilities are overcrowded; the problem can be easily linked to the penchant of the courts to overuse detention instead of alternative sentences. A report by the African Network for the Prevention and Protection against Child Abuse and Neglect declared that the most popular penalties invoked by juvenile judges were custodial sentences.[54] Overuse of detention is also apparent in the findings of the Human Rights Watch investigation of Kenyan juvenile justice. More than half of the children interviewed were subjected to some form of detention. Almost one quarter of the children were imprisoned rather than sentenced to alternate facilities. Of the few that escaped custody, two were punished with physical measures.[55] If a shift in sentencing were to occur, the conditions of prisons, remand homes, *borstal* institutions, and specialized schools could be limited.

Overall, the treatment of youths in Kenya is in serious violation of human rights conventions. Children should be afforded special protections, not locked up, beaten, and forced to work. The overuse of detention has led to horrendous conditions for children behind bars, detrimental to both their physical health and emotional well being.

GHANA

Ghana, like South Africa, was under colonial rule. Great Britain imposed the laws of the United Kingdom on the nation for decades. "Prior to the advent of British imperial rule, traditional law, which sought to maintain social equilibrium and to ensure communal solidarity, governed social relations among Ghana's peoples."[56] The British were the first to install a written penal code. The influence of British law is notable foremost in the extremely low age of criminal responsibility. Following the footsteps of its former ruler, Ghana has set the age at which children are liable for their actions at seven years.[57]

But in 1998, Ghana made an effort to further protect juvenile offenders. The Parliament amended the Criminal Code of 1960 to include raising the age of criminal responsibility from seven years to twelve.[58] It is quite notable that a nation notorious for discrimination against women has not made a distinction in criminal liability between male and female offenders. For example, in rural regions, "women can be punished with banishment by traditional village authorities for teenage pregnancy or suspected witchcraft."[59] While women are often subject to protectionist legislation and there is little equality under the law between the genders, there is no difference between the commissions of crime for children based on their gender. Finally, the range of age in which a child has limited liability is seventeen. Until an offender's eighteenth birthday, all offenses are heard before the juvenile court.[60]

In Ghana, the lower courts have jurisdiction over all juvenile cases that involve criminal charges for juveniles, and often involve a separate juvenile court. But, these courts are usually not permanent, because according to the government there are not enough juvenile delinquency issues to hold proceedings on a regular basis. The court panel consists of two magistrates that are assisted by two laypeople, one male and one female. The courts convene approximately ten times a year and usually only in the larger cities.[61]

Ghana also employs an alternative court rather than the juvenile court through a process entitled community tribunals, particularly in regions that are far from cities.

> Act 459, the Courts Act 1993 designated community tribunals as courts to try juvenile cases and provides that the community tribunals must include a social welfare officer. This is being queried by the Department of Social Welfare, as it is potentially a fusing of judicial and executive powers. This reform means that now juvenile courts are available at district level rather than at a regional level.[62]

The purpose of the alternative juvenile tribunals is to involve the social welfare approach to juvenile justice instead of forcing a youth offender to face criminal proceedings. In addition, it provides an easier alternative to regional juvenile courts, which as mentioned, only meet in certain areas and make it difficult for all offenders to attend.

While the Criminal Procedure Code of 1960 was the original law that dealt with Ghanian juveniles in conflict with the law, the Ghana National Commission on Children felt that it was both unacceptable and incomplete. Their work allowed for the 1998 passage of the Children's Act, but further review felt that many of the special protections for juvenile offenders were still not considered. The most recent change to the law comes under the Juvenile Justice Bill. While it is still being debated, the bill outlines a number of additional protections for children.

First, the new Juvenile Justice Bill proposes a much more in-depth and uniform system for juvenile courts across the nation. Among the major changes is the proposal to nationalize the idea of social inquiry already present in the community tribunals. The bill states that the court must account for the circumstances of the juvenile's life. This must occur before any sentence is handed down, and if the sentence deviates from the general guidelines of what that offense usually carries, the court is required to make a written explanation. The report is to ensure that whatever sanctions are given to the youth are in his best interest.[63] In the explanation of the need for the social inquiry report, the bill further highlights the system in which the material can and cannot be used:

2. The social enquiry report shall be prepared by a probation officer who shall visit the home of the juvenile.
3. The social enquiry report shall include particulars on the background of the juvenile, the present circumstances of the juvenile, the conditions under which the offence was committed and recommendations for sentence.
4. The court shall ensure that the contents of the report are made known to the juvenile and a copy shall be made available to the juvenile or the legal representative of the juvenile.
5. The court may request an oral report from the probation officer in addition to the social enquiry report.
6. If the court does not follow the recommendations given in the report, written reasons shall be given as to why the recommendations have not been complied with.[64]

Other additional changes from the new legislation will include the implementation of a diversion process, or the possibility of keeping the minors out of juvenile court altogether by mediating criminal charges with the juvenile rather than subjecting the offender to the formalities of the court system. The bill also includes a system of formal juvenile courts that will replace the regional and ad hoc courts presently found in Ghana. The bill states: "juvenile court shall sit either in a different building or room from that in which sittings of other courts are held or in different days from those on which sittings of other courts are held."[65] Finally, the bill outlines the need for expedited juvenile hearings in the hope that if the case is not complete within six months of the initial contact with the court, the case will be dismissed. Ghana's present system has not lived up to international standards for the administration of juvenile justice, but there has been a genuine attempt to make necessary changes that will benefit a child in conflict with the law. The bill came up for debate in the 2003 session in the Parliament.[66]

In regard to the privacy of the juvenile offender, the juvenile has the following right during all stages of contact with the justice system, including the investigation and any formal court proceedings: any individual who publishes the name or any identifying information about a youth in conflict with the law has committed a criminal offense, and will be formally charged. Until the bill becomes law, however, juveniles continue to have identifying information released about them, and the government recognizes that it has led to social ostracizing that has not helped the rehabilitation of the youth.[67]

Another right ignored in the Children's Act but outlined in the Juvenile Justice Bill is the privilege of parental involvement in all proceedings. While it was previously not a concern of legislation, the Juvenile Justice Bill allows parental involvement from the moment of initial contact with the police.

> Clause 11 stipulates that at least one parent, guardian or a close relative is to be informed of the arrest of the juvenile by the police. Close relative has been defined in the Bill and if such a person cannot be traced, a probation officer or social worker is to be informed. The presence of a parent, guardian, close relative or probation officer is also required at the interview.[68]

The aid of parents is not simply emotional support, but also includes an expectation of financial help. For instance, if a child will remain in detention unless bail is met, the parents have the right to pay the bail for him. If a child is sentenced to a fine for his actions, the parents can provide the funds. Finally, the juvenile also has a right to parental presence throughout formal court proceedings, and it is the responsibility of the judiciary to explain this to the youth. "The presiding officer shall, at the commencement of proceedings in court, inform the juvenile in language that the juvenile understands of the following . . . the right to have a parent, guardian close relative or probation officer present at the proceedings."[69]

Possibly because much of Ghanian criminal law is based on British codes, the Criminal Procedure Code of 1960 guaranteed the right to counsel for a defendant of any age. In an independent report presented by the Country Information and Policy Unit, Immigration and Nationality Directorate, Home Office, researchers found that the right was outlined in the criminal code, but more importantly, was implemented during court proceedings. "Defendants are presumed innocent until proven guilty, trials are public and defendants have a right to be present, to be represented by an attorney, to present evidence and to cross examine witnesses. The authorities respect and observe these rights in practice."[70] While the amendments to the Juvenile Justice Bill reiterate the importance of legal representation for juveniles, it is notable that neither the latest version of the law nor the earlier Criminal Code provides for a defense attorney when the juvenile and/or his or her family are unable to afford it.

The laws of Ghana allow for capital punishment for serious and violent crimes, but not for juvenile offenders. The Criminal Procedure Code of 1960 holds that capital punishment cannot be inflicted on any citizen under the age of eighteen, and unless an offender is seventeen, it is a contravention of law to imprison him or her.[71] Ghana's initial report to the Committee on the Rights of the Child discusses other secure establishments that will house and reform a youth offender. Like Kenya, youths can be remanded to either a *borstal* institution or a reform school depending on their age and crime. Both establishments are required to provide education similar to what the offender would receive if free, and rehabilitative treatment aimed at altering criminal tendencies. Usually, offenders are in custody for approximately three years. Although this means that a youth will be subject to measures for a longer time frame than if they committed the same crime as an adult, the differentiation is that adult sentences are meant to be punitive while youth sanctions are for reform. One section of the code prohibits juvenile integration with adult criminals.[72] Finally, juveniles are expected to have contact with various social welfare workers that will aide in psychological and social development.

The Juvenile Justice Bill outlines a number of other options that judges could implement beside detention. Possible sanctions against minors are relatively similar to present law. They include the dismissal of charges against an offender, dismissal with a formal warning from the court, probation, supervision by an appropriate family member, detention in a reform school or *borstal* institution, or fines that can include the costs incurred from damages caused by criminal actions. If none of these measures are acceptable for an individual case, the court reserves the right to create alternate sentences of its own choosing.[73]

Both the present and proposed juvenile laws declare that youths under the age of seventeen cannot be incarcerated with adult offenders at any cost. But, inspections of national penal institutions show that Ghana is in violation of its own laws. The acting Chief Justice His Lordship in Ghana, Mr. Justice E. K. Wiredu and Mr. Ernest Owusu have publicly acknowledged the problem and agreed that the practice of confining youths with adult criminals must end. According to these officials, the separation of youths will be the first step in recognizing that youth offenders must be afforded reformatory measures rather than harsh penalties.[74]

An American State Department report found that prisons were in terrible condition, and that juveniles could be found on the premises. Utilizing an independent report issued by the Committee on Human Rights and Administrative Justice, the State Department noted that by all accounts, overcrowding led to unhygienic conditions, including unclean facilities and a lack of proper ventilation. Inmates receive little food during their incarceration; the approximate value of allotment per prisoner on a daily basis is US$0.35. There are no medical services unless the inmate can afford to pay. While the original report caused quite a stir, the United States noted that government response was minimal. Some prisoners were released, but no major changes have taken place.[75]

When juveniles are instead committed to institutions reserved for their own age group, their care is placed under the jurisdiction of the Ministry of Employment and Social Welfare. This department oversees both detention centers and probation homes, equivalent to American halfway houses, in a variety of cities across the nation.[76] Few studies, however, have been able to document the conditions of these centers to ascertain whether they are protecting the rights of children and making every effort to rehabilitate them.

Youth justice in Ghana, particularly sentencing, can only benefit from the passage of the detailed Juvenile Justice Bill. At present, there is no legislation outlining the rights of juveniles in detention, and thus, it is difficult to hold detention centers and rehabilitation facilities to any standards. First, the bill calls for the construction of separate establishments, senior and junior detention centers, which take into consideration the age and criminal history of the offender. This dichotomy is to further protect younger, nonviolent offenders from the bad influences and/or abuse of violent, older juveniles. Even after release from detention, juveniles are expected to remain in contact with center staff so that rehabilitation processes can continue after release.

It is important to note that the proposed legislation makes no statements regarding rights and guarantees that will be provided to youths in confinement. There is no mention of education, health care, or any promise against physical punishment.[77] All in all, sentencing procedures in Ghana are both understudied and unregulated. Sentencing for juveniles ranges from probation to detention in juvenile facilities to incarceration in adult prisons. Little is known about the care received post-sentence, and whether any rehabilitation occurs for the offender to avoid recidivism.

NIGERIA

Nigeria, like Ghana, was also under colonial rule by the British. The Children and Young People's Act was originally passed by the British in 1943, and it listed the age of criminal responsibility at seven. When Nigeria became an independent state, it revised much of the British penal code, but the Nigerian government allowed the age of criminal responsibility to remain at seven. Between seven and twelve years of age, the government has the additional burden of proving that juveniles have the capacity to understand the implications of their actions.[78]

But the government apparently does not always adhere to its legal policy. In August 2002, a news story broke about the arrest of a four-year-old
child in Lagos, Nigeria's capital. According to the article, police "had arrested a four-year-old boy for breaking the windscreen of a neighbour's
car. The law enforcers not only kept the infant in the police station for two
days, but also forced him to do manual labor."[79] Under Nigerian criminal
statutes, the child should not have been held responsible because his age
deemed him too immature to understand the crime that he committed.
While the child was not officially charged, he was still subjected to legal
processes. He was informally detained and punished, though this was
done without court sanctions. It was in total violation of Nigeria's age of
criminal responsibility.

The age of criminal responsibility is listed at seven, yet the Children and
Young Person's Act defines a child as any person who is under the age of
fourteen, and any individual over the age of fourteen is instead considered
a young person. There is no specific definition of a juvenile in Nigerian penal code. Nigeria also falls short in regard to international standards by
which offenders should be incorporated under the juvenile justice system.
The unmentioned "juvenile" is any individual who has not attained the
age of seventeen years. A further requirement for children prosecuted under the law is that any juvenile offender will be charged as an adult if the
commission of crime occurs with an adult.[80] Though Nigeria has ratified
the United Nations standards on rights of the child that deems anyone under eighteen as a juvenile, Nigeria prosecutes all offenders that have
reached seventeen years of age in the adult penal system.

Unlike other European colonies, the juvenile court in Nigeria is directly
adapted from the British system. Nigeria did not have a juvenile court until the British installed one in the mid-1940s. After independence from
Great Britain in 1960, the nation adopted a system similar to the one already in place, and entitled the governing legislation the Children and
Young Person's Act. All that is required for the various states in the nation
is that they have a separate court for juvenile offenders that oversees both
delinquents that are deemed children and young persons. The court proceedings are administrated by a magistrate who is appointed by the Chief
Justice in the area.[81]

Presently, most Nigerian states have a juvenile justice system similar to
Ghana's system. It is an informal and ad hoc setup, not a permanent fix-
ture in the court system. In the temporary courts, Nigerian law requires
that all cases are heard by a magistrate and two laypeople—one male and
one female.[82] Nigeria also reported to the United Nations in regard to
their courts that: "[J]uvenile courts are supposed to be held outside the
view of the public and in separate buildings from where the normal court
proceedings are held, but a lack of facilities has prevented the implemen-

tation of these provisions."[83] In reality, both of these policies apply; the administration of juvenile justice differs in the various states in Nigeria, depending on location. "The different states of the Federation have adopted two approaches to the establishment and operation of the juvenile courts. In a few states (especially Lagos State), a visible structure of juvenile justice administration is on the ground. But in most states, such structures are not readily visible."[84]

In somewhat of a variation of standard diversion practices, the Nigerian government allows the police to play a huge role in determining which children are sent to a court and which are otherwise dealt with. The police also reserve the right to make the decision to discharge the youth without formal charges instead of mandating a court appearance, all completed without any involvement from a magistrate or court personnel.[85] But, according to reports from independent investigators, the Nigerian police often abuse their power in regard to juvenile courts. A "study on juvenile justice administration conducted by the CRP with the assistance of Penal Reform International (PRI), found that police officers often falsified the age of juveniles to pass them off in court as adults, in order to avoid adhering to the legal requirements for their treatment."[86]

Nigeria's policies regarding juvenile justice are not up to par with international human rights standards because a separate system with trained juvenile jurists is not in place. The purpose of having a juvenile court is to provide additional protections to minors who are considered to have a limited liability as well as a lesser capacity for understanding and accepting the consequences of their actions. When the police circumvent the system for whatever reason, the children suffer.

The Children and Young Person's Act of Nigeria details the right to a shield from public scrutiny. Part II, Arts. 5 and 6 hold:

5. In a juvenile court no person other than the members and officers of the court and the parties to the case, their solicitors and counsel, and other persons directly concerned in the case, shall except by leave of the court, be allowed to attend so however that *bonafide* representatives or news agency shall not be excluded, except by special order of the court.
6. No person shall publish the name, address, school, photograph, or anything likely to lead to the identification of the child or young person before the juvenile court, except with the permission of such court or in so far as required by the provisions of this Act and a person who acts in contravention of the provisions of this subsection is liable to a fine of one hundred Naira.[87]

Parents and guardians of Nigerian youth offenders have an extraordinarily high level of liability for crimes. The Children and Young Person's Act mandates that a parent must be present at all stages of proceedings, with court-enforced attendance. In addition, if the offense is less serious and fine or payment of damage is levied against the child, the court may order the parents to provide funds. The parents can also be ordered to give security that their child will behave henceforth. If the parents refuse to attend or pay the charges imposed by the court, the parents can be sentenced to imprisonment for the crime of the juvenile. Interestingly, all of the alternative measures levied against parents or appropriate guardians can occur as a substitute for the finding of guilt or conviction of the youth.

Conversely, one would expect that parents were provided some rights in the juvenile court. But, they are few and far between. While parents reserve the right to appeal any sentence against them made by the juvenile court, they have little say in how the court treats their child: "Where the child is brought before a juvenile court for any offense other than homicide the case shall be finally disposed of in such court, and it shall not be necessary to ask the parent whether he consents that the child shall be dealt with in the juvenile court."[88] It is ironic that the parents have excessive liability for the actions of their child, including the possibility of imprisonment, but also have very little power to oppose the court. Not only are these rules in violation of the international standards of due process rights, they also forge an exacerbated class-based system. Wealthier parents can easily pay off the court for any fines ordered, yet poorer parents may be imprisoned for a crime that they did not commit.

Nigeria's guarantee of the right to legal representation is another instance in which national policy is not met in practical implementation. Chapter four of the Nigerian Constitution guarantees that the juvenile offender has the right "to be informed promptly or directly of the charges against him or her, and if appropriate through his or her parents or legal guardians, and then have legal or other appropriate assistance in the preparation and presentation of his or her defence."[89]

During a study completed by the Centre for Law Enforcement Education in Nigeria, independent researchers surveyed judicial officers and learned that the right to legal defense is often ignored. One hundred and fifty-six juvenile officers in Nigeria responded anonymously to a survey on the protection of rights in the juvenile justice system. Only 8.5 percent of the respondents stated that they felt that juveniles realized "very well" their rights to legal aid. Conversely, almost three times the respondents, 23.2 percent, stated that juveniles' knowledge of their right to an attorney was very poor.[90] Again, the rights of juvenile offenders explicit in both international standards and Nigerian law are ignored. Juveniles are the most vulnerable defendants to face the court, and for this are afforded decreased liability and understanding for their actions. This occurs because youths are generally considered less mature than adults. It is sad that the defendants most in need of protection, particularly legal advice when facing a judicial body, have their rights habitually disregarded.

Nigeria's report to the Committee on the Rights of the Child outlines the types of sanctions that a minor may be sentenced to if convicted of criminal action. They include dismissing of all charges, releasing the offender with a warning after exacting a promise for good behavior, requiring supervision by a relative or other appropriate adult, being supervised in an appropriate institution, or ordering fines and costs that must be paid by the parent or guardian of the offender. Custodial measures include placement in a reform establishment, which includes the provision that it must be for less than six months, placement in a *borstal* institution, or imprisonment.[91]

Independent researchers have learned that the primary goal of sentencing in Nigeria is punitive rather than rehabilitative, and that detention is utilized far more often than any alternate sentences. "The nations emphasize punishment and custody of offenders and where reformation is prescribed, it is incidental. Idada (1972) argued that: from the attitude of the courts, at least in this country, there is clear evidence that punishment is the primary aim of the sentencing process."[92]

Thus, when juveniles are convicted of crimes, they are most likely remanded to either rehabilitation homes or *borstal* institutions. Like other nations, the initial overcrowding leads to a slew of other problems. For instance, population statistics of the Borstal Training Institution in Kakuri have constantly risen over the past few decades. In the late 1970s, the establishment exceeded its capacity by approximately twenty juveniles. However, in the mid-1980s, the number of children that could live comfortably in the facility remained at 120, but inspectors found over 500 youths. While the latest figures from 2001 are lower, the institution still remains incredibly overcrowded.[93]

Through surveys of both inmates and officials at juvenile detention facilities in Nigeria, researchers from the Centre for Law Enforcement Education learned that all involved parties felt that conditions in both rehabilitation centers and *borstal* institutions were inadequate for the health and development of youth offenders. First, surveys revealed that an overwhelming number of staff felt that juvenile facilities were lacking in resources for food, bedding, medicine, educational classes, and vocational training. In addition, many officials noted that youths were given little time or space for exercise and rest.[94]

Instead of providing youths with proper care after requiring their removal from their home and families, the government further harms children by denying them proper care. Children, particularly those experiencing any emotional or physical difficulties, require adequate nutrition and medical care. In addition, if the purpose of confinement is meant to reform youth offenders, education and skills training should be a top priority. The detention facilities in Nigeria are failing juvenile offenders by refusing to provide them with adequate means to survive or any rehabilitative measures.

Interestingly, juvenile responses to queries about physical conditions of detention differed from the statements of officials. A majority of juveniles, albeit small, claimed that they had sufficient sleeping facilities and food. However, many of the children involved in the Nigerian juvenile justice system originally come from states of dire poverty. For youths who are used to have nothing to eat, any amount of nourishment may seem adequate.

Worse than the care provided to juveniles is the abuse experienced by minors in custodial settings, as evidenced from the responses of institutionalized offenders. Almost half of the youths reported that they had been subject to some form of verbal and/or physical assault. At least one-third of the youths experienced mental abuse as well, and were threatened with violence, had their sentence extended, and were denied sustenance.[95] However, children in detention facilities like *borstal* institutions reported lower levels of abuse than their institutionalized counterparts. Almost three-quarters of offenders stated that they were protected from physical and sexual abuse at the hands of other inmates or staff. Over three-quarters of inmates felt that they had appropriate means of complaining about conditions, and could easily interact with both staff and other inmates.[96]

Finally, forms of physical punishment are not considered abuse under the laws of Nigeria, and are often used in custody of juveniles. The legality of corporal punishment might explain why some interviewed juveniles expressed disagreement when asked if they were physically assaulted. In reality, corporal punishment occurs often and in a variety of forms. Youths can be forced to "frog jump," be subjected to harsh exercise regiments, or beatings. These penalties are often for minor infractions of the rules, and show that youth establishments in Nigeria are more punishment oriented than concerned with youth reform.[97] At present, the administration of juvenile justice and institutionalization is better than that of Kenya, for instance, but still needs revamping. Children should always be fed and cared for, and should experience no fear of torture or physical abuse.

NOTES

1. United Nations Committee on the Rights of the Child. "Consideration of the Reports Submitted by State Parties Under Article 44 of the Convention." 23 Feb. 2000, 23rd Session. [Online] Available: http://www.unhchr.ch/tbs/doc.nsf/9c663e9ef8a0d080c12565a9004db9f7/6e861f881eca1b1e8025687f005a805b

2. Luyt, William F. M. "The Deprivation of Liberty of Children in South Africa. Technikon SA. [Online]. Available: http://216.239.33.100/q=cache:opNkH3Nbp MkC:www.tsa.ac.za/corp/research/papers/2ndEcnf%2520paper%2520Luyt.doc+%22south=africa%22+AND+%22juveniles%22&hl=en&ie=UTF-8

3. "Crime." *World Factbook of Criminal Justice Systems: South Africa.* 1993. [Online]. Available: http://www.uaa.alaska.edu/just/just490/justice/factbook93/crime.html.

4. U.S. Department of State Commission on Human Rights. "Human Rights Reports for 2000: South Africa." Washington, D.C.: Feb., 2001. [Online]. Available: http://www.humanrights-usa.net/reports/southafrica.html.

5. South African Law Commission. "Report on Juvenile Justice," Project 106. [Online]. Available: http://wwwserver.laew.wits.ac.za/salc/report/project106.html.

6. National Council of Family and Juvenile Court Judges. Newsletter: Summer 2000. [Online]. Available: http://www.ncjfcj.unr.edu/homepage/today/Today-Summer%2000.pdf.

7. "Report on Juvenile Justice." 2.

8. Parliament of the Republic of South Africa. "National Assembly: Order Paper No. 9." Fifth Session, Second Parliament. 6 Mar. 2003. [Online]. Available: http://www.parliament.gov.za/pls/portal/web_app.utl_output_doc?p_table=papers&p_doc_col=paper&p_mime_col=mime_type&p_id=584170.

9. United Nations "Initial Reports Due to State Parties in 1997: South Africa." Committee on the Rights of the Child. 22 May 1999. [Online]. Available: http://www.unhchr.ch/tbs/doc.nsf/385c2add1632f4a8c12565a9004dc311/d2c94c67c4df8870802567ef0035d7c8?OpenDocument.

10. "Initial Reports Due to State Parties in 1997: South Africa."

11. Report on "Juvenile Justice."

12. Report on "Juvenile Justice."

13. Report on "Juvenile Justice."

14. "Initial Reports Due to State Parties in 1997: South Africa."

15. "Initial Reports Due to State Parties in 1997: South Africa."

16. "Initial Reports Due to State Parties in 1997: South Africa."

17. "The Deprivation of Liberty of Children in South Africa."

18. "The Deprivation of Liberty of Children in South Africa."

19. "Initial Reports Due to State Parties in 1997: South Africa."

20. "The Deprivation of Liberty of Children in South Africa."

21. "Pollsmoor Inmates Complain of Assault." South African Press Association. 20 Mar. 2002. Westlaw. [Online]. Available: http://web2.westlaw.com/search/default.wl?Action=EditQuery&CFID=0&CiteListOnly=False&DB=SAPASSN&DocSample=False&EQ=search&Method=TNC&n=4&Query=%22juvenile+detention%22&RLTDB=CLID%5FDB434313&RP=%2Fsearch%2Fdefault%2Ewl&Service=Search&SS=Doc&Tab=Cite+List&TF=10&TC=8&RS=WLW2.84&VR=2.0&SV=Split&FN=_top&MT=Westlaw.

22. "Initial Reports Due to State Parties in 1997: South Africa."

23. "South Africa." *Info-Please Atlas.* 2002–2003. [Online]. Available: http://www.infoplease.com/ipa/A0107983.html.

24. "The Deprivation of Liberty of Children in South Africa."

25. Africa News Service. "Kenya; Children Make Up 70 Percent of Workforce in Some Sectors." 28 Sept. 2001. LexisNexis. [Online]. Available: http://80-web.lexis-nexis.com.proxyau.wrlc.org/universe/document?_m=535d7e153269e954, accessed 15 Oct. 2002.

26. Human Rights Watch. *Juvenile Injustice: Police Abuse and Detention of Street Children in Kenya*. June, 1997, 32. [Online]. 21 Nov. 2002. Available: http:.// www.hrw.org/reports/1997/Kenya.

27. *Juvenile Injustice*, 35.

28. *Juvenile Injustice*, 26–27.

29. "Juvenile Justice in Kenya." Reprinted from Article 40, a publication of the Children's Rights Project of the Community Law Centre at the University of the Western Cape. CYC Online. Sept. 1999. [Online] Available: http://www .cyc-net.org/cyc-online/cycol-0999-youthjusticekenya.html.

30. *Juvenile Injustice*, 5.

31. *Juvenile Injustice*, 5.

32. *Juvenile Injustice*, 26.

33. *Juvenile Injustice*, 29.

34. *Juvenile Injustice*, 29.

35. *Juvenile Injustice*, 4.

36. "Juvenile Justice in Kenya."

37. United Nations: Committee on the Rights of the Child. "Consideration of Reports Submitted By State Parties Under Article 44 of the Convention—Initial Reports of State Parties Due in 1992: Kenya." 13 Jan. 2000. [Online]. Available: http://www.unhchr.ch/tbs/doc.nsf/385c2add1632f4a8c12565a9004dc311/a8d883 af803683a8c1256a96002f5004/$FILE/G0140557.pdf.

38. "Consideration of Reports Submitted By State Parties Under Article 44 of the Convention—Initial Reports of State Parties Due in 1992: Kenya."

39. "Juvenile Justice in Kenya."

40. "Consideration of Reports Submitted By State Parties Under Article 44 of the Convention—Initial Reports of State Parties Due in 1992: Kenya."

41. "Consideration of Reports Submitted By State Parties Under Article 44 of the Convention—Initial Reports of State Parties Due in 1992: Kenya."

42. "Consideration of Reports Submitted By State Parties Under Article 44 of the Convention—Initial Reports of State Parties Due in 1992: Kenya."

43. "Consideration of Reports Submitted By State Parties Under Article 44 of the Convention—Initial Reports of State Parties Due in 1992: Kenya."

44. "Consideration of Reports Submitted By State Parties Under Article 44 of the Convention—Initial Reports of State Parties Due in 1992: Kenya."

45. *Juvenile Injustice*, 4.

46. *Juvenile Injustice*, 5.

47. Orr, David. "Street Children." International Children and Youth Care Network. Jun. 2000, Number 17. [Online]. Available: http://www.cyc-net .org/cyc-online/cycol-0600-nairobi.html.

48. *Juvenile Injustice*, 23.

49. Stockman, Farah, "Juvenile Hall Instead of School: Kenya Faces Obstacles in Aiding its Poorest Children" *Christian Science Monitor*, 23 Mar. 2000.

50. *Juvenile Injustice*, 43.

51. *Juvenile Injustice*, 44.

52. *Juvenile Injustice*, 46.

53. *Juvenile Injustice*, 48.

54. *Juvenile Injustice*, 35.

55. *Juvenile Injustice,* 35.

56. Library of Congress: Country Studies. From http://www.AllRefer.com. "Ghana: Criminal Justice." November, 1994. [Online]. Available: http://www.1up-info.com/country-guide-study/ghana/ghana168.html. Accessed March 24, 2004.

57. Partnership for Global Good Practice. *International Standards for the Administration of Juvenile Justice and Examples of Good Practice.* London: Partnership for Global Good Practice. 2002. [Online]. Available: http://www.restorativejustice. org/asp/details.asp?ID-2262.

58. AFROL Gender Profiles. "Ghana," 3 [Online]. 27 Oct. 2002. Available: http://www.afrol.com/Categories/Women/profiles/Ghana_women.html.

59. "Ghana," 1.

60. "Ghana: Criminal Justice," 2.

61. Ebbe, Obi N. I. *"Ghana."* *World Factbook of Criminal Justice Systems:* U.S. Department of Justice: Bureau of Justice Statistics. [Online]. Available: http://www.ojp.usdoj.gov/bjs/pub/ascii/wfbcjgha.txt.

62. United Nations Committee on the Rights of the Child. "Initial Reports of State Parties Due in 1992: Ghana." 20 Nov. 1995. [Online]. Available: http://www.unhchr.ch/tbs/doc.nsf/385c2add1632f4a8c12565a9004dc311/a4d75 fbb3234e377c125635b003355de?OpenDocument&Highlight=0,Ghana.

63. Legal Resources Centre: "Juvenile Justice Bill: Ghana." 18 Jan. 2002. [Online]. Available: http://www.lrc-ghana.org/legal_rights/juvenile_justice_bill.rtf.

64. "Juvenile Justice Bill: Ghana."

65. "Juvenile Justice Bill: Ghana."

66. "Legislative Business: In the Third Session of the Third Parliament of the Fourth Republic of Ghana the Following Bills Will be Presented to the House for Consideration and Passing Into Law." The Parliament of Ghana. [Online: 23 Mar. 2003]. Available: http://www.parliament.gh/hmeP/legibusPag/pendLegis.htm.

67. "Juvenile Justice Bill—Ghana."

68. "Juvenile Justice Bill—Ghana."

69. "Juvenile Justice Bill—Ghana."

70. "Ghana: Country Assessment." Country Information and Policy Unit. Apr., 2002. [Online]. Available: http://www.ecoi.net/pub/mv64/uk-gha0402.htm.

71. "Ghana: Criminal Justice."

72. "Initial Reports of State Parties Due in 1992: Ghana."

73. "Juvenile Justice Bill—Ghana."

74. "Ghana: Isolate Juvenile Offenders." *Africa News.* 12 Apr. 2001. Lexis Nexis. [Online]. Available: http://web.lexis-nexis.com/universe/document? _m=4fced2aff6f00f5b1947ffa96df5b29&docnum=28&wchp=dGLbVtb-1S1V& _md5=e4f0c83c3253d9f2a91243a45a6833a7.

75. U.S. Department of State, Bureau of Democracy, Human Rights, and Labor. "Country Reports on Human Rights Practices 1996: Ghana." 30 Jan. 1997. [Online]. Available: http://www.usis.usemb.se/human/1996/africa/ghana.html.

76. "Ghana: Criminal Justice."

77. "Juvenile Justice Bill—Ghana."

78. "Nigeria: Focus on the Administration of Juvenile Justice." IRIN. Lagos, Nigeria: 26 Aug. 2002, 3. [Online]. Available: http://www.irinnews.org/ report.asp?ReportID=29531, accessed 16, Oct. 2002.

79. "Nigeria: Focus on the Administration of Juvenile Justice," 1.

80. Alemika, E. E. O., and I. C. Chukwuma. *Juvenile Justice Administration in nigeria: Philosophy and Practice.* Lagos, Nigeria: Centre for Law Enforcement Education, 2001, 36–38.

81. Alemika and Chukwuma. 37.

82. Ebbe, Obi N. I. "Nigeria." *World Factbook of Criminal Justice Systems.* U.S. Department of Justice: Bureau of Justice Statistics. [Online]. Available: http://www.ojp.usdoj.gov/bjs/pub/ascii/wfbcjnig.txt.

83. "Nigeria: Focus on the Administration of Juvenile Justice," 1.

84. Alemika and Chukwuma, 37.

85. "Nigeria."

86. "Nigeria: Focus on the Administration of Juvenile Justice," 2.

87. Alemika and Chukwuma, 79.

88. Alemika and Chukwuma, 80–82.

89. Alemika and Chukwuma, 30.

90. Alemika and Chukwuma, 45.

91. United Nations Committee on the Rights of the Child. "Initial Reports of State Parties Due in 1995: Nigeria." 21 Aug. 1995. [Online]. Available: http://193.194.138.190/tbs/doc.nsf/385c2add1632f4a8c12565a9004dc311/f5c4157 cf6f755abc125635d005157e2?OpenDocument&Highlight=0,Nigeria.

92. Alemika and Chukwuma, 16.

93. Alemika and Chukwuma, 41.

94. Alemika and Chukwuma, 47.

95. Alemika and Chukwuma, 55.

96. Alemika and Chukwuma, 57.

97. Alemika and Chukwuma, 61.

8

Asia

A sia, more than any other continent in the world, has diversity in religious, political, and cultural ideals. Many Asian countries are also
known for their avoidance of Western culture, adhering instead to long-
standing traditional values, including the importance of the family. These
values have an enormous impact on the criminal law statutes in each
country, and while many regulations are considered stricter than those of
the Western world, the effect on each nation is a lower crime rate than
America and Europe.

INDIA

India is known for strong family values, an exploding population, and a
permeating caste system that differentiates between the rights of economic classes. The caste system decides what occupations an Indian may
pursue as well as who they are allowed to marry. These regulations are
not mandated by law, however, and although there might be differentiations in the application of criminal statutes, there is equality under the
penal codes for all Indian citizens. The Human Rights Watch released a report that discussed the situation of children in India in 1996. The ambigu-
ity in penal statutes makes it somewhat difficult to pinpoint at exactly
what age a child can become criminally liable for his actions. "Under Indian Penal Code, anyone over the age of twelve is considered an adult,
and ambiguities in the code concerning the ability of the child to be cognizant of a crime have made it possible for children as young as seven to

be treated as adults under the law."[1] India was also under British colonial rule before independence, and it is likely that the young age of criminal responsibility, seven, was adopted from British criminal law. The *World Factbook of Criminal Justice Systems* is more succinct in describing India's age of criminal responsibility. While seven is the actual age listed for liability, offenders between the ages of seven and twelve can only be prosecuted if there is proof that "the child had attained the sufficient maturity of understanding to judge the nature and consequences of his or her conduct on the occasion in question."[2]

The Indian Penal Code lists anyone over the age of twelve as an adult, but children up through the age of eighteen who commit criminal offenses are dealt with in the juvenile court setting. But, instead of providing special protections to children aged seven to eighteen, the courts habitually remand children as young as six to detention centers. The Human Rights Watch reported, "Rather than provide custodial care like parents provide, juvenile homes have denigrated into jail-like custodial centers . . . [a number] of these children were between the ages of six and ten years. A shocking revelation about our penal system is that such small children should be detained at all!"[3]

In response to these changes, India launched a campaign to alter the Juvenile Justice Act of 1986 and adjust the age of criminal responsibility. The union minister of state for social justice and empowerment, Maneka Ghandi, has started the National Initiative for Child Protection (NICP). The NICP would like to fully "incorporate all guarantees in the UNCRC [United Nations Convention on the Rights of the Child] . . . with the minimum age of criminal responsibility raised from seven to twelve and no child under the age of twelve should be prosecuted under any legislation."[4] Somewhat due to the work of advocates, the nation amended its juvenile justice laws in 2000. The latest law, the Juvenile Justice (Care and Protection of Children) Act, makes no change to the age of criminal responsibility. The only reference the law makes to age is to note that any citizen under the age of eighteen is considered a juvenile.[5]

In relation to juvenile courts, the Juvenile Justice Act of 2000 claims: "the State Government may, by notification in the Official Gazette, constitute for a district or a group of districts specified in the notification, one or more Juvenile Justice Boards for exercising powers and discharging the duties conferred or imposed on such Boards in relation to juveniles in conflict with the law."[6] The bill later becomes more detailed in regard to the actual actors involved. The juvenile bench includes a metropolitan or judicial magistrate who is appointed by the state government for his or her particular skills in juvenile issues. In addition, an assistance panel is made up of honorary social workers, also appointed by the government—one of whom must be female and one who must male.[7]

Unlike other nations, the juvenile court in India is kept separate from the Juvenile Welfare Board that hears cases regarding mistreated and abused juveniles. But, when circumstances are such that a delinquent juvenile has been placed under the jurisdiction of the Welfare Board or vice versa, the two juvenile justice systems reserve the right to transfer a child to the other system. Other connections between the courts and the welfare system are that neither system can act if any of the members of their respective panels are absent, and that no person shall be appointed to serve in the court or the welfare system unless they have special knowledge of psychology and welfare of children.[8]

Internal researchers and media personnel report that the present situation for the juvenile courts is more of a paper farce than an implemented truth. Apparently, very few Indian juveniles are actually sent to juvenile courts rather than adult courts. First, police will treat mature-looking juveniles as adults rather than follow the process to ascertain their age. Parents with little money are often unable to do anything as their child gets tied into the court process. Even judicial officers have been found guilty of ignoring the pleas of juveniles that they should be prosecuted in the juvenile court. *The Times of India* reported in 2000 that the fate of a juvenile depends on "whether the juvenile appears under age. If he looks older and has facial hair, despite his protestations the police may book him as an adult offender. Which means that he will be tried in a regular court instead of a juvenile court."[9]

Further, even in formal proceedings the court can deny the juvenile's right to trial in a court of lowered liability: "It is then entirely up to the magistrate's discretion, whether he or she is convinced that the offender is indeed a juvenile. If the parent or guardian is not educated then simply filling in the bail application the right way may take time. Court staff have been known to pick faults with the applications time and again."[10] While the outline of the Indian juvenile court seems to provide protections to youth offenders, in practice many children are denied the right to a juvenile court appearance. It seems that all of the court actors, whose jobs are based on the protections of rights, are consistently working against juveniles and their families.

Ironically, regardless of government representatives' claims, the children arrested for criminal offenses are not treated as if they were corrupted innocents, but instead are denied basic legal rights guaranteed by international standards for adults and children alike. The present law insists that youths are afforded the right to an attorney. For instance, in regard to the right to legal defense, "'Under the law, it is also the duty of the magistrate to ensure that the offender has legal representation," says joint commissioner of police (training) Kiran Bedi. "Several NGOs also offer free legal advice but not many people are aware of these counseling centres."[11] Thus, while there are legal guidelines for the right to representation and legal aid centers that provide services to those who cannot afford representation, many Indian citizens have not been fully informed of their rights or of the free services, and never take advantage of them. A 1996 Human Rights Watch Report regarding homeless children in India released similar findings. "Legal representation is rare and there are few facilities existing for the detention of juveniles separate from adults."[12]

In regard to the right to protection from public scrutiny, the Indian government clearly outlines the laws and underlying explanations as follows: "No report in any newspaper, magazine, news-sheet or visual media of any inquiry regarding a juvenile in conflict with the law under this Act shall disclose the name, address, school or any other particulars calculated to lead to the identification of the juvenile nor shall any picture of any such juvenile be published."[13] However, as previously noted, many juvenile offenders are charged as adults as court actors ignore their assertions that they are under the age of criminal majority. For youth offenders arbitrarily tried in adult settings, no protection against public knowledge occurs and youths are subjected to social stigmatization when they are finally released from the system.

Both the original Juvenile Justice Act of 1986 and its 2000 amendments require the involvement of parents in judicial proceedings from the moment of arrest. "Where a juvenile is arrested, the officer-in-charge of the police station to which the juvenile is brought shall, as soon as may be after the arrest, inform the parent or guardian of the juvenile, if he can be found, of such arrest and direct him to be present in the Juvenile Court before which the juvenile will appear."[14] But, the original dissemination of information to parents may never take place if the police choose not to do so. In April 2002, juveniles arrested by police were sent to adult jails while their parents frantically tried to locate them. The boys spent more than three weeks in jail while their parents canvassed police stations to find their children. The police were legally required to notify the parents about their children's whereabouts, and the youths should have been treated as juveniles until documentation of their true age took place.[15]

If the information on the whereabouts of the youth is actually presented to the parent, the judicial body reserves the right to require their presence once formal proceedings begin: "Any competent authority before which a juvenile is brought under any of the provisions of this Act may, whenever it so thinks fit, require any parent or guardian having the actual charge of, or control over, the juvenile to be present at any proceeding in respect of the juvenile."[16] Finally, India holds parents liable in a unique way once sentencing commences. If the child is found to be too unruly and requires detention, the court reserves the right to force the parent to contribute to the maintenance of the offender while he or she is imprisoned. Parents are expected to provide funds for the food, shelter, and clothing of their child while in detention, as if the child was residing in their home.[17]

India claims that its juvenile laws are guided by the underlying values of rehabilitation for the juvenile delinquent. The purpose of the law is to care for youth offenders and resocialize them. These objectives apply to youths in conflict with the law as well as children in situations of neglect. All measures regarding youths in all circumstances are meant to integrate them into their communities. Through community bonds, children will develop into a life free of deviance and crime.[18] Instead of punishing youth offenders, India has a policy of protecting them.

India, however, continues to allow the death penalty for youth offenders charged as adults. Executions have not occurred in the nation for some time, but the option of capital punishment as a punishment remains. Representatives from India reported to the United Nations that capital punishment was not an available option for juvenile offenders, and neither was life imprisonment.[19] But, the Committee on the Rights of the Child listed the use of capital punishment for minors as one of their main concerns with India's system of juvenile justice, declaring that executions must be fully abolished.[20] The use of the death penalty for juvenile offenders conflicts directly with India's stated policy to protect children in conflict with the law.

Besides the option of capital punishment, the Juvenile Justice Act outlines a variety of alternate sentences that a judge may impose on a youth. These include: freedom with an admonition and warning by the court; release to parent including the order for some form of family therapy; release to parent or any available and fit guardian combined with probation for a period of less than three years; probation through a specified public office for a period of no more than three years; an order for community service; detention in a special home; or order the youth to pay a fine as long as the juvenile is over fourteen years of age and is using his own funds. If the offender is under fourteen, his parents can provide the funds for the fine. The Act elaborates further rules regarding the use of detention. If the offender is seventeen, the detention order cannot be for more than two years. However, for all other youth offenders, the detention order can last until a child reaches the age of eighteen. The court retains some flexibility in choosing the length of sentence of confinement. The judge takes the individual offender's circumstances and all other relevant facts into consideration and can increase or decrease the length of punishment.[21]

It is noteworthy that the recommended periods of confinement are extremely long. Although the court retains a measure of flexibility in the length of the sentence, a young juvenile could remain in detention for years if the court chose to utilize this sanction. For instance, because the age of criminal responsibility in India remains at seven, if an eleven-year-old female was convicted of a criminal offense, the judge could legally sentence her to seven years of detention in a juvenile institution.

A number of independent researchers have been unhappy with the conditions of juvenile detention facilities. These "special homes" are decrepit and employ staff that often abuse young inmates. The Human Rights Watch found that juvenile facilities were more like prisons than adequate establishments of learning and growth. Worse, the government department responsible for the condition of juvenile establishments has turned a blind eye to the problems. The majority of the children subjected to these homes are actually children in need rather than youths who have committed crimes.[22] This is in direct conflict with the stated purpose of all forms of detention under Indian law. Instead, any place of detention is supposed to act like substitute parents, caring and loving the youth.[23]

Detention as a sentence seems to be the most likely ordered punishment by Indian courts, even for nonviolent and minor offenses. In one prison, investigators learned that over four-fifths of detainees were in custody for theft. In another center, the majority of youths present were confined because of vagrancy and "suspicion."[24] If these minors actually committed crimes at all—and many of them did not—they were immediately contained. Instead of investigating whether youth crime would drop if social welfare groups were able to provide more food, India would rather lock up its youth. International standards on juvenile justice require that detention should only be used as a last resort, and when all other attempts at rehabilitation for a minor have failed. Across India, children are being confined in jail-like settings against their will, at times for nothing more than their state of poverty and having nowhere else to go but the streets.

Numerous studies have proven that conditions in these facilities are substandard. In reality, the homes are more like prisons than educational institutions. There is a lack of staff, facilities are dilapidated, and no forms of rehabilitative treatment are offered. Interviewees at all levels, including inspectors, children, social workers, and staff admitted that sexual and physical abuse were serious problems.[25] Studies of adult facilities have shown that juveniles sentenced to correction or imprisonment, although such sanctions are technically illegal under Indian law, are not always separated from adult criminals. In particular, youths in rural areas have to be held in prisons because there is simply nowhere else to place them.[26] Many inspections have led independent organizations to conclude that juveniles are not separated from adults in penitentiaries and offer recommendations that the government begins to do so. Evidence of abuse and mistreatment by the Indian juvenile justice system for youth offenders or neglected children must lead the government to instill rapid change. Hopefully, alterations will be more in line with the stated policy of legislation to protect and care for youths.

CHINA

China often tops the lists of human rights organizations as one of the worst nations in terms of crimes against humanity. Executions in the nation are rampant, yet China's definition of a child is closer to compliance with international standards than the majority of nations in this study. The lowest age in which a child can be prosecuted under the law is fourteen. "Article 14 of the Criminal Law of the PRC [People's Republic of China] states: 'A person who has reached the age of sixteen who commits a crime shall bear criminal responsibility. A person who has reached the age of fourteen but not the age of sixteen who commits the crime of killing another, serious injury, robbery, arson, habitual theft, or crimes seriously undermining social order shall bear criminal responsibility.'"[27]

In addition, any offender over the age of fourteen but under the age of eighteen has limited liability for their crimes. In a comparison with surrounding countries that accord full criminal responsibility for offenses to children at the age of twelve, Chinese policy states that an offender is not mature enough to face the consequences of his or her crime until age eighteen.[28]

But, Chinese policy is not completely in line with its actions. When Amnesty International investigated criminal law in Tibet—controlled by China—they found that, of the offenders arrested for political crimes in December 1994, twenty-six of the detainees were under the age of eighteen. Two of the offenders were only twelve, and thirteen were under the age of sixteen.[29] While China's policy on paper is commendable, the actions of the government are unacceptable. The law provides for flexibility only in the most serious of crimes, and even then, the youngest age that an individual can be liable for an offense is supposedly fourteen. But, the children arrested were guilty of little more than nonviolent protest, and were also under the age at which children are expected to have the capacity to understand their actions.

Chinese control of press releases and human rights investigations within the country make it somewhat difficult to ascertain the actual situation of juvenile justice. Numerous and conflicting reports have been released in regard to specific juvenile courts: "Juvenile courts do exist in China, but their establishment appears to have been relatively recent and there is no available report of their activities. A Chinese press article stated in 1991 that Zhejiang province has had special courts for juveniles since 1988. . . . In 1994, another article in the Chinese press stated that 3,000 courts protecting the rights of children under the age of 16 had been set up since the introduction of the law on minors in 1992."[30]

Interestingly, the latter press release coincided with the initial report that China submitted to the Committee on the Rights of the Child. In the report, China held that, "According to figures from the Supreme People's Court, by the end of 1993 China had established 3,135 special agencies (juvenile courts) to hear criminal cases involving juveniles, including 317 independent juvenile tribunals; it had 9,322 juvenile judicial officers, and basically all criminal cases involving minors were heard in juvenile courts."[31] The stated purpose of the separate courts is to promote the rehabilitation and education of children in conflict with the law. The children's emotional and intellectual capacities must be taken into account, but also balanced with the public desire for safety from crime. Procuratorates are also involved in the court system basically with the function of overseeing the juvenile courts and insuring that the special rights of the juvenile are protected.[32] Thus, in addition to courts, China has a unique method of ensuring that courts act within the rights afforded to minors. Procuratorates are almost like additional guardians for youths in conflict with the law, specialists who use their legal knowledge to help the juveniles advocate their own cases.

While the policy presented by China to both the United Nations and domestic press makes it appear that China is vigilantly protecting human rights, the actual reality of the situation is the distinct opposite. China has a history of human rights violations worse than many nations in the world. Both juveniles and adults are often subjected to punishment and sentences without a chance to protest or have an impartial trier of fact make a decision regarding their case. The Law of Protection on Minors and the report to the United Nations reflect this issue. China describes a system of juvenile courts, but never mentions that it is a requirement for any juvenile offender to be processed by the juvenile justice system. Their lack of statement on this matter combined with evidence from independent investigators brings to light the Chinese alternate that is used in lieu of a court.

The court itself is not a required component of justice in China, for juveniles or adults. In 1995, the same year that China released its initial statements to the United Nations, Amnesty International released a report condemning the nation. "Juveniles under investigation, like adults, may be put in detention by the police without any judicial decision. . . . Without being tried, juvenile detainees may simply be issued an administration detention order and sent to a labour camp to serve their term."[33] There is no greater violation to international standards regarding the rights of children than to have the individuals most in need of protection under the law facing harsh sentences without any method of redress. If juveniles can be sentenced without ever seeing a judge, or at least be given an opportunity to express their account of the incident for which they have been detained, then numerous innocent juveniles throughout China are punished for crimes that they did not commit.

The Federal Republic of China, at least in stated policy, employs basic criminal procedure in line with the standards required by the United Nation's Convention on the Rights of the Child. Chinese law has incorporated these rights into their Criminal Procedure Law. For instance, Article 27 holds, "In cases in which the defendant is deaf, mute, or a minor and has not authorized anyone to be his defender, the People's Court shall designate a defender for him."[34] Again, if the youth is never actually afforded the opportunity to participate in court proceedings, they have no need for legal assistance. It is interesting to note that the policy of legal aid differs from the right of the adult offender because there is no requirement for legal aid unless there are special circumstances. If the offender does not choose an attorney, the court is given the option to, but is not required to, appoint one.[35]

Independent researchers have learned that for adult offenders, the option to acquire legal representation is often ignored. Loopholes aid the authorities in prosecuting cases without representation for the offender. For instance, Article 110 of the Criminal Procedure Law states that, "the defendant is given notice of his right to no less than seven days before trial. . . . The investigation, during which period the detained defendant has no right to legal counsel, may take up to two months. The increase in lawyer's fees, although still under strict statutory control, has put representation beyond some people's means."[36]

The situation for juveniles varies little. In reaction to amendments to the Criminal Procedure Law in 1996, which guaranteed that a child in conflict with the law is guaranteed legal aid free of charge, a national movement has begun to set up centers to respond to the need for lawyers: "Lawyers, experts and legal aid centres across the country are working to better protect the nation's teenagers and young adults. Experts say an informal legal aid network for teenagers and young adults has been established in areas across China comprised of local branches of the Legal Aid Centre at the Ministry of Justice, local governments, law firms and other legal service providers."[37]

While the standards for legal representation appear to be better for juvenile offenders than adults, one group of juvenile offenders continues to have rights to legal representation denied by the government. Tibetan political prisoners include a number of juveniles, often punished for little more than protesting in opposition to the Chinese government. Unfortunately, legal representation for these children is not the only violation against their rights. One researcher writes, "What can the Chinese authorities do to the children if they speak out against their situation? Plenty. There are at least twenty-five known juvenile political prisoners in Chinese jails in Tibet. They are kept in adult prisons, denied legal representation, cut off from contact with their families, and forced to do the same hard labor that the adults in prison perform."[38] While China has made advances that guarantee the rights of juveniles required by international standards, the government continues to deny these rights to an ethnic minority.

Chinese law considers the right to remain free of public scrutiny a necessity for the rehabilitation of children. Article 111 of the Criminal Procedure Law states, "no cases involving the commission of crimes by minors aged fourteen or over but under sixteen are to be heard in public. Cases involving the commission of crimes by minors aged sixteen or over but under the age of eighteen are also generally not to be heard in public."[39] The differentiation in age groups is a reflection of the liability assigned to children arrested for crimes. The law affords limited liability for all children under eighteen, but those over sixteen have a greater capacity for criminal understanding than any younger offender.

In comparison to adult offenders, the Chinese policy on keeping trials closed to the public is somewhat unique. Until recently, all trials, including those of adults, were closed to the public. Changes in the law as the nation begins to recognize more legal rights have altered this, while also continuing the previous policy of keeping information about juvenile offenders private. "In recent years the practice of opening trials and police procedures to the public [has] been adopted in China. All initial cases, except those concerning State secrets, individual privacy or juvenile delinquency, should be tried publicly."[40]

Again, however, Chinese officials deviate from stated laws when prosecuting Tibetan juveniles. The right against public information applies to police contact as well, in an effort to limit social stigmatization in education and work. But when one human rights organization interviewed Tibetan juveniles released from police custody, they learned that information regarding them was released to the public. In one instance, this led to consequences that were detrimental to the child: "Former Detainee A was aged thirteen at the time of his arrest in 1987 after a violent demonstration in Lhasa. . . . After a few days in detention, he was released after his family and teachers intervened. He learned later that he had been expelled from his school. Many of his friends had also been expelled."[41] If Chinese authorities had adhered to their stated policies, Detainee A would never have been ostracized or expelled.

Chinese parents are allowed to attend all criminal proceedings and are expected to play a role in the reform of the juvenile. Article 10 of the Criminal Procedure Law states that, "In cases in which a minor under the age of 18 commits a crime, the legal representative of the defendant may be notified to be present at the time of interrogation and adjudication."[42] From the first moment of contact with police, parents or guardians are notified so that they may participate. In addition, in their original report to the United Nations Committee on the Rights of the Child, authorities stated that divisions responsible for handling youth offenders are particularly concerned with education. Parents and guardians continue to have a role at all stages of interaction with the justice system. Parents, as well as educators and social workers, are asked to participate in reform sessions with the youths, or arrange lectures, group projects, and cultural events.[43] Thus, while parental involvement in all stages of government contact with juvenile offenders is not required, all departments involved recommend that parents take a role, in the hope that they will aid in rehabilitation.

Like India, China also reported to the United Nations that the underlying principles of juvenile justice administration were meant to be rehabilitative. Juvenile courts are expected to continue education in their sentencing and keep in mind the objectives of reform rather than punitive action. In addition, the physical and emotional circumstances of a minor must be considered.[44] Also like India, China violates its own stated policy in allowing the execution of juvenile offenders. In regard to the legislation regarding juvenile justice, the Protection of Minors code, China has prohibited any capital punishment for offenders who were under eighteen during the commission of the crime.[45] The Committee on the Rights of the Child, however, later chastised China for allowing capital punishment for any offender who has reached the age of sixteen, through an indirect violation of their own law. China accomplishes this tactic by sentencing minors over sixteen to death, but waiting to implement punishment until the offender is eighteen. The United Nations recognizes that this procedure is not only a violation of juvenile justice standards, but also constitutes cruel and unusual punishment.[46] China technically adheres to its own policy by delaying execution for minors until they reach eighteen, however, international standards require that youth offenders are never be sentenced to death.

Chinese law also includes rather strict provisions for alternate punishments. Life imprisonment can be utilized as a sanction for minors above the age of fourteen. The government attempts to explain the sensibility of such sanctions by adding that life imprisonment carries the possibility of early release. Any child who has reached fourteen years can be penalized with life imprisonment. However, the law allows for these offenders to be afforded the possibility of early release if they can prove that they have made progress in rehabilitation and regret their criminal activity. This policy applies to both youths and adults, but is acted upon more for young offenders. The juveniles must take responsibility for their actions, alter their conduct, continue their education while in confinement, and complete all tasks they are assigned to meet the qualifications for reversal of the initial sentence. If a youth manages to have his or her sentence commuted, the youth remain on parole for a time period after release.[47] The government of China lists no sentencing alternatives; there is no mention of possible probation, community service, or release into the care of a fit guardian.

The only involvement in rehabilitative activities supposedly occurs in conjunction with imprisonment. Juveniles are expected to continue their education while in confinement, and parents and relevant social welfare organizations are expected to remain in contact with youths to ensure that they are beginning the path to a legal lifestyle. Parents, educators, and community leaders are asked to come and lead educational activities with confined minors. Activities can range from artistic and cultural events to helping with course work and lectures. Even when behind bars, Chinese youth are expected to remain intellectually engaged. The purpose of interaction with numerous members of the community is to show the youths that people care about them, and that they have an obligation to become law-abiding citizens.[48] The contact with families and the range of therapeutic treatment is commendable, but these should stand as alternate sentences rather than incorporated into detention.

Instead, the government violates international standards by using confinement in almost all juvenile cases, rather than as a last resort. Government authorities have outlined the conditions of confinement, and have noted that youth facilities have armed staff and electric fences. All types of physical punishment are prohibited. Females are separated from male offenders in all aspects of detention and are supervised by female guards.[49] While detained, juveniles are legally mandated access to familial visits, a legal representative on a regular basis to assist youths with any official issues, and a combination of political, cultural, and vocational education.

The purpose of each type of "education" sentence is to reform the criminal ways of the youth. Communist ideology plays a huge role; the government is convinced that youths who are exposed to the intellectual side of laws will learn to value a legitimate lifestyle. Children are also expected to work hard to reverse their immoral habits of the past. More than two-thirds of the time that juveniles are incarcerated, they learn vocational skills and Chinese culture, with a portion of time reserved for compulsory education.[50] Again, many of these reform activities could take place while a youth remained at home; children on probation in other nations are required to participate in certain activities beyond contact with an officer of the law, but are also allowed to return home on a daily basis.

The Regulations on Sanctions and Administration of Public Order, unlike China's statements to the United Nations, does list a few possible alternate sentences for children under the age of fourteen. Instead of allowing state control, minors are reprimanded by the court and then turned over to their parent or guardian for punishment. If the conviction of the minor is for the least serious offenses, a sentence can be served in a work-study school rather than a detention facility. This sanction is reserved for the most minor of crimes, only those that legally cannot carry criminal punishment. And remand to a work-study school, although not like traditional imprisonment, still involves a form of detention against the will of the youth. The overuse of detention is so widespread in China that it spreads to actions that are not criminally punishable, and juveniles who have broken no law are subject to court-ordered containment.

It seems somewhat ridiculous to commend China's behavior in regard to juvenile justice in any way, but unlike many other nations, China has actually abided by its policy of not integrating juveniles into adult prison facilities. The most recent Human Rights report from the U.S. State Department holds that youths are unequivocally separated from adult inmates and females are housed separately from males.[51] While the policy of imprisonment for most crimes remains in violation of international standards, it has an impact on the separation of juveniles from adult criminals. Other nations present a policy in which juveniles can only be detained as a last resort, which means that the numbers of juvenile facilities constructed are few. But, when courts continue to remand children to confinement, justice authorities quickly run out of space for youth offenders, and children end up in adult penitentiaries.

China's policy also states that in addition to housing children separately from adult criminals, youth offenders will be treated differently during confinement.[52] But the life of juveniles imprisoned throughout China is instead indistinguishable from the experience of adult inmates. Overall, it is difficult to get trustworthy data regarding juvenile detention in China because of the ongoing policy of censorship and suppression of government information. "[T]here is little publicly available information about the juvenile justice system. Ministry of Public Security regulations state that local and national figures for the number of juveniles in correctional facilities and Reeducation through Labor '[that] have not been published or approved for release' should be considered state secrets."[53]

Most of the information regarding the treatment of juveniles under Chinese policy comes from investigations of mistreatment of Tibetan youths by authorities. While there are provisions against torture of juvenile inmates, political activists of all ages have been severely assaulted. Deprivation of sustenance is a popular punishment while detained, as is the use of electric torture devices and long-term isolation.[54] While there are virtually no studies of juvenile detention conditions in China, the nation's history of human rights abuses can only lead to the interpretation that abuse is rampant for Chinese children as well. The situation for Tibetan youths is further exacerbated by the fact that this ethnic minority is not afforded the right of separation from imprisoned adults.

Finally, China violates both its own legal standards and international principles for juvenile justice through its practice of administrative sentences of neglected youth. China does not consistently make a separation between youth who are in conflict with the law and youth who, because of their economic circumstances, are forced to make the streets their home. Homeless individuals of all ages are routinely shuffled into Custody and Repatriation ("C&R")centers, where overcrowding, abuse, and disease are rampant. In one overcrowded cell, Human Rights in China found that authorities made no distinction between youths and adults.

Almost mockingly, researchers noted that juveniles in detention are almost better off than children in custody who have committed no crime. For instance, one detainee told the researchers that he was housed in a cell with seventy people, including seven children under the age of twelve, and two babies under the age of two. While the baby's father was present in the center, he was housed separately from his child.[55] It is shocking that the nation actually affords more protections to youths who have committed crimes than children who are homeless. At least children who commit crimes are certain to be separated from the adult criminal population.

Conditions are deplorable in the "C & R" centers. In each one visited by inspectors, lack of light and water, overcrowding, poor ventilation, unsanitary conditions that led to bad hygiene make detention more than uncomfortable. Food is usually not of good quality, and abuse and mistreatment by captors is ongoing. A number of inmates alleged abuse by staff and inmates who had managed to attain power. One inmate recounted his knowledge of another inmate who was beaten to death. Children do not escape similar fates because of their age. Instead, they too are assaulted and forced to labor under threat of further abuse.[56] Children barely old enough to speak are held in detention in horrendous conditions for no reason other than their lack of wealth. China needs to investigate and make changes to the many forms of detention centers throughout the country.

JAPAN

Though unlike China in that Japan is a democratic nation, both nations have the same age listed for criminal liability. No one under the age of fourteen can be held responsible for illegal offenses. The Japanese penal system has undergone numerous changes since the end of World War II, but the age of criminal responsibility has not been altered since the Juvenile Law of 1948. In 1951, the code was amended and the definition of juvenile, or offenders who have less liability for their actions, was increased from fourteen to twenty. Delinquents under the age of twenty can be remanded to the Juvenile Court if they meet the following requirements: "Juveniles who committed offenses were, of course, within the scope of the law, which also embraced juveniles who are 'prone to commit an offense' on the basis of not subjecting themselves to the reasonable control of guardians, staying away from home without good reason, associating with people of criminal propensity or immoral character."[57]

While the law states, however, that children under the age of fourteen can be held criminally liable for their actions, children under that age who commit crimes are still under the jurisdiction of the court.[58] Like many other nations, Japanese policy regarding criminal liability for children who have not reached puberty is not in line with the reality of the juvenile justice system. If a child under the age of fourteen cannot be held liable for his or her actions, shouldn't the child be subject to alternative measures other than court involvement? Even if the child has more limited liability under the law than juveniles over fourteen, the present and legally mandated age of criminal responsibility should deny the court jurisdiction over children under that age.

Japan is similar to the United States and other Western nations in its application of juvenile law. A rise in juvenile crime after World War II led Japan to institute a uniform system for the administration of juvenile justice. From the passage of the 1948 Juvenile Law onward, Family Courts were founded on the principles of *parens patriae*, the notion that the court becomes an additional guardian for a minor. The Juvenile Law includes important tenets in relation to the rights of juveniles. First, the family Court is given jurisdiction over any juvenile offender between the ages of fourteen and nineteen, children who break the law but are under the age of fourteen, and juveniles up to the age of twenty who have not committed any crimes but are considered by the court and other actors in the justice system to be prone to commit such an offense.[59] This extension of jurisdiction over juveniles above and beyond the age of criminal responsibility reflects a desire by Japan to prevent crime by children of all ages.

The judges in the Family Court are professional jurists appointed by the national cabinet from recommendations by the Supreme Court. They are chosen because of a national expectation that they will always act in the best interests of the child. The probation officer is another important actor within the juvenile court. The officer is originally trained in social sciences to qualify for the position, and holds the responsibility of providing background research into the juvenile's life to ascertain relevant information regarding the circumstances of the life of the juvenile rather than just the actual criminal incident. "The Family Court Investigation Officer [is] to make an investigation of the behavior, background, character, and surrounding environment of the juvenile, the parents and guardians and other relevant persons, using medical, psychological, educational, sociological and other specialized knowledge. In practice, the investigation involves gathering information from parents, schools, employers, physicians, and others with relevant information."[60]

Interestingly, the police have little discretion about which cases may and may not face the court. Under law, "The police must refer all cases of juvenile offenders directly or via public prosecutors to the family court. . . . The public prosecutors [also] do not have discretion in screening cases. Therefore, after an investigation they must refer all cases to the family court."[61] Because prosecutors and police have little discretion in dismissing the case of a child without formal charges, the Family Court judges retain all power over juvenile offenders. This body has made great strides in the protection of youths, even without the assistance of other authorities. First, "the essential focus of the Family Court in juvenile matters remains protective and restorative rather than punitive. . . . Of a total of 164,327 such cases [of juveniles under investigation] disposed of in 1997 for instance, fully 66.6 percent resulted in noncommencement (fukaishi, or dismissal without hearing.)"[62]

Japanese law operates with the help of multiple court actors to insure a fair, rehabilitative, and protective juvenile court system. It is a system that surpasses the goals of international rights organizations, both avoiding punishment while simultaneously looking into the root factors and circumstances of the offender's life to find an explanation for his or her actions.

The Japanese Constitution guarantees that juveniles in conflict with the law and/or their parents have the right to secure representation during court proceedings. But, cases in Japan rarely reach the court stage, as authorities choose to divert offenders away from the system. While the right to legal aid is offered, it is in fact often not utilized, because hearings involving a judge are often not inclusive of a child's denial of guilt: "The proceedings will only in very rare instances deal with disputed matters of fact, which is to say denial of guilt, and juveniles will again only rarely be represented by counsel (the latter fact is obviously related to the first; why would one need an attorney unless one were disputing the facts?)"[63]

However, the rise of juvenile crime and the influence of the U.S. juvenile justice system have led to a number of amendments to try to make legal representation in certain criminal cases a requirement for youth offenders. These efforts, however, have been unsuccessful:

Japanese academics and attorneys, obviously aware of Gault and its aftermath, began to press for law reform from the 1970s and draft amendments to the 1948 Juvenile Law incorporating more due process features, including greater use of legal counsel for juveniles, were proposed and discussed. . . . Change however has been slow to say the least. . . . Those introduced in the 145th Diet session (1999) include granting the Court discretion, when it deems necessary, to have a prosecutor participate in proceedings with respect to offences punishable by more than three years imprisonment, and, when a prosecutor so participates, to ensure that the juvenile is represented by an attorney, appointing one if necessary.[64]

One possible explanation for the lack of desire of Japanese legislators to consider the right to representation is the cultural focus on familial responsibility. In the way that many nations expect a lawyer to act as the advocate of child offenders, Japanese courts apply this duty to parents and other relatives. Judges in the Family Court often call upon parents to hear statements regarding the offender, or send the Family Court investigator to hear statements from parents. The visual description of the courtroom further connects parents to the role of advocate: "[T]he juvenile sits facing the judge in a room marked by quasi-informality (tables and chairs with no raised dias), flanked by parents or guardians, with the Family Court Investigation Officer who handled the case at a table to the left."[65]

Court officers also follow procedures in which the parent is admonished and informed that it is partially their responsibility to aid in the offender's rehabilitation. Japanese authorities reported to the United Nations that their main goal is to protect and rehabilitate the juvenile, and that parents must take part in this objective. The court and the parents work together to prevent further crime. Sanctions that are noncustodial often additionally require involvement by probation officers with the family to ensure that they are working with the child.[66] While Japanese parents are not criminally liable as compared to other nations, the court holds them responsible and expects them to play a serious role in all proceedings and rehabilitative measures.

Finally, Japanese law recognizes the right of the juvenile to have all hearings closed to the public. Only those with valid investment in the case are allowed to attend court. In 1995, authorities reported to the United Nations that:

> In the case of juvenile trials, the procedure is not made public and certain restrictions are imposed on perusal and copying of records. Furthermore, the Juvenile Law forbids the carrying in newspapers or other publications of articles or photographs containing the name, age, occupation, house, looks, etc. [that] may identify who has been brought to proceedings in the Family Court or prosecuted for an offence [that] he/she committed while he/she was a juvenile. The Family Court makes efforts to keep confidentiality in juvenile cases while considering the social demand for disclosure of information. For example, they try to avoid expressions [that] would identify the accused or the injured juvenile, and use brief and abstract expressions to describe the motive and details of the crime to protect the juvenile's feelings and not to obstruct his/her rehabilitation. Through these measures, the Family Court tries to respect the privacy of juveniles.[67]

Through this outlook, Japan has achieved the perfect balance between the desires of the public to know about crime and the right of the offender to remain shielded from public scrutiny. By releasing nonidentifying information about each case, all interested parties can be satisfied.

Japanese law allows for goals of care and rehabilitation to play a role in sentencing juvenile offenders. For instance, government representatives have stated that youths are considered immature and in need of special treatment. Their lack of capacity to fully understand their crime affords them protection instead of fault for their actions. The Court uses sanctions in an effort to alter their criminal path by ensuring that their living circumstances are healthy. According to national law, any offender under the age of eighteen must be sanctioned differently than adult offenders. First, juveniles cannot be subjected to the death penalty or to life imprisonment. However, if a youth commits a crime that can be punished with life imprisonment or execution and the youth are over the age of sixteen, he or she continues to retain protection against the harshest sentences, but will be tried and charged as an adult. In addition, while fines can be levied on juveniles and adults alike, there is a legal mandate against forced labor by juveniles who are unable to pay their fine.[68]

Japan, in response to a lessening of juvenile crime, began a trend in which family court justices meted out very slight punishments for juvenile offenders. "Unlike other countries, Japan is experiencing a trend toward milder punishments in juvenile cases, with many youths receiving a suspended sentence. For example, in 1993, only fifty youths were sentenced to juvenile prisons."[69] If a judge instead sanctions a youth with some form of detention, Japanese children can be sent to one of two types of establishments. Juvenile training schools are reserved for youths in need of rehabilitation, and are subdivided into four sections: primary, middle, special and medical, and treatment. Each of these schools is divided by youths who will be present over a short period of time and those who will be present for longer periods.

The purpose of a juvenile training school is explained as a place that provides compulsory education as well as special skills training. Juveniles are also placed in contact with guidance counselors and doctors to measure their intellectual and physical growth. The eventual goal is that children will leave these establishments and reenter their communities as law-abiding citizens. They are taught respect for others by group living, and learn to value both themselves and the people around them. During the confinement, staff are expected to take the actual age of the offenders and their stage of development into account to determine the best methods of treatment.[70]

More serious and violent offenders are sent to juvenile prisons. Family Courts have often refrained from utilizing these institutions, and open spaces have led authorities to use the facilities for the younger and immature adult criminals who would benefit from separation from more hardened criminals. Young adults below the age of twenty-six can be placed in juvenile centers if they are nonviolent and will not become a corrupting influence on younger offenders.[71] In regard to the life circumstances of such establishments, the government notes that prisons are very similar to the training school. Guidance and compulsory education combined with skills training are imperative in these facilities. In addition, medical care is offered, and all treatment is meant to help the youth become an active community member with good connections to peers and fellow citizens. They are taught about the value of their lives and respect for others.[72]

Probation is utilized in all three circumstances, pending release from either type of institution or accompanying release by the Family Court without any form of detention. All juveniles placed under supervision can remain so until they reach age twenty. Probation includes additional programs of rehabilitation above what detention centers offer, and ongoing care upon release. Juveniles remain under the guidance of appropriate social welfare workers and officers of the law. They are constantly reminded of the importance of following social and legal rules. Even after release from custodial settings, youths are required to participate in ongoing programs related to their offenses.[73]

Juvenile sentencing provisions seem better in Japan than elsewhere, but both government authorities and independent researchers have found instances of abuse against juvenile inmates. First, a Human Rights Watch investigation into all Japanese prisons uncovered allegations by former youth inmates that guards resorted to physical violence to retain control.[74] The government itself had to discipline juvenile detention staffers for years of abuse on youth inmates. For instance, at the Nara Juvenile Prison, nine staff members were disciplined for allegations of slapping thirteen inmates. The officers were formally reprimanded, because physical punishment is outlawed in Japanese detention centers, regardless of the infraction.[75]

The reports of abuse appear to be more of an anomaly than general procedure, unlike what has been seen in other nations in this study. Japan limits the practice of detention only to the most serious cases, and all measures of sentencing are meant to be rehabilitative. Juveniles are separated from adults, and while conditions may not be luxurious, they are sufficient to provide for the care of youths. Abuse seems to occur infrequently, and the government effectively disciplines those responsible for actions against minors.

NOTES

1. Human Rights Watch. by "Abuse and Killing of Street Children in India Police." Nov. 1996. [Online]. Available: http://www.hrw.org/reports/1996/India4.htm.

2. Raghavan, R. K., "India." *World Factbook of Criminal Justice Systems.* [Online]. Available: http://www.ojp.usdoj.gov/bjs/pub/ascii/wfbcjind.txt.

3. "Abuse and Killing of Street Children by India Police."

4. Vackayil, Joseph. "Juvenile Justice Pleads for Caring Redressal." *Indian Express Newspapers, 2000.* [Online]. Available: htttp://www.expressindia.com/fe/daily/20000703/fco02025.html.

5. The Juvenile Justice (Care and Protection of Children) Act of 2000. New Dehli: Universal Law, 2001. [Online]. Available: http://gendwaar.gen.in.text/list/.5%Carticles%5Cacts%5CJuvenile%20Justice.html.

6. The Juvenile Justice (Care and Protection of Children) Act, 2000 (56 of 2,000). [Online]. Available: http://socialwelfare.delhigovt.nic.in/juvenilejustice1.htm. Accessed March 24, 2004.

7. The Juvenile Justice (Care and Protection of Children) Act, 2000.

8. The Juvenile Justice (Care and Protection) Act, 2000: Sections 6–7

9. Chatterjee, Sudeshna. "Know the Juvenile Justice Act." *The Times of India.* 9 Apr. 2002. Westlaw. [Onlin] Available: http://web2.westlaw.com/search/default.wl?Action=EditQuery&CFID=0&CiteListOnly=False&DB=TIMESINDIA&DocSample=False&EQ=search&Method=TNC&n=2&Query=%22Juvenile+Justice+Act%22+%26+defense&RLTDB=CLID%5FDB46723&RP=%2Fsearch%2Fdefault%2Ewl&Service=Search&SS=Doc&Tab=Cite+List&TF=10&TC=8&RS=WLW2.83&VR=2.0&SV=Split&FN=_top&MT=Westlaw.

10. Chatterjee, 1.

11. Chatterjee, 1.

12. "Abuse and Killings of Street Children in India."

13. The Juvenile Justice (Care and Protection of Children) Act of 2000

14. "The Juvenile Justice Act—1986

15. "Courts Tell Police to Explain Arrest of Boys." *The Times of India.* 9 Apr. 2002. Westlaw. [Online] Available: http://web2.westlaw.com/search/default.wl?RS=WLW2.83&VR=2.0&SV=Split&FN=_top&MT=Westlaw&RecDB=TIMESINDIA&RFFrom=%2FDirectory%2FDefault%2Ewl.

16. "The Juvenile Justice Act—1986"

17. The Juvenile Justice (Care and Protection of Children) Act of 2000

18. United Nations Committee on the Rights of the Child. "Initial Reports of State Parties Due in 1995: India."

19. "Initial Reports of State Parties Due in 1995: India."

20. United Nations Committee on the Rights of the Child. "Concluding Observations of the Committee on the Rights of the Child: India." 23 Feb. 2000. [Online]. Available: http://www.unhchr.ch/tbs/doc.nsf/385c2add1632f4a8c12565a9004dc311/6bfe919a361e8a498025687f005c9062?OpenDocument&Highlight=0,India.

21. The Juvenile Justice (Care and Protection of Children) Act of 2000

22. "Abuse and Killing of Street Children in India."

23. The Juvenile Justice (Care and Protection of Children) Act of 2000

24. "Abuse and Killing of Street Children in India."

25. "Abuse and Killing of Street Children in India." (emphasis added).

26. U.S. Department of State—Bureau of Democracy, Human Rights, and Labor. "Country Reports on Human Rights Practices 2002: India." 31 Mar. 2003. [Online]. Available: http://www.state.gov/g/drl/rls/hrrpt/2002/18311.htm.

27. Amnesty International. "People's Republic of China. Persistent Human Rights Violations in Tibet." 1995. [Online]. Available: http://amnesty.org/ailib/aipub/1995/ASA/171895.ASA.txt.

28. "People's Republic of China. Persistent Human Rights Violations in Tibet" Appendix A.

29. "People's Republic of China. Persistent Human Rights Violations in Tibet," 2

30. Information Office of the State Council of the People's Republic of China. "The Situation of Children in China." Beijing, 1996. [Online]. Available: http://chinesculture.about.com/library/china/whitepaper/blskids.htm. Accessed March 24, 2004.

31. United Nations: Committee on the Rights of the Child. "Initial Reports of States Parties Due in 1995: China." 1 Aug. 1995. [Online]. Available: http://www.unhchr.ch/tbs/doc.nsf/385c2add1632f4a8c12565a9004dc311/d0f6 d82c145d1ee3412562d7004e4c0f?OpenDocument&Highlight=0,China.

32. "Initial Reports of States Parties Due in 1995: China," Section 211–215.

33. "People's Republic of China: Persistent Human Rights Violations in Tibet," Section III.

34. Amnesty International. "People's Republic of China, Gross Human Rights Violations Continue," appendix 1: "Persistent Human Rights Violations in Tibet." 1996. (ASA 17-18-95, May 1995.) [Online]. Available: http://www.amnesty.org/ailib/intcam/china/china96/hrv.htm. Accessed: March 24, 2004.

35. "Criminal Law and the Procedure of the People's Republic of China." Provided by Lectic Law Library. [Online] Available: http://www.lectlaw.com/files/int01.htm.

36. "Criminal Law and the Procedure of the People's Republic of China."

37. Zongwei, Shao. "Legal Teams and Young People." *China Daily*. 25 Oct. 2002. Westlaw. [Online]. Available: http://web2.westlaw.com/search/default.wl? Action=EditQuery&CFID=0&CiteListOnly=False&DB=CHDY&DocSample=False &EQ=search&Method=TNC&n=2&Query=%22JUVENILE%22++%26++% 22LAW%22&RLTDB=CLID%5FDB415233&RP=%2Fsearch%2Fdefault%2Ewl& Service=Search&SS=Doc&Tab=Cite+List&TF=10&TC=8&RS=WLW2.83&VR=2.0& SV=Split&FN=_top&MT=Westlaw.

38. Dispatch, Andrew. "Tibetan Odyssey Part II: There's No Place Like Home— But Tibetan Exiles Make Do in Dharamsala." *The Odyssey: India and China Stage*. 20 May 2000. [Online]. Available: http://www.worldtrek.org/odyssey/asia/052000/052000andrewtibettwo.html.

39. "People's Republic of China Gross Human Rights Violations Continue."

40. "China: Legal Principles Guarantee Human Rights." *China Daily*. 19 Oct. 1999. Westlaw. [Online]. Available: http://web2.westlaw.com/search/default.wl? Action=EditQuery&CFID=0&CiteListOnly=False&DB=CHDY&DocSample=False &EQ=search&Method=TNC&n=4&Query=%22JUVENILE%22+%26+%22public% 22&RLTDB=CLID%5FDB492233&RP=%2Fsearch%2Fdefault%2Ewl&Service= Search&Tab=Cite+List&TF=10&TC=8&RS=WLW2.83&VR=2.0&SV=Split&FN= _top&MT=Westlaw.

41. "People's Republic of China Gross Human Rights Violations Continue."

42. "People's Republic of China Gross Human Rights Violations Continue."

43. "Initial Reports of State Parties Due in 1995: China."

44. "Initial Reports of State Parties Due in 1995: China."

45. "Initial Reports of State Parties Due in 1995: China."

46. United Nations Convention on the Rights of the Child. "Concluding Observations of the Committee on the Rights of the Child: China." 7 Jun. 1996. [Online]. Available: http://www.unhchr.ch/tbs/doc.nsf/385c2add1632f4a8 c12565a9004dc311/d26a86d517d48050c125636300424a98?OpenDocument& Highlight=0,CRC%2FC%2F11%2FAdd.7.

47. "Initial Reports of State Parties Due in 1995: China."

48. "Initial Reports of State Parties Due in 1995: China."

49. "Initial Reports of State Parties Due in 1995: China."

50. "Initial Reports of State Parties Due in 1995: China."

51. U.S. Department of State—Bureau of Democracy, Human Rights, and Labor. "Country Reports on Human Rights Practices 2002: China." 31 Mar. 2003. [Online]. Available: http://www.state.gov/g/drl/rls/hrrpt/2002/18239.htm.

52. "The Situation of Children in China." Beijing: Information Office of the State Council of the People's Republic of China. Apr. 1996. [Online]. Available: http://www.fmprc.gov.cn/eng32287.html#2.

53. China Rights Forum—Human Rights in China. "'Protections' Fail to Protect China's Implementation of the Convention on the Rights to the Child." Spring, 1996. [Online]. Available: http://iso.hrichina.org/iso/article.adp? article_id=82&subcategory_id=17.

54. "People's Republic of China Gross Human Rights Violations Continue."

55. "Not Welcome At the Party: Behind the 'Clean-Up' of China's Cities—A Report on Administrative Detention Under 'Custody and Repatriation.'" *Human Rights in China*. Sept. 1999. HRIC Arbitrary Detention Series, No. 2.

56. "Not Welcome At the Party: Behind the 'Clean-Up' of China's Cities—A Report on Administrative Detention Under 'Custody and Repatriation.'"

57. Salzberg, Stephan M. "A Century of Juvenile Law in Japan." University of British Colombia. [Online] Available: http://www.finearts.uvic.ca/~capiexec/ jplawconf/salzberg-repwk.htm.

58. Winterdyk, John (ed.). *Juvenile Justice Systems: International Perspectives*, 2nd ed. Toronto: Canadian Scholars' Press, 2002. 6.

59. Winterdyk, 6.

60. Salzberg, 11.

61. Winterdyk, 16.

62. Salzberg, 11.

63. Salzberg, 13.

64. Salzberg, 14.

65. Salzberg, 15.

66. United Nations Committee on the Rights of the Child. "The Second Report of Japan: Under Article 44, Paragraph 1, of the Convention on the Rights of the Child." Nov. 2001. [Online]. Available: http://193.194.138.190/html/menu2/6/ crc/doc/report/srf-japan-2.pdf.

67. United Nations: Convention on the Rights of the Child. "Committee on the Rights of the Child: Initial Reports of State Parties Due in 1996—Japan. 30 May 1996. [Online]. Available: http://www.hri.ca/fortherecord1997/documentation/ tbodies/crc-c-41-add1.htm.

68. "Committee on the Rights of the Child: Initial Reports of State Parties Due in 1996—Japan."

69. Winterdyk, 17.

70. "Committee on the Rights of the Child: Initial Reports of State Parties Due in 1996—Japan."

71. Winterdyk, 17.

72. "Committee on the Rights of the Child: Initial Reports of State Parties Due in 1996—Japan."

73. "Committee on the Rights of the Child: Initial Reports of State Parties Due in 1996—Japan."

74. Human Rights Watch. "Prison Conditions in Japan." Mar. 1995. [Online]. Available: http://www.hrw.org/reports/1995/Japan.htm.

75. "Nara Juvenile Staff Disciplined for Beating Inmates." *Kyodo News Online*. 19 Jan. 2003. [Online]. Available: http://home.kyodo.co.jp/all/display.jsp?an=20020119010.

9

Australia

Like much of Africa, Australia was under British colonial rule from the late eighteenth century through the early years of the twentieth century, not gaining independence until 1901.[1] The long-standing Western occupation forged a modern society with a large population of citizens of either British or Irish heritage. Australia also has a small indigenous population that has retained many of its traditional cultural values even in the face of modern innovation. The merger of British laws in a land quite far away from the European continent with traditional aboriginal values has produced a legal system somewhat discriminatory against the indigenous population, although written policies reflect equality for all citizens under the law.

The age of criminal responsibility in Australia is ten years. Again, like many former British colonies, the impact of European statutes has remained although the colonizing power has disappeared. In addition, the prosecution has the burden of evidence in all criminal trials to prove that any child between the age of ten and fourteen could distinguish between right and wrong during the commission of the crime.[2] Australia is often considered an extremely liberal nation; nonetheless, the age of criminal responsibility is not as high as might be expected. The minimum age of criminal responsibility for juvenile offenders between the age of ten and fourteen is flexible based on the following assumption in penal codes: there is a "gradual imposition of criminal responsibility depending on a young offender's appreciation of the wrongness of his or her act."[3]

It is important that Australia is willing to make changes to the juvenile justice system in regard to the age at which children can be held criminally liable. The country has only recently instituted the uniform age of criminal responsibility, and did so at the recommendation of the United Nations. In the 1997 Committee on the Rights of the Child Country Report, U.N. representatives chastised Australia: "The Committee is deeply concerned that the minimum age of criminal responsibility is generally set at the very low level of 7 to 10 years, depending upon the state."[4] Shortly thereafter, Australia amended its penal codes to reflect a uniform age of criminal responsibility at the higher side of the low age spectrum in all of the states.

Australia has also instituted a cap on the age in which juvenile offenders that have a limited criminal liability can still be brought to juvenile court. While the age of criminal responsibility is uniform across the nation, the maximum age associated with limited liability differs in separate states. In the Commonwealth, Australian Capital Territory, the Northern Territory, New South Wales, South Australia, Western Australia, and Tasmania, the age in which an offender is fully prosecuted as an adult is eighteen. In both Queensland and Victoria, the age is lower, and any offender over seventeen is processed through the adult justice system. But, as of 2000, the federal government has made requests to both states to review their juvenile laws and to raise the age at which offenders are still considered juveniles.[5]

Like Nigeria and the United States, Australia has a number of different regions that implement juvenile justice differently. In the territories of Australia, Western Australia, and Queensland, juvenile justice matters are presided over by a special judge of the district court. In addition, offenses with a range of severity and punishments are handled by the children's court, although juveniles reserve the right to have their cases heard by an adult court instead. South Australia differs slightly, because while there is a juvenile court in existence, the public prosecutor, the police prosecutor, the court, and the severity of the crime allow cases to be transferred to adult court. The remaining territories of New South Wales, Victoria, Tasmania, the Northern Territory, and the Australian Capital Territory have magistrates rather than formal juvenile judges under the jurisdiction of the children's court. Like the district court territories, the magistrate territories also employ a children's court and allow for delinquents charged with the most serious crimes to be transferred to the adult court.[6]

The juvenile justice system in all regions of Australia seems to meet the standards of international rights groups by having a different judge oversee the case in a separate court system than adult offenders. Australia also employs diversion schemes across the nation, involving the police and social workers in an effort to keep youths out of the criminal justice process. The first contact with a juvenile justice actor is with the police. "Many children's involvement with police results in a police caution rather than further involvement in the juvenile justice system. Cautioning schemes can be informal and at the discretion of individual police, or formal and connected with formal diversionary processes."[7] The ideology behind the implementation of diversion is that the younger offenders will eventually grow out of their criminal tendencies, and that it would be more mentally and emotionally detrimental to subject a juvenile to formal court proceedings.

Before the 1990s, the territories of Western Australia and South Australia utilized children's panels, made up of both police and social workers, to determine alternatives for the youth. But, over the past decade, police have begun to caution offenders more, as well as employ the unique implementation of a process called Family Group Conferences. The Conferences bring together the offenders with their family to meet the victim, and also includes important community members. The purpose is to help the juveniles understand the impact of their crime and to show remorse for their actions.[8]

Australia also differs greatly from other nations in that police used to hold the responsibility for prosecution of juvenile crimes. But, a recent public uprising in response to an escalation in juvenile crime gave the power of prosecution of juveniles to lawyers.

> Reflecting concerns that juveniles are often only slapped on the wrist despite serious crimes, the government is making trained lawyers prosecute them instead of police officers. . . . Attorney General Jim McGinty . . . said juveniles were increasingly engaging experienced defense lawyers, and police were no match for senior counsel. . . . "People who have been the victims of serious crimes committed by juveniles have a right to expect the state to provide the legally trained and the best prosecutors available."[9]

Australia is within its rights to alter the process of juvenile justice. It is important to note however, that the transformation to a stricter prosecution is a response to a rise in juvenile crime, the same shift that has already occurred in both North America and Western Europe.

The rights of juveniles vary throughout Australia, because like the United States, federal law is superceded by state law in certain instances. The opening line of the nation's initial report to the United Nations in 1996 states, "In general the administration of juvenile justice is a matter that falls within the jurisdiction of the States and Territories."[10] The differentiation in state laws has specifically had an impact on the juvenile's right to representation. "Most Australian jurisdictions now have specialist youth legal aid and legal representation services and most Australian children's courts operate duty counsel schemes. However, the quality and accessibility of specialist legal representation is variable between and within jurisdictions."[11]

Australian law does not require legal assistance for anyone, and although the right to have assistance is respected and often advised for more serious matters, it is not a necessity for the commencement of legal proceedings.[12] Juvenile justice administration follows the same legal requirements. A juvenile is allowed to have legal representation, but it is not a guarantee. Even national authorities expressed concern about this, and promised the United Nations that they would attempt to rectify the lack of legal services available to all children. The report claims, "[T]here are, however, currently very few community legal services, as distinct from mainstream services provided by legal aid commissions, that operate specifically to serve the legal needs of children and young people. This is so despite the fact that children and young people under the age of 18 years of age make up just over 25 per cent of the Australian population and encounter legal problems in areas such as family law, juvenile crime and child protection."[13]

While federal law is responsible for the basic administration of rights, states differ on whether the right to legal representation is mandatory. For instance, in the Northern Territory, juvenile legal representation can be ordered if the trier of fact feels that it is necessary: "The Juvenile Justice Act [of] 1983 empowers the Juvenile Court or the Supreme Court to give the juvenile such advice as he or she needs to obtain legal representation or to order legal representation be given to the juvenile, if the Court is of the opinion that such representation is necessary and has not been arranged."[14] New South Wales has a different approach, allowing offenders to enjoy the right to an attorney for free: "In New South Wales, all children appearing in the Children's Court are entitled to free legal aid. Legal assistance is available from the Legal Aid Commission, the Aboriginal Legal Service, or from private legal practitioners."[15] Again, the right to legal representation in Australia varies depending on the state, and no federal law provides overall guidelines that a state must follow in regard to juvenile justice.

In addition, Australia as a whole has made little change in the availability of representation for juveniles since the release of its initial report to the United Nations. In fact, the use of diversionary processes, in which offenders are never subjected to formal court proceedings but are instead provided a warning by police and similar authorities, includes stipulations that legal representation for the minor does not have a role. "As an initial response to minor offending, jurisdictions have shifted away from children's panels to police cautioning programs. Such schemes are the most cost effective and minimally intrusive . . . legal representation is not a part of these diversionary procedures."[16] While national authorities made claims to the Committee on the Rights of the Child that greater access to legal aid, regardless of state variation in law, was going to become a priority, juvenile justice administrations have instead sidestepped the issue by keeping children away from formal criminal procedure.

Differentiations in state procedure also impact a juvenile's right to a closed trial. Some states require that the court be closed, and only parties with an investment in the offender may participate, while other states hold that all proceedings must be open to the public. The Australian Capital Territory, for instance, follows this rule: "Where the Children's Court is sitting, the hearings are in camera, and only interested parties are allowed in the courtroom. The magistrate may give special permission for the press to be allowed into the courtroom, but they may not report the names of the child or children concerned. Permission is given to the press very infrequently."[17]

Queensland law is similar to the Australian Capital Territory, but the severity of the crime allows for closed trials to become public hearings. "The right to privacy is safeguarded for young people who commit, or who are alleged to have committed, offences under the Juvenile Justice Act [of] 1992 and the Children's Court Act [of] 1992. Children's Courts are closed to the public except where a young person is being dealt with by a Children's Court Judge for a serious offence (e.g. murder)."[18] The juvenile law of the Northern Territory, on the other hand, leaves the decision regarding public involvement in youth court proceedings to the discretion of the magistrate: "The Juvenile Justice Act [of] 1983 provides for proceedings to be undertaken in open court. But, the magistrate may order that the court be closed. The Act stipulates that a magistrate is empowered to restrict the publication or reports of the proceedings."[19]

The involvement of parents and their rights under juvenile law also varies depending on the state. Some states only require the notification of parents while other states call for the involvement of parents and hold them liable for the actions of their children. The Australian Capital Territory keeps parents updated on juvenile contact with authorities: "Under the Children's Services Act [of] 1986, when a child (that is, a person under the age of 18 years) is charged with an offence the police must forthwith take all reasonable steps to notify a parent of the child of the charge, of the child's location and of the time and place when the child will be brought before a court."[20] In this state, the burden is on the authorities to involve the parent.

New South Wales is quite different, placing the burden on parents that they must be involved:

On 13 March 1995 the Children (Parental Responsibility) Act [of] 1994 came into force. The legislation enables courts to require parents to be present during criminal proceedings against children, to require children to give undertakings to submit to parental supervision and to require parents to be present at court in the event of a breach of such an undertaking.The court may also require parents to give undertakings concerning the future behaviour of children and other matters or to give security (whether by the deposit of money or otherwise) for the good behaviour of the child until the child attains the age of 18 years or such other period as appropriate. The legislation further enables a court to require a child that has been found guilty of an offence and the child's parents to undergo family counseling and makes it an offence for a parent, by willful default or by neglect to exercise proper care and guardianship, to contribute to the commission of an offence by a child.[21]

In this state, a parent is punished for the guilt and repetitive illicit offenses of their child. Parents are considered accomplices when their children will not end their deviant behavior. New South Wales, in an attempt to control juvenile crime, infringes on the right of parents.

Victoria, on the other hand, utilizes the requirement of parental involvement to avoid formal court proceedings by issuing formal cautions. This form of justice can only occur with parental knowledge: "The Victorian Police cautioning process provides for the cautioning of young people in preference to arrest or prosecution for offences. A caution may only be given if an offender admits to committing an offence. It may be issued without attending court, but only in the presence of a parent or guardian."[22]

Australian law in regard to the rights of children has no cohesiveness. Children in one state are afforded rights that offenders in the state next door are denied. The Australian government must begin to pass legislation that supercedes state administration of juvenile justice. Certain rights, such as the right to legal representation, the right to parental involvement without assigning liability to guardians, and the right to closed trial should become uniform across the nation. With each state operating with respect to its own legislative goals, the underlying need for juvenile justice to work toward rehabilitation is not being met.

National law regarding options of sentences also varies from state to state in Australia. In most jurisdictions, the range of penalties includes fines, community service, supervision by an appropriate adult or in a custodial setting, or probation.[23] The only major federal guideline directing sentencing is the United Nation's treaty on punishment, which was incorporated into law upon ratification. The government's report to the Committee on the Rights of the Child states that guidelines for corrections were ratified in 1989 at the Conference of Correctional Administrators. The guidelines were taken directly from the United Nations Standards for Treatment of Prisoners and apply to youth and adult offenders.[24]

It is the courts' practice to take the relevant circumstances of a child's life into account when they are making sentencing decisions. Judges look at previous history, including mental and emotional disorders or family problems. At times, however, the lack of federal guidelines regarding how a juvenile should be sentenced allows for certain judges to overlook significant information:

> All children's courts in Australia generally take account of the particular circumstances of the offender. The immaturity or inexperience of the child may affect the commission of the offence and courts are generally aware of this. Matters such as a prior record or a background report that discusses the likelihood of reoffending play a large part in sentencing children. Some jurisdictions provide explicit sentencing principles. Nevertheless, submissions expressed concern that courts do not always have sufficient regard to the totality of relevant circumstances when deciding sentences. Magistrates often do not take sufficient account of social factors such as homelessness, family circumstances, educational needs, and so on in determining sentences for children.[25]

After ascertaining facts about the life of the juvenile, magistrates have an assortment of choices concerning sentencing. A child can be made to pay a fine, be reprimanded and released on the promise of good behavior, ordered to participate in community service, put on probation, required to participate in mental health services, serve detention at home or on weekends, serve detention in a juvenile detention center, or serve detention in a youth training establishment. Like other nations, Australia's states employ multiple forms of secure detention, using factors such as seriousness of crime and violence, as well as past history to decide where a youth will be placed. Other sentencing options include the use of conferencing, which can occur with a victim and the offender or the offender and his family. These meetings are run by different organizations in the various jurisdictions, but are meant to allow the offender to take responsibility for his actions without experiencing formal sentencing.

The lack of national cohesion in juvenile justice also applies to the use of detention. While some districts prefer the more rehabilitative approach of alternate sentencing, other regions find that detention is the most popular option when penalizing young criminals. For instance, juveniles in Queensland can only be sentenced to detention if all other measures have been tried and found to be insufficient. On the other hand, legislators and authorities in New South Wales are convinced that detention is the only available penalty for offenders convicted of felonies and youths who have extensive criminal histories. This ideology is more concerned with the protection of the community rather than the needs of the young offender.[26]

Some of the regions in Australia are now turning to mandatory sentencing, even for juveniles, in the face of rising crime rates. Western Australia, for instance, has passed the Crime (Serious and Repeat Offenders) Sentencing Act. This act fixes a certain length of detention that stands as the minimum requirement for conviction of specific crimes if the offender has a criminal past.[27] Western Australia is not alone in its use of compulsory penalties. The Northern Territory designated that all juvenile offenders should have a punitive work order incorporated into their sentence. The purpose of such work is shame, which negates the international standard of rehabilitation in sentencing. Young convicts are expected to wear a certain uniform or identifying piece of material while they perform the work so that bystanders will recognize them as delinquents.

Federal guidelines have been implemented that states and territories in Australia are required to conform to when confining a youth. The National Quality of Care Standards (QOC Standards) and Design Guidelines for Juvenile Justice Facilities in Australia and New Zealand were ratified by all the states in 1996 and apply to all forms of juvenile detention.[28] But, the wide range of experiences with juvenile crime in different jurisdictions has led to great deviation in the types of juvenile detention employed by the regions. Some states require only small juvenile centers specifically for males, while other regions require more than one facility and a greater capacity. Living conditions within the centers also vary based on states. For instance, South Australia is known by researchers for its excellent conditions for and high standard of juvenile care. But Brisbane's establishments mirror the conditions of prisons.[29]

On the other hand, education and learning of a skill is considered very important in each of the jurisdictions in Australia. All detention centers have some form of either vocational learning or compulsory education classes. The centers vary in what they offer, but include compulsory courses like reading and math, guidance on social skills, and in some cases, an opportunity to pursue higher education.[30] Children under fifteen years of age are required to participate in education, similar to the laws regarding schooling for nonoffending minors. From the age of fifteen, youths can choose whether to continue their education, but many detention centers base the award of privileges on whether a youth has decided to continue schooling.

The use of punishment for minors in detention has also been regulated by federal guidelines. Again, many of the decisions regarding youth offenders are left to the individual jurisdiction, but general principles have been instituted that all detention centers must abide. Standards relating explicitly to the implementation of care in juvenile facilities remain in draft form, but in many cases are already adhered to. Staff and supervisors are not allowed to use any form of physical violence as punishment and cannot penalize youths by denying them access to food, medical care, treatment, or education. All forms of verbal and psychological intimidation and abuse are also outlawed. Children should never be humiliated, particularly with any references to their race or gender. In addition, adults must be specifically trained staff members to administer any form of discipline to youths.[31]

Specific regions of Australia have defied international guidelines by transferring youth offenders to prison before they reached eighteen years of age. While some states hold juveniles either until the end of their sentence or until they turn twenty-one, many push youths convicted of serious crime and disciplined with long sentences into adult penitentiaries. While there is differentiation between the jurisdictions, children can be moved to adult facilities if they have attacked other youths or staff, committed a crime while confined, or have attempted to escape. Generally, all behavior that youth facilities are unable to control require a transfer. But, the requirements in some regions are less stringent. For instance, one state allows youths to be moved to adult prisons if they consistently corrupt other offenders and lead them to misbehave.[32]

The issue of discriminatory sentencing of aboriginal youths can be found in each of the states. For instance, in 2000, the detention rate for indigenous youth in Western Australia was extraordinarily high. Aboriginal youths were thirty times more likely to be placed in custodial settings than their white counterparts.[33] This situation is by no means an anomaly. In 1996, minorities were approximately twenty times more likely to be restricted in detention facilities than nonindigenous youth. These numbers simply represent the average; in some jurisdictions, the situation is much worse. In Queensland, minorities are overrepresented forty to one, and in Western Australia, by about thirty to one.[34]

Racism is found in more than mere numbers. A recent inquiry into Kariong Detention Center on the Central Coast, a facility usually reserved for violent and older offenders, uncovered serious allegations of racially motivated abuse by staff on inmates. Wayne Armytage is the director of a nonprofit organization dedicated to helping young aboriginal youths in detention. After meeting with youths at the facility, he wrote a letter including their complaints: "In a letter Armytage later wrote to the then Minister for Juvenile Justice, Faye Lo Po', he listed examples of the racial abuse the youths alleged they had been subjected to. 'You black c——, you got no ticker.' 'Come on, you black gronk, hit me.' And 'Shut up, you black mutt.'"[35] Australia's methods of sentencing are more in line with international standards than other nations, but the country would benefit greatly from two improvements in punishment. First, aboriginal youths should be treated equally to children of nonindigenous descent. Second, stronger federal guidelines will lead the jurisdictions with abusive and failing sentencing policies to the level of the more successful regions.

NOTES

1. "Australia," Microsoft® Encarta® Online Encyclopedia, 2003. [Online]. Available: http://encarta.msn.com.

2. Urbas, Gregor. "The Age of Criminal Responsibility." *Australian Institute of Criminology: Trends and Issues*, No. 81. Canberra: Nov. 2000, 1.

3. Urbas, 2.

4. United Nations. "Committee on the Rights of the Child, Concluding Observations: Australia." 10 Oct. 1997. University of Minnesota: Human Rights Library. [Online] Available: http://www1.umn.edu/humanrts/crc/australia1997.html.

5. Urbas, 3.

6. Winterdyk, John (ed.). *Juvenile Justice Systems: International Perspectives*, 2nd ed. Toronto: Candian Scholars' Press, 2002. 37.

7. The Australian Law Reform Commission. "A Statistical Picture of Australia's Children: Juvenile Justice Systems." [Online]. Available: http://www.austii.edu.au/au/other/alrc/publications/reports/84/02.html#Head-31.

8. Winterdyk, 40–42.

9. Day, Selina. "Lawyers to Prosecute Juveniles" [Online]. Available: http://www.news.com.au/common/story_page/0,4057,4412222%255E2761,0.html.

10. United Nations Convention on the Rights of the Child. "Initial Reports of State Parties Due in 1993: Australia's First Report Under Article 44(1)(a) of the Convention on the Rights of the Child." 1 Feb. 1996 [Online]. Available: http://www.bayefsky.com/reports/australia_crc_c_8_add.31_1996.php.

11. Winterdyk, 38.

12. "Australia's Third Report Under the International Covenant on Civil and Political Rights." Australian Law Online. Mar. 1987–Dec. 1985. [Online]. Available: http://www.law.gov.au/agd/Department/Publications/publications/ICCPR3/Welcome.html

13. "Initial Reports of State Parties Due in 1993: Australia's First Report Under Article 44(1)(a) of the Convention on the Rights of the Child."

14. "Initial Reports of State Parties Due in 1993: Australia's First Report Under Article 44(1)(a) of the Convention on the Rights of the Child."

15. "Initial Reports of State Parties Due in 1993: Australia's First Report Under Article 44(1)(a) of the Convention on the Rights of the Child."

16. Winterdyk, 41.

17. "Initial Reports of State Parties Due in 1993: Australia's First Report Under Article 44(1)(a) of the Convention on the Rights of the Child."

18. "Initial Reports of State Parties Due in 1993: Australia's First Report Under Article 44(1)(a) of the Convention on the Rights of the Child."

19. "Initial Reports of State Parties Due in 1993: Australia's First Report Under Article 44(1)(a) of the Convention on the Rights of the Child."

20. "Initial Reports of State Parties Due in 1993: Australia's First Report Under Article 44(1)(a) of the Convention on the Rights of the Child."

21. "Initial Reports of State Parties Due in 1993: Australia's First Report Under Article 44(1)(a) of the Convention on the Rights of the Child."

22. "Initial Reports of State Parties Due in 1993: Australia's First Report Under Article 44(1)(a) of the Convention on the Rights of the Child."

23. Australian Law Reform Commission Report #84. "Seen and Heard: Priority for Children in the Legal Process." 1997. Australia: Australian Law Reform Commission.

24. "Initial Reports to State Parties Due in 1993: Australia's First Report under Article 44(1)(2) of the Convention on the Rights of the Child."

25. "Seen and Heard: Priority for Children in the Legal Process."

26. "Seen and Heard: Priority for Children in the Legal Process."

27. Winterdyk, 46.

28. "Seen and Heard: Priority for Children in the Legal Process."

29. "Seen and Heard: Priority for Children in the Legal Process."

30. "Seen and Heard: Priority for Children in the Legal Process."

31. "Seen and Heard: Priority for Children in the Legal Process."

32. "Seen and Heard: Priority for Children in the Legal Process."

33. "Crime and Justice Statistics for Western Australia, 2000." University of Western Australia—Media Statement. 12 Dec. 2001. [Online]. Available: http://www.uwa.edu.au/media/statements/2001/12/crime_and_justice_statistics_for_western_australia,_2000_(12_december).

34. "Seen and Heard: Priority for Children in the Legal Process."

35. Horin, Adele. "Giving it the Hard Cell." *The Sydney Morning Herald*. 21 Apr. 1999. Westlaw. [Online].

10

Conclusion

The minimum age of criminal responsibility and the maximum age at which juvenile offenders can still be treated as youths varies widely across the world. Some nations utilize a system based purely on age, while others take into account the mental capacity of the offenders to understand the implications and wrongness of their actions. Many nations reflect, through their penal treatment of juvenile offenders, decades of colonial rule. In addition, what some countries claim as their policy is not what is actually instituted in regard to how young children that commit illegal actions are treated. Across the world, children who cannot read or care for themselves are held liable for actions as simple as begging for food or theft to support themselves in impoverished times.

It seems that most nations are more interested in lowering the age of criminal responsibility and instituting harsher penalties for juveniles by processing them through the adult court rather than making an effort to learn the roots of child crime. While the United Nations and other international organizations have called for a uniform and fair standard of ages and mental capacity in which criminal liability can be applied, many nations are still in gross violation of these requests.

Many countries from a variety of regions in the world have shown more of a willingness to follow the United Nations' standards regarding the need for a juvenile justice system than to raise the age of criminal responsibility. While some nations are better than others, the majority of nations investigated for the purposes of this study have some form of policy in place to provide additional protections to children in conflict with the law, generally with the underlying values of a desire to rehabilitate and educate juvenile offenders rather than punish them.

But, a number of nations are not only in gross violation of international standards in regard to the appropriate methods of administration of juvenile justice, they also are in violation of many of their own domestic laws. Juvenile justice workers, from police to judges, in countries like China, Nigeria, and Kenya need to be held accountable for their actions in regard to youth offenders. Allowing children to be sent to adult court and circumventing the justice system altogether violates the inherent rights to life afforded by the International Declaration of Human Rights.

Rather than holding juveniles to the same standards as adult criminals and instead treating them as children with a lesser liability for the crimes and a smaller capacity to understand the consequences of their crimes should return nations around the world to more progressive notions. It should be the project of every country in the world to involve social welfare workers to understand the causes leading the child to commit offenses, and the responsibility of the juvenile justice system to balance the protections of society with the need to help the offender begin a new path of legally and socially acceptable behavior.

Many of the nations involved in this study also state the importance of special rights for juveniles in conflict with the law, and differentiate those rights from the privileges afforded to adult offenders. While a variety of countries codify the rights to parental involvement, legal representation, and closed proceedings, nations are often in violation of their own stated laws. The infringement upon guaranteed rights for the most vulnerable population of offenders, as well as the most easily rehabilitative, crosses class, ethnic, and racial lines. For instance, the United States considers itself the leader of the Western world and decries nations for their breach of human rights, but has sent youth offenders to trial without competent legal aid. On the other side of the world, Japanese families are relied upon to give legal advice to their children.

It is sad to say that the support and administration of the specific juvenile rights meant to ensure the most comfortable process with authorities, as well as the most successful rehabilitative experience, are constantly denied around the world. While most nations have met international guidelines by incorporating these privileges into their legal codes, national and local justice systems continue to ignore the rights of minors. The youth offenders are often taken advantage of because of their age and vulnerability, and the underlying rationale for the assignment of such rights is disregarded.

Overall, abuse of minors rages across the world. No nation involved in this study fully used detention only as a last resort, attempted to rehabilitate the offender, and never resorted to physical violence against youths.

A number of nations continue to allow juvenile capital punishment. Other nations prohibit corporal punishment in policy, but utilize it liberally in practice. Young children are detained in deplorable, unhealthy, and dangerous physical conditions. They receive substandard education and learn more from the hardened adult criminals whose populations they are often integrated into. The state of juvenile detention across the world leaves much to be desired. Organizations like the United Nations and international human rights organizations must join in an effort to overthrow the present system of punishment, and help nations realize that many youth offenders commit crimes because of emotional, mental, and social problems. The only way to halt delinquents from developing into serious adult offenders is to provide them with proper psychological care and an opportunity to succeed in a secure and loving environment.

Appendix A

Table A.1. Age of Criminal Responsibility

Country	Minimum Age of Criminal Responsibility*	Maximum Age of Juvenile Status*
United States	depends on state	depends on state
Canada	12	14–18
Chile	10	16–18
Colombia	12	18
United Kingdom	10	18
Ireland	12	18
France	13	18
Germany	14	18–21
Sweden	15	21
Russia	14–16	18
Poland	15–17	17
Romania	14–16	16
Hungary	14	18
Israel	12	18
Egypt	7	18
Iran	9–15	9–15
Syria	7	15
South Africa	7	14–18
Kenya	8	18
Ghana	12	18
Nigeria	7–12	14–17
India	7–12	18
China	14–16	18
Japan	14	18–20
Australia	10–14	18

*Age in years

Appendix B

Table B.1. Juvenile Rights When in Conflict with the Law

Country	Right to An Attorney?	Right to Privacy?	Right to Parental Involvement?
United States	yes (not in practice)	depends on state	no
Canada	yes	depends on case	yes
Chile	no	no	yes
Colombia	yes	yes	no
United Kingdom	yes	yes	yes
Ireland	yes	depends on case	no
France	yes	yes	yes
Germany	yes	yes	yes
Sweden	yes	yes	yes
Russia	yes	no	depends on case
Poland	yes	yes	yes
Romania	yes	yes	yes
Hungary	yes	yes	yes
Israel	depends on case	yes	depends on case
Egypt	yes	yes	yes
Iran	yes	yes	no
Syria	yes	yes	depends on case
South Africa	yes	yes	yes
Kenya	yes (not in practice)	yes (not in practice)	yes (not in practice)
Ghana	yes	yes	no
Nigeria	yes (not in practice)	yes	yes
India	yes (not in practice)	yes	yes
China	yes	depends on case	yes
Japan	no	yes	yes
Australia	depends on state	depends on state	depends on state

Index

abuse of juveniles, 182–83; in Egyptian detention facilities, 103; in Indian detention facilities, 150; in Israeli detention facilities, 99; in Japanese detention centers, 163; in Kenyan detention facilities, 128, 129, 130; in Nigerian detention facilities, 140; in Polish detention facilities, 78; and racism in Australian detention facilities, 177; in Romanian detention facilities, 82–83; in Russian detention facilities, 73–74; in South African detention facilities, 122–23; of Tibetan political prisoners in China, 157; in U.K. detention facilities, 44; in U.S. juvenile detention facilities, 14

Act on Proceedings Concerning Juveniles (Poland), 75

adults, youth treated as: in Australia, 170; in Canada, 16, 20; in Chile, 25–26; in Egypt, 100; in Ghana, 134; in India, 147; in Iran, 106–7; in Ireland, 45; in Kenya, 124, 127; in South Africa, 118; in U.K., 41; in U.S., 9–10, 11–12. *See also* juvenile court systems; waivers for juvenile jurisdiction

Africa, 117–44; Ghana, 130–35; Kenya, 123–30; Nigeria, 135–40; South Africa, 117–23

African Network for the Prevention and Protection against Child Abuse and Neglect, 130

age of criminal responsibility, 2–3, 181, 185; in Australia, 169–70; in Canada, 16; in Chile, 25–26; in China, 151; in Colombia, 30–31; in Eastern Europe, 68; in Egypt, 99–100; in France, 49–50; in Germany, 53–54; in Ghana, 130–31; in Hungary, 83; in India, 145–46; in Iran, 103–4; in Ireland, 44–45; in Israel, 93–94; in Japan, 158–59; in Kenya, 123–24; in Nigeria, 135–36; in Poland, 74–75; in Romania, 78–80; in Russia, 68–69; in South Africa, 118; in Sweden, 59; in Syria, 108–9; in U.K., 39–40; in U.S., 7–8

"Ages at Which Children Are Legally Entitled to Carry Out a Series of Acts in Council of Europe Member Countries" (Centre for Europe's Children report), 49, 53

alternate sentencing, 5. *See also* sentencing

189

About the Authors

Paola Zalkind is a recent graduate of American University.

Rita J. Simon is University Professor in the School of Public Affairs and the Washington College of Law at American University.